Planning,
Teaching and Evaluating

Planning, Teaching and Evaluating: A Competency Approach

124291

Clifford H. Edwards
Howard G. Getz
Franklin G. Lewis
Michael A. Lorber
Walter D. Pierce

 Nelson-Hall, Chicago

Library of Congress Cataloging in Publication Data
Main entry under title:

Planning, teaching and evaluating.

    Bibliography: p.
    Includes index.
    1.   Teacher, Training of. 2.   Lesson planning.
I. Edwards, Clifford H.
LB1715.P55   370'.732   76-41903
ISBN 0-88229-204-8

Manufactured in the United States of America

Contents

Introduction

Teacher education programs in the United States have been criticized for many years in terms of their effectiveness in producing qualified personnel. This criticism has more recently reached a new pitch of intensity, with special interest groups asking that teachers be made accountable for pupil achievement. There is no doubt about the seriousness of this new challenge as evidenced by the growing number of states where certification is now dependent upon the demonstration of competency rather than the usual completion of a series of courses. The teacher-education profession has attempted to meet the challenge of accountability by supplanting existing programs with competency-based programs. The effort has been an extensive one, and is being accomplished with as much of a united front as any modern movement in the preparation of teachers. Among other things, competency-based teacher education has received the endorsement of the American Association of Colleges for Teacher Education with its vast membership of teacher preparation institutions.

This book is designed to be used in competency-based teacher-education programs. Trainees who successfully meet the competency levels specified herein will acquire most of the tools which are needed to increase student learning.

Most of these materials have received extensive field-testing during nearly five years' use in the teacher preparation program at Illinois State University, Normal. During the last five years, approximately 5,000 students have been successfully involved in this program.

The book is composed of fourteen chapters, each of which forms a separate self-instructional package. Each self-instructional unit is organized to follow the general model of instruction (GMI) containing objectives, preassessment, instructional procedures, and evaluation. These components have been organized into an integrated whole for the purpose of maximizing learning to foster teaching proficiency.

Even though each chapter is self-contained, the fourteen chapters form a systematic and integrated approach to the development of skill in planning, teaching, and evaluating. Skills are developed sequentially and gradually presented within more complex repertoires of behavior.

Chapter 1 gives a description of the general model of instruction along with its rationale and empirical support. There is some evidence that using the model can bring about increased achievement in the classroom.

Chapters 2 through 7 deal with lesson planning. Chapter 2 gives trainees practice in writing instructional objectives in the behavioral format, while Chapter 3 helps to increase their competency in formulating behavioral objectives in the three domains of knowledge, namely, cognitive, affective, and psychomotor.

The subject of Chapter 4 is preassessment. Once objectives have been developed, the next task of the teacher is to determine the extent to which his or her pupils can already achieve the objectives as well as to identify any deficiencies which may limit the meaningfulness of the learning activities which must be engaged in to accomplish the objectives. Preassessment provides the answers to these instructional problems.

Chapters 5, 6, and 7 focus upon instructional procedures. Once the teacher understands the relationship between goals and the present capabilities of students, he or she is ready to formulate strategies for helping students achieve those objectives. The task here lies in providing experiences which capture student interest, and engaging them in activities that they are able to perform successfully and which constitute appropriate practice for the objectives to be achieved. The goal is to be able to produce an appropriately written plan which can be used to teach a well-organized lesson.

The objectives of Chapters 8 through 13 are to develop

competency in teaching a series of simulated lessons. In this series of
six packages, specified teaching skills must be exhibited by trainees as
they attempt to help their pupils achieve objectives at different levels
in the various domains of knowledge. The major focus is on helping
the trainee engage pupils in higher-order cognitive processes rather
than on the mere acquisition of information. Trainees are expected to
analyze their teaching performance as they proceed and make adjustments based upon their analyses. Even though the program may be
used as a self-instructional tool (with students performing self-
analysis) it is also designed to incorporate supervisory feedback.

The final chapter, Chapter 14, is about evaluation. Evaluation
requires criterion-referenced rather than norm-referenced evaluation. This necessitates an adjustment not only in the way grading is
perceived, but also in the way tests are formulated. It is particularly
critical to develop evaluative tools that accurately measure a competency rather than using norm-based testing practices. In addition, it is
imperative that evaluation procedures fit the competency being
measured. Paper-and-pencil tests will not suffice in measuring some
proficiencies. These must be determined by a different kind of skill
demonstration.

It may be noted that the format used for the different chapters in
the book may vary somewhat. The purpose of this is, in part, to
illustrate different ways in which to organize a learning package. For
example, in the learning activities section of some chapters, exercises
are incorporated within those portions of the section which the
student reads. In others the exercises appear at the end of the reading
material.

The evaluation section of the different chapters also illustrates
how this aspect of a learning package may vary. In some chapters the
evaluation consists of a self-test which is equivalent to the test which
will later be taken as a final evaluation. In other packages the
evaluation section consists of instructions regarding how to proceed
in demonstrating a particular competency.

chapter 1

The General
Model of
Instruction—GMI

OBJECTIVES

1. When given a diagram of the general model of instruction, you will be able to assign the proper label for each part from a list provided with 80 percent accuracy. *(Knowledge)*

2. After studying the material covering the GMI, you will be able to demonstrate comprehension of each part of the GMI by correctly answering at least 80 percent of a series of objective questions. *(Comprehension)*

3. When given a series of statements about certain aspects of the GMI, you will be able to classify 80 percent of the statements as to their related step within the GMI. *(Comprehension-Analysis)*

4. When presented with a hypothetical teaching situation, you will (after studying both this chapter and Chapter 5) be able to design a teaching strategy that incorporates each of the four steps in the GMI in conformity with the principles described. *(Synthesis)*

PREASSESSMENT

You should make use of the questions below to guide your study so that a minimum of time is spent on familiar material. Each question is followed by a number that links it to the *Instructional Procedures* included in this chapter. If you can answer the questions without referring to the Instructional Procedures section, you should be ready to demonstrate that proficiency immediately by successfully passing the objective examination at the end of this chapter.

1. What is the name of each part of the GMI? *(1, 2)*

2. Why is each chapter in this text a model of the GMI? *(1, 2)*

3. What levels of education and what length of teaching unit can the GMI be used for? *(1)*

4. What men have contributed to the development of the various segments of the GMI? *(1)*

5. What was the result of the Levine[1] study? *(1)*

6. What is the basic question answered by the Instructional-Objective stage of the GMI? *(3)*

7. Why does stating objectives precisely help in the selection of appropriate objectives? *(4)*

8. Why do some instructors have more freedom than others in the selection of objectives? *(4)*

9. What is meant by the classification of objectives? What purpose does it serve? *(5)*

10. What four models for the classification of objectives could be used by teachers? Which model is used in this text? *(5)*

11. What are the three parts of a behavioral objective? Which part proves that the objective is truly behavioral? *(6)*

12. What does each part of a behavioral objective answer? *(6)*

13. What is preassessment? What purpose does it serve? *(7)*

14. What stage follows preassessment? *(8)*

15. Describe each of the following psychological principles.

    a. revelation of objectives *(9)*

    b. perceived purpose *(10)*

    c. equivalent practice *(11)*

    d. analogous practice *(12)*

    e. knowledge of results *(13)*

    f. individualized instruction *(14)*

16. Why and when should objectives be revealed to students? *(9)*

17. Why should students be included in initial goal-setting for a course? *(10)*

18. What problem is encountered in equivalent practice for objectives evaluated by objective tests? *(11)*

19. How may knowledge of results take place if the student's effort is original? *(13)*

20. What are the purposes of the evaluation section of the GMI? *(15)*

21. What are possible explanations if the evaluation shows learning did not take place? *(15)*

INSTRUCTIONAL PROCEDURES

LEARNING ACTIVITY 1: *1. General Model of Instruction* In this volume, each chapter is a miniature example of what is commonly called the General Model of Instruction (GMI). Over the years, educators have endeavored to find a model that could be adapted to almost every teaching-learning situation. It would describe a theoretical and philosophical base that would provide any age group, any length of unit of study, and any subject with a solid base from which to design sound instructional strategies.

Through work done in military training, programmed instruction, and experimental psychology, an amalgamation evolved that is now known as GMI. It has subsequently proved to be an important tool in curriculum development, teaching self-improvement and analysis, in addition to providing one of the most succinct approaches to planning for teaching and learning. In a recent study by Martin Levine[1], preservice teachers were randomly assigned to experimental and control groups. The experimental group was trained in the use of the GMI while the control group was trained in the more traditional methods. When both groups taught youngsters, the experimental group significantly outperformed the control group.

2. GMI Overview We are now ready to examine the instructional model. First, we will present an overview; second, we will examine each of its parts. Concurrently, we will also refer to how it can be used in instructional design, and touch briefly on its use in curriculum development and improvement of teaching. Examine the following diagram carefully.

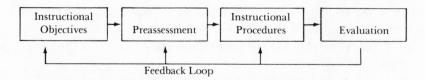

FIGURE 1—1 — GENERAL MODEL OF INSTRUCTION

3. Instructional Objectives Figure 1—1 describes the steps in designing and implementing a complete sequence of instruction. The first stage implies that there has been the structuring of a precise set of goals for the unit. In its simplest form, the instructional objectives should answer the initial question, "What are my students going to be able to do after the course is completed?" Writing clear and concise objectives is crucial to using the GMI effectively. Just being able to write objectives appropriately and distributing them to your students can aid in increasing learning. There are several studies that serve to substantiate that the revealing of objectives is a powerful tool to aid in our attempts to maximize learning.[2,3,4,5,6] This skill is so important that Chapters 2 and 3 are devoted to it exclusively.

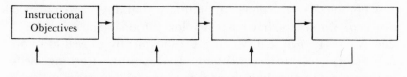

FIGURE 1—2

4. The Selection of Instructional Objectives As you begin to pinpoint with specificity what it is that you expect of your students (often using input of the students in the determination of the objectives), a much clearer picture of that particular objective's relationship to others emerges. The questions concerning the value of the objective are more easily dealt with. The problems of what the student is already able to do and what is to follow are crystallized in the process. Any problems about the feasibility of instructional accomplishment are also brought more clearly into focus.

In short, by clearly stating your instructional intent, you are able to judge more adequately which objectives to select as part of the course. For some teachers (i.e., preservice mathematics, foreign language teachers), the problem of selection is not as great because of pressures to have students at a prescribed level. For other teachers (i.e., English, art, music, and social studies), there is a much greater variety of possible goals. In any case, the use of precise objectives will assist teachers in both situations to clarify objectives and to maximize learning.

5. *Classification of Objectives*   One of the charges that has been laid at the feet of the educator is that he or she does not insure that much more goes on in classrooms besides a dispensing of information by the teacher and its subsequent return in the form of a student test or paper. This charge, unfortunately, is all too often true. How can the teacher insure that there is a development of a variety of intellectual, attitudinal, and physical growth of individual students? One excellent way is to formulate objectives that have been deliberately structured to attain such goals.

There are several models that can assist you in classifying your goals into categories that will insure cognitive variety. Albert Upton[7] has suggested these three broad categories—sensory (psychomotor); affective; and logical (cognitive). Within the logical component, the categories of qualification, operations analysis, structural analysis, and classification can be used to make sure that the students engage in various intellectual endeavors. Robert Gagné[8] has suggested an analysis of intellectual operations that moves from "response differentiation" to strategies based on a behavioral modification approach to learning. J. P. Guilford's[9] well-known "structure of intellect" model also provides a basis for classifying objectives.

However, the best-known scheme for classifying objectives is the work of Benjamin S. Bloom and his associates.[10] Because of its wide acceptance, it is included in this volume as the basis upon which objectives are classified and formulated.

6. *Essential Parts of Behavioral Objectives*   Behavioral objectives have been broken down into their essential parts by many, but historically, the work of Robert M. Mager[11] seems to describe these elements as succinctly as any other. There are three key components to any objective. (Only an overview will be presented here. Chapters 2 and 3 deal specifically with the skills necessary to formulate and classify objectives.)

The first (and fundamentally essential) component of a behavioral objective is a statement of the observable behavior. Sometimes called the terminal behavior, it describes the observable competency that the student must be able to perform. It answers the question, "What is the student going to be able to do after the instruction is completed?"

The second important component of a well-written objective is a minimum acceptable standard. Often called the criterion level, this element in the objective should answer the question, "How well will the student have to perform the required competency?"

The third component of an appropriately written objective is a statement of conditions. This answers the question, "Under what circumstances will the student demonstrate his competency?"

As an example, we might begin with the notion that it would be good if all youngsters could acquire the skill of discerning fact from opinion in news columns and editorials. The terminal behavior is then, "The student will be able to identify both fact and opinion in editorials." In order to set up the circumstances, we might add sufficient conditions in order to observe the activity clearly. We therefore add, "When given editorials," and "underline the factual content in red pencil and opinion in regular pencil." Further, in order to answer the question, "How well will the student be able to discern fact from opinion?" we add a criterion level: "Underline at least four opinions and five facts."

Putting the parts together, we have a complete behavioral objective: "Given a copy of an editorial, the student will be able to underline at least four opinions in regular pencil and five facts in red pencil."

7. *Preassessment*   After formulating the precise objectives for the unit or lesson, the next step is an assessment of the extent to which students already have the psychological and intellectual (and in some cases physiological) skills called for. This process is called preassessment.

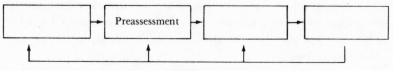

FIGURE 1—3

Preassessment procedures will be dealt with in depth in Chapter 4, but let's take a quick look at preassessment in relation to the total GMI. One of the primary functions is to maximize the speed of learning. One basic reason the GMI can assist in that maximization is because it provides for adjustment *at the outset of instruction* to handle possible learning problems.

a. Some students may already know portions of the lesson. Proper use of preassessment will keep these students from being bored and from wasting time.

b. If there are some students who do not have sufficient background, a remedial program may be in order, and/or other adjustments in the learning activities may also be made so as to cope with the varying skill levels of the pupils.

c. If a majority of students are not ready for the material, the objective may be modified so as to be more suitable.

If teachers would really use preassessment, enormous gains could be made in the learning process.

8. Instructional Procedures Stage After setting up the objectives and making an assessment of students in relation to those goals, you are now ready to design and implement your teaching strategies. At this point, the range of possibilities is limited only by the imagination and skill of the teacher. Chapters 5 through 13 of this book are designed to assist you in building greater competency. At this point, however, there are several psychological principles that are more relevant to the GMI and they should be kept in mind as you build up your specific teaching skills.

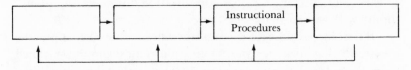

FIGURE 1—4

9. The Principle of Objectives All of us are familiar with the following experience as students. The first day of class we gather information about our new teachers, listen to what they say, and then attempt to guess what the teacher *really* wants. It is because we have guessed well in the past that we have gone as far as we have in school.

Occasionally, a student will be fortunate enough to encounter a teacher who lets everyone know early in the course just exactly what will be expected, and then proceeds to follow exactly what he or she stated. This instructor will usually be deemed superior to one who conceals or doesn't really know what goals to pursue.

As pointed out previously, there is empirical evidence that substantiates the position that if the teacher will reveal the objectives for the course, and the pupils realize how to use the objectives, the amount of learning increases. [2, 3, 4, 5, 6] Students don't have to make guesses regarding the competencies they must display; they know precisely and don't waste time on irrelevancies.

In order to insure that the pupils do indeed know what is expected of them, the teacher may need to teach the objectives with just as much vigor as any other part of the lesson, and arrange strategies so that the objectives are revealed initially in a lesson and subsequently reviewed as often as necessary to maintain a correct perspective of the instructional intent.

10. The Principle of Perceived Purpose   As pointed out by James Popham and Eva Baker, "the learner should be shown the value of what he is studying. In the first place, an effective description of *what* the learner is supposed to accomplish is most helpful. If, in addition, the learner can be shown *why* these objectives are worthwhile, he is far more likely to achieve the desired goals."[12]

Almost every teacher who teaches at the secondary level has confronted the question (often asked at a particularly inopportune moment, and accompanied by an antagonistic sneer) "Hey, teacher, why do we have to learn this?" Answers such as "You'll need it for college" and "Because the board of education thinks it's important" simply will not satisfy the questioner.

If the objectives are revealed and modified with student input, the question is less likely to arise. Motivation is most simply generated through the involvement of students in the initial goal-setting. When this seems impossible, the teacher must initiate techniques wherein the students arrive at the conclusion that the objectives are worthwhile, in a way that generates some internal commitment.

This problem, of course, could lead to the realization on the part of the teacher that the goals adopted are indeed irrelevant to the needs of the students. If that turns out to be the case, then the teacher would do well to abandon them post haste.

11. The Principle of Equivalent Practice This principle is probably the most obvious and yet the most neglected principle in the use of GMI. It is obvious that if the student knows exactly what he is to be able to do after instruction, and we know that he is ready for such instruction because of preassessment, then the most logical thing to do is to practice the exact skill that he will later have to demonstrate. For instance, if the student is to be able to measure metal bars of less than one inch with micrometers with accuracy to within a .002 of a inch, then we should have him measure metal bars with micrometers. Any other activity *may* be helpful, but actual measuring practice is the quickest and most valid way to accomplish the objective.

When the final skill to be exhibited is to demonstrate comprehension through responses to test items, then it may be necessary to build practice test items for equivalent practice purposes. They may not be the exact items, but may cover the same content. Many trial or practice tests included in this volume use this principle.

12. The Principle of Analogous Practice As the name implies, analogous practice is practice that is deemed helpful in accomplishing the objective. Suppose that ultimately we wish the students to be able to measure the height of buildings and trees and the distances across rivers using trigonometric functions. Analogous practice could be exercises where students solved problems from diagrams using trigonometric functions. Such practice would be helpful to our ultimate objective.

When we combine both equivalent and analogous practice, they are often labeled "appropriate practice." Through the use of both types of practice, the teacher is able to develop unlimited possibilities for instructional activities.

13. The Principle of Knowledge of Results If you, as a student, have ever spent time practicing, turned in a product that demonstrated that practice, and then were unable to find out whether that practice was done correctly or incorrectly, you felt the frustration of not having knowledge of results. Adjustments by the human mind can be made much more quickly if a person is told immediately whether or not his or her responses are correct.

The teacher need not be confined to a singular technique in providing such feedback. There are many possible procedures available that will let the student know quickly how he or she has performed on a particular learning task. If the work is a product or synthesis of material, however, feedback procedures may involve the use of models as illustrations and individual reporting by the teacher, because efforts of this kind do not have clear right or wrong answers.

14. The Principle of Individualized Instruction   Once a thorough preassessment has been accomplished, there is often an implication for individualization of instruction. The reason for this is obvious. It is seldom that every member of an entire class will be ready for a specific lesson at the same time. If it is possible to tailor the activities to the student's specific status, then it should be done. This basic psychological principle has been demonstrated time and again as a sure way to help maximize learning. Unfortunately, teachers of today were most likely reinforced during four years of college in direct opposition to this principle. Students are all taught the same way and then "graded" on the basis of their relative position in the class. Is it any wonder that so few individualize their instructional techniques when they return to the secondary schools as teachers?

There are many techniques for individualizing, some of which are discussed in Chapters 5 and 6. In addition, Chapter 7 is devoted entirely to the individualized technique of self-pacing.

15. Evaluation   The fourth step in a sequence of instruction is the evaluation.

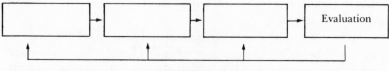

FIGURE 1—5

There is little point in utilizing the GMI to build objectives, preassess, and implement instruction without a final evaluation to determine if the instruction was successful. Evaluation in the GMI serves a much broader function than to merely assign marks. When instruction is successful as demonstrated by pupil learning, the teacher can take credit for this success. If the instruction was not successful, the evaluation helps determine the cause of the learning breakdown. The following questions are helpful in determining the nature of the learning problem.

1. Were the objectives inappropriate and do they need modification?

2. Was the preassessment inadequate? Did it fail to tell the instructor the real status of the pupil?

3. Were the learning activities ineffective? Did they need redesigning?

4. Was the evaluation a true reflection of the competency developed in the objective and taught in the learning activities?

5. Are the procedures and materials sufficient for most students, with only a few students needing to recycle and repeat one or more stages?

The evaluation, then, is the key for ultimate success as a teacher.

Properly used, the GMI can be used by teachers in a cycle for continuous teaching self-improvement. When the objectives are appropriate for the learners as predetermined by preassessment, you are free to manipulate the learning environment to maximize learning.

LEARNING ACTIVITY 2: OPTIONAL ACTIVITIES If you feel that you wish to study this area further, or wish to amplify the material explored herein, the following two books are recommended.

1. James Popham and Eva Baker, *Systematic Instruction.*

2. Robert Kibler, Larry Barker, and David Miles, *Behavioral Objectives and Instruction.*

EVALUATION

After you have read and studied the above materials, use the following self-test to ascertain whether or not you have a solid grasp of the GMI. This test is similar to the one which will be provided by the instructor to determine your proficiency in this area.

TRUE-FALSE

_____ 1. The GMI is a useful tool, but generally only applicable to larger units of study. *(1)*

_____ 2. The classification of objectives used in this text can be accomplished by using any of several classification schemes. *(5)*

_____ 3. The question asked by the conditions in a behavioral objective is "How well does the student have to perform the competency described in the objective?" *(6)*

_____ 4. Perceived purpose is the principle that students are likely to learn more if they can see value in what they are studying. *(10)*

_____ 5. The principle of analogous practice is to practice exactly the behavior described in the objective. *(12)*

_____ 6. When a teacher uses both equivalent and analogous practice the terms "appropriate practice" can be used for both. *(13)*

_____ 7. Most new teachers will individualize instruction through training received during teacher education. *(14)*

_____ 8. The second stage of the GMI is preassessment. *(1)*

_____ 9. The terms "terminal behavior" and "observable behavior" can be used interchangeably. *(6)*

_____ 10. Evaluation in the GMI is primarily for purposes of assigning marks to students. *(15)*

11-15 Label each part of the following diagram from memory.

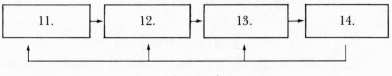

(15.)

To which stage in the GMI does each of the following relate?

16. Equivalent practice
17. Conditions
18. Determining objective achievement

Answers

1.	F	6.	T
2.	T	7.	F
3.	F	8.	T
4.	T	9.	T
5.	F	10.	F

11. instructional objectives
12. preassessment
13. instructional procedures
14. evaluation

15. feedback
16. instructional procedures
17. instructional objectives
18. evaluation

NOTES

1. Martin Levine, "The Effect on Pupil Achievement of Criterion-Referenced Instructional Model Used by Student Teachers," *The Journal of Teacher Education*, Vol. XXIII, No. 4, Winter 1972, pp. 477–487.

2. Robert Kibler, Larry L. Barker, and David Miles, *Behavioral Objectives and Instruction*, (Boston: Allyn and Bacon, 1970).

3. G. V. Harrison, "The Instructional Value of Presenting Explicit Versus Vague Objectives," *California Educational Research Studies*, 1967.

4. R. R. Mager and J. McCann, *Learner Controlled Instruction*, (Palo Alto, Calif.: Varian Associates, 1961).

5. R. M. Verhaegen, "The Effect of Learner-Controlled Instruction in a Fourth-Grade Biology Curriculum," unpublished Master's thesis, University of California, Los Angeles, 1964.

6. Joseph R. Jenkins and John T. Neisworth, "The Facilitating Influence of Instructional Objectives," *The Journal of Educational Research*, Vol. 66, No. 6, February 1973, pp. 254–256.

7. Albert Upton, *Design for Thinking*, (Palo Alto, Calif.: Stanford University Press, 1961).

8. Robert Gagné, "The Analysis of Instructional Objectives for the Design of Instruction," in *Teaching Machines and Programmed Instruction*, ed. Robert Glaser (Washington, D.C.: National Education Association, 1967).

9. J. P. Guilford, *The Nature of Human Intelligence*, (New York: McGraw-Hill, 1967).

10. B. S. Bloom, D. R. Krathwohl, and B. B. Masia, *Taxonomy of Educational Objectives—The Classification of Educational Goals*, (New York: David McKay, 1961).

11. Robert F. Mager, *Preparing Instructional Objectives*, (Palo Alto, Calif.: Fearon, 1962).

12. James Popham and Eva Baker, *Systematic Instruction*, (Englewood Cliffs, New Jersey: Prentice-Hall, 1970), pp. 80–81.

chapter 2

Instructional
Objectives

OBJECTIVES

1. You will be able to demonstrate the ability to recall and relate information concerning the components, functions, advantages, and disadvantages of precise instructional objectives well enough to achieve a score of at least 80 percent correct on the objective test at the end of this chapter.

2. Given a series of instructional objectives and a list of weaknesses common to such objectives (such as omission of an observable terminal behavior or omission of a minimum acceptable standard of performance), you will be able to identify, with at least 80 per cent accuracy, those weaknesses, if any, that apply to each objective.

3. Given two improperly stated instructional objectives, you will be able to rewrite them so that they contain an observable terminal behavior, conditions under which that behavior is to be demonstrated, and a minimum acceptable standard of performance.

4. Given a topic in your teaching field, you will be able to write three precise instructional objectives, each of which calls for a

different kind of behavior, and each of which contains an observable terminal behavior, conditions under which that behavior is to be demonstrated, and a minimum acceptable standard of performance.

PREASSESSMENT

The following questions and tasks reflect the information presented here. Each question is followed by a number which links it to the *Instructional Procedures* in this chapter. If, after looking through this section, you are sure that you already possess this information, you may want to attempt to demonstrate the above objectives immediately. If so, go directly to the evaluation section at the end of this chapter.

If you find that you are not sure of the information, you may either refer to the particular section indicated or, preferably, read the entire chapter.

1. Why, with respect to objectives, are many taxpayers unhappy with public education as it now stands? *(Introduction)*

2. What is a precise instructional objective? *(1)*

3. How can precise instructional objectives comprise a "job description?" *(1)*

4. Who first popularized precise instructional objectives, and when? *(1)*

5. What term was first used to label what is now commonly called a precise instructional objective? *(1)*

6. What are the three main components of a precise instructional objective? *(2)*

7. What is an observable terminal behavior? *(2)*

8. Write three examples of unambiguous terminal behaviors and three examples of behaviors which are ambiguous. *(2)*

9. How, if at all, can ambiguous terms be properly used when stating precise instructional objectives? *(2)*

10. Why is it usually necessary to state conditions in a precise instructional objective? *(2)*

11. Should all conditions be stated for all objectives? Why or why not? *(2)*

12. What are some typical conditions you might find in a precise instructional objective? *(2)*

13. Why should conditions such as "as given in class" be avoided? *(2)*

14. Write two examples each of quantitative and qualitative standards. *(2)*

15. When specifying lengths of answers, should minimum or maximum lengths be indicated? *(2)*

16. What is the major problem in trying to specify qualitative standards? *(2)*

17. How can "parameters" be used to facilitate the writing of standards? *(2)*

18. Should all minimum acceptable standards be specified for all objectives? Why or why not? *(2)*

19. Why should terms such as "major points" be used with great care in objectives? *(2)*

20. How can the utilization of precise instructional objectives help to improve the teaching-learning process? List at least six ways. *(3)*

21. What are some of the disadvantages associated with the use of precise instructional objectives? List at least three. *(4)*

22. How are precise instructional objectives misused? List four ways. *(4)*

23. Is the use of precise instructional objectives increasing or decreasing? *(5)*

24. What are the three ways you will most likely come into contact with precise instructional objectives? *(5)*

25. Why is it not usually possible to convert general objectives to precise instructional objectives on a one-to-one basis? *(5)*

26. How should you go about writing and using precise instructional objectives? *(6)*

27. List at least six steps you should follow in the proper writing and utilization of precise instructional objectives. *(6)*

28. List at least three sources to which you can turn for ideas for precise instructional objectives. *(6)*

29. What are three ways by which you can check to see if the objectives you write clearly convey your instructional intent? *(6)*

30. What are some of the common errors made when writing precise instructional objectives? How can you avoid them? *(6, 7)*

31. What is the relationship between the cognitive and the affective domains? *(8)*

32. Describe the concerns of each of the three taxonomic domains. *(8)*

33. What are at least two difficulties unique to the writing of objectives in the affective domain? *(8)*

34. How does the utilization of cognitive and affective domain objectives differ? *(8)*

35. Can the affective domain be safely ignored? Why or why not? *(8)*

INSTRUCTIONAL PROCEDURES

LEARNING ACTIVITY 1: *Introduction*   Prior to discussing the nuts and bolts of precise instructional objectives, let us look first at a very basic reason they are being used.

Many Americans are unhappy with the results of public education. Each year taxpayers pour at least $50 billion into the nation's schools, and each year they complain more bitterly that the money is being wasted because the schools are "not doing their job." When educators rush to their own defense, they frequently make matters worse by voicing such meaningless cliches as "We are turning out students who will be ready to take their places in society," and "We are concerned with developing well-rounded individuals." Such rhetoric prompts many parents to say to themselves, "Baloney! If I want my kid 'well-rounded,' I'll feed him lots of cookies and cake at home. Your job is to teach him something!"

The crux of the problem is that until recently, educators have not had to spell out exactly what they were attempting to achieve. Without precisely stated goals, there was no way to evaluate empirically what was being accomplished with the billions of dollars being spent for education, and there was no way either to repudiate or substantiate the charge that the schools were not doing their job. During the past few years, taxpayers have finally forced educators to admit the need for educational objectives that are clear, meaningful, and amenable to empirical evaluation, and the resulting wave of interest in increased accountability among educators is sweeping the nation.

The following information focuses on a number of questions commonly asked by people interested in using precise instructional objectives to improve the educative process. It is hoped that the information will be complete enough not only to enable you to write precise instructional objectives, but also to make you cognizant of the variety of benefits accruing from their use. At the very least, the information will give you a basis upon which to argue the relative merits of this instructional tool.

1. What is a Precise Instructional Objective? A precise instructional objective is a statement of instructional intent. It states, in terms of observable activities, just what a student will be able to do after instruction, under what conditions he will be expected to do it, and the degree of proficiency he will be expected to demonstrate.

A whole set of carefully conceived and precise instructional objectives can also be thought of as a kind of teacher job description. As each teacher develops his own set of precise instructional objectives, he is not only specifying what his students will be able to achieve, but is also directly implying that he considers it his prime responsibility and function to help students achieve at least those particular objectives. The job description aspect of precise instructional objectives is becoming more and more important as teachers find it increasingly necessary to justify their own professional existence in terms of student benefits.

One further point should be remembered. The term "precise instructional objective" is just one label among many for the same thing. When Robert Mager's book, *Preparing Instructional Objectives,*[1] was published in 1962, he used the term "behavioral objective." Unfortunately, over the years, it has taken on the connotation of the stimulus-response learning theories of behaviorists such as B. F. Skinner. To avoid misconceptions, writers have tried a number of different labels including "instructional outcomes," "behavioral goals," and "instructional objectives." The term "precise instructional objective" is used here because it seems to be the most descriptive of our instructional intent.

2. What are the Three Main Components of a Precise Instructional Objective? Robert Mager identified an observable terminal behavior, conditions, and a minimum acceptable standard as the three main components of a precise instructional objective.[2] Although we will examine each of these components separately, keep in mind that *all three parts together* comprise a precise instructional objective.

An observable terminal behavior describes, in terms of activities that you can actually see, exactly what a student will be able to do at the end of instruction. Experience has shown that terms such as "define, in writing," "underline," and "diagram" are much more effective in describing terminal behaviors than are terms such as "know," "learn," and "understand." This is so because the former terms are directly observable and have only one meaning whereas the latter terms are not directly observable and can be interpreted in a number of ways. Which terms give you the clearest mental picture of what you will be expected to do, "The student will write," "The student will underline," or "The student will learn?" Certainly the first two terms are more exact and are therefore more useful in describing terminal behaviors.

Consider the following objectives:

1. The student will know the difference between analogous and equivalent practice;

2. The student will be able to define, in writing, the terms analogous and equivalent practice and illustrate each definition with at least one appropriate example.

Since the word "know" in the first objective represents a behavior that is not directly observable, students cannot determine how the teacher expects them to demonstrate that knowledge. As the objective now stands, neither the teacher no the student can describe exactly how the terminal behavior is to be demonstrated and therefore the teacher will be unable to ascertain when, or if, the objective is achieved. With no observable behavior, the objective is meaningless.

The second objective contains an observable behavior—"define, in writing." Since the teacher and the student can now describe how achievement of the objective is to be demonstrated it is a simple matter to determine when, in fact, the objective has been achieved.

It should be noted that words such as "know," "learn," "understand," "grasp," and "appreciate" do not necessarily have to be avoided when writing precise instructional objectives. If it is your opinion that such words are necessary to communicate your instructional intent, then use them, *but be sure to include an explanation of how the implied behavior is to be demonstrated.* For example, the objective: "The student will demonstrate his understanding of the terms 'analogous' and 'equivalent practice' by writing their definitions and illustrating each with an appropriate example," is an acceptable objective from a purely technical standpoint, but may be unnecessarily wordy. In virtually all instances you will find that words such as "learn," and "understand" are superfluous to good objectives and tend to confuse, rather than clarify, the instructional intent.

Some terms, such as "identify," "differentiate," and "solve," while certainly less ambiguous than terms such as "know," "learn," and "understand," still leave some room for misinterpretation because they are insufficiently descriptive of the behavior being sought. This is so because terms such as "identify" and "solve" represent purely mental activities. In order for you to be certain that a student has, in fact, "identified" or "solved" something, it is necessary that the results of the mental activity be reported or demonstrated in some observable form. Therefore, to clarify insufficiently descriptive terms one should add to them behavior qualifiers such as "identify by writing," "differentiate by checking," and "show, in writing, the step-by-step procedure for solving." These qualifiers enable you to communicate more clearly to students first the real behavior you are seeking, and second, the overt means by which that behavior is to be demonstrated. This further explanation sharpens the mental picture the student has of what is expected and thereby tends to reduce his anxiety.

The important point to remember is that the precise instructional objective should enable both you and your students to describe, prior to instruction, just what the instructional goal is and how its achievement is going to be demonstrated. If behavior qualifiers are needed, be sure to use them.

Another point to keep in mind is the inherent disadvantage in having students orally demonstrate a competence. If an objective requires a student to "orally state" something, the reliability of the demonstration is compromised if other students hear the recitation. It would be illogical, for example, to write an objective such as "The student will be able to list orally three measures of central tendency," unless provisions were made for each student to demonstrate the competency privately. If the competence were to be demonstrated in a class setting, you would be unable to differentiate between those students who actually knew the material and those who were merely mimicking what they heard others say.

The conditions component of a precise instructional objective further describes the terminal behavior. Conditions tell the students

what kinds of freedoms or restrictions are going to exist when they are
asked to demonstrate achievement of the objective. Conditions frequently refer to time limits or to the use of aids or special equipment,
but they can refer to whatever factors you consider important to the
demonstration of the terminal behavior. A physical education
teacher, for example, might consider it necessary to specify "using a
regulation baseball" in an objective concerning the hitting of line
drives in order to avoid any question as to whether a baseball or a
softball is to be used. The function of conditions in a precise
instructional objective, again, is to clarify the student's mental
picture of what is expected of him by informing him of specific
freedoms, constraints, or other conditions.

Consider these:

1. The student will be able to describe, in writing, at least two
possible advantages and two possible disadvantages associated
with the use of precise instructional objectives.

2. Using only his notes, the student will be able to describe in a
paper of no more than two pages, at least two possible advantages and two possible disadvantages associated with the use of
precise instructional objectives.

The first objective contains an observable terminal behavior,
"describe, in writing," but the student does not know if he will be
expected to memorize the required information or if he can simply
open a text and copy what he needs. In the second objective, all doubts
are removed. The condition that notes may be used is clearly stated
and there is little room for misunderstanding. Likewise, the specification of length, "in a paper of no more than two pages," gives the
student an even more complete description of what is expected of
him.

While statements of conditions are usually quite helpful and are
sometimes absolutely necessary to avoid misunderstandings, some
care must be taken in their use. Conditions such as "after a lecture,"
"given in class," and "as discussed in class" can actually weaken an
objective by limiting the sources from which a student may draw
information in formulating responses. Certainly it would not be your
intention to penalize a student for having acquired information or
skills outside of your class, and yet conditions such as those just
mentioned imply such a penalty. A precise instructional objective

describes an observable terminal behavior. It does *not* describe how the student will acquire the knowledge or skill to demonstate that behavior. The means by which students will be helped to acquire information and skills lie in the realm of teaching-learning activities and should *not* be included in the precise instructional objectives.

Another point to remember is that it is unwise to attempt to state all conditions each time. For example, the condition "with no aids" will probably be common to a large percentage of the objectives you write. To include the words "with no aids" in each and every objective, however, would be repetitive and would tend to become distracting. A more logical solution would be to state any conditions which will be common to most objectives (such as "with no aids," "in writing," and "within one class period") at the beginning of the list of objectives and to discuss them with your students prior to instruction. Any conditions which vary from these conditions would, of course, be specified in the appropriate objective(s).

As a general rule, you should state conditions whenever there is the slightest possibility that doubts or misunderstandings may arise, and omit them otherwise. If, however, there is any doubt at all in your mind as to whether or not conditions are needed in a particular objective the safest course is to include them. *Keep in mind the fact that if no conditions are specified in the objective, it is unfair to impose them at the time the behavior is to be demonstrated.*

The minimum acceptable standard of performance completes the student's mental picture of what is expected by specifying the *degree of proficiency* with which the terminal behavior is to be demonstrated. This last component is absolutely necessary if the objective is to have any meaning to either the teacher or the student because without it, neither will be able to determine the difference between acceptable and unacceptable terminal behavior. Unless the minimum acceptable standard is crystal clear and removes any and all doubts concerning exactly how well the terminal behavior is to be demonstrated, the objective should not be used.

Depending upon the kind of behavior called for, the minimum acceptable standard can be stated in quantitative terms, qualitative terms, or both. As the name suggests, quantitative terms specify amount or numbers. The following are some examples of objectives using quantitative minimum acceptable standards.

The student will be able to:
1. Underline all nouns in any given paragraph.
2. Given four sets of symptoms, diagnose, in writing, the correct disease in at least three of the cases.
3. List, in writing, the three primary colors.
4. Write at least three precise instructional objectives, each of which contains an observable terminal behavior, conditions under which that behavior will occur, and a minimum acceptable standard.

The first three of the above objectives utilize only quantitative standards (all, at least three, and three). The fourth example combines a quantitative standard (at least three) with a qualitative standard (contains an observable terminal behavior, conditions under which that behavior will occur, and a minimum acceptable standard). More will be said concerning qualitative standards shortly.

A common misconception concerning quantitative standards is that the specification of allowable time or lengths of answers is, by itself, sufficient to convey a minimum acceptable standard of performance. *Generally speaking, this is not true.* Consider the following examples:

The student will be able to:
1. Describe, in a paper of no more than two pages, the results of World War II.
2. Type at least two letters in one class period.

In the first objective the student could logically assume that the answer "The Allies won" would be quite sufficient. In the second objective, the student could turn in two messy, error-filled pages at the end of the period and be justifiably angry if they were not accepted. In neither objective did the quantitative standard, alone, convey the true instructional intent. Qualitative standards were also needed.

Another important point is that lengths of answers, such as "in a paper of no more than two pages," are usually best described in terms of maximum, rather than minimum, lengths. This is so because you want to give students some idea of how extensive their answer should be, but you also want them to say what they have to say and then stop. You do not want students to pad answers with irrelevant data simply to fill up a required number of pages. Sometimes, although not often, a statement of approximately how many pages are expected, for example, three to five, is even more descriptive than a maximum number of pages. If so, use this option. Remember, however, that it is not the number of pages that is important, it is what is on those pages that really matters.

As you have probably surmised, qualitative as well as quantitative standards are usually necessary to communicate instructional intent. Qualitative standards may imply subjective judgments but should describe the particular attributes or characteristics that must be included in the terminal behavior demonstration if that demonstration is to be declared acceptable. For example, the previously stated objectives could be improved by restating them as follows:

The student will be able to:

1. Describe, in a paper of no more than two pages, the results of World War II in terms of the economic development of France, Germany, and the United States.

2. Within one class period, type a personal letter and a business letter, each of which is error-free and no more than one page in length.

As rewritten, the above objectives communicate instructional intent more clearly and minimize the chances of misunderstandings occuring.

One problem in attempting to establish qualitative standards is that in judging a terminal behavior such as the two above, you will undoubtedly consider many factors such as logical organization, completeness, relevancy, neatness, spelling, and punctuation errors, which are either too common or too nebulous to specify. The common kinds of standards, as the common kinds of conditions, can be stated at the beginning of the list of objectives thus relieving you of the obligation of stating them for each separate objective. Common standards such as "all papers will be typed or written in ink and contain fewer than six spelling and/or punctuation errors," are sufficient to inform students that these standards will be applied to all appropriate objectives.

The task of specifying standards regarding logical organization, completeness, relevancy, and similar nebulous factors is one that many teachers find extremely difficult. In order to reduce the difficulty of stating complex or nebulous standards, some teachers have found that specifying particular points to be included in the paper or skill demonstration successfully communicates to the student what is expected of him.

In the first objective above, the parameter "in terms of the economic development of France, Germany, and the United States" gives the student a clear picture of how he is to orient his answer and what the minimum points to include are.

Since it would be impractical to include all possible qualitative standards, an acceptable alternative is to specify as many of the parameters as necessary to communicate instructional intent. The fact that all possible standards are not included in each objective should not be taken as an abdication of your right or your professional obligation to make judgments concerning overall quality. You are simply acknowledging the fact that certain behaviors are highly complex and are therefore attempting to convey instructional intent by specifying as many important parameters as possible.

One further point concerning qualitative standards. If you want students to refer to particular ideas, points, or aspects when demonstrating a terminal behavior you should identify those points in the objective. Terms such as "main ideas," "most important points," and "major aspects" should be used only when you are willing to accept the student's opinion regarding these matters. If you are not precise in describing a terminal behavior, you should not make students bear the consequences of misinterpretation.

As a brief review, the three components of a precise instructional objective are: an observable terminal behavior; conditions under which that behavior is to be demonstrated; and a minimum acceptable standard of performance.

3. How Can Precise Instructional Objectives Improve the Teaching-Learning Process? By exposing educational goals to critical analysis and by utilizing precise instructional objectives, not only does the question of "are schools doing their job" become answerable, but all those concerned can examine exactly what that job is and can make suggestions regarding the addition, deletion, and modification of objectives to help bring the schools' job more in line with what they believe it should be.

There is no doubt that stating precise instructional objectives and allowing all who want to see and criticize them to do so is a trying experience. The give and take regarding why this is taught and why that is not, however, generally serves to strengthen education by forcing educators to assess very carefully the merits of each course offered and/or each objective set forth.

By delineating clear and definite goals for teachers and students, the teaching-learning process is also improved. Stating instructional goals in terms of observable and measurable activities enables both you and your students to pinpoint those instructional goals deemed especially important and provides a way of determining when those goals have been accomplished.

If one compares formal education to the acquisition of knowledge from a vast storehouse, stating precise instructional objectives is comparable to planning a route through the storehouse and specifying a set of minimum acquisitions. Since both the time and money available for exploration of the storehouse is limited, the alternative to the above—allowing students to wander aimlessly through the storehouse acquiring bits and pieces of information at random, if at all—is not acceptable to either students, teachers, or taxpayers.

One should no more engage in teaching-learning activities without stating a specific instructional goal than one should set out on a trip without first deciding upon a destination. In either case, since you do not know exactly where you want to go, you can do little more than name a general direction of travel. Precisely stated instructional objectives act as a road map enabling you to specify your destination(s) and telling you how you will know when you arrive. Sometimes detours are necessary but they should be made for rational reasons.

Just as specifying a destination prior to embarking upon a trip enables you to select the best routes and means of travel and to avoid needless delays, stating instructional goals precisely enables you to select those particular materials and procedures which are most likely to help your students achieve the stated goals. Consider the following example:

—The student will be able to recite, without error, any given segment of the multiplication tables (1-12).

The objective itself suggests the means to its achievement. For example, there is no doubt that at some point in your planned instruction you will have to deal with multiplication tables. Since the objective specifies recitation as the observable terminal behavior, you know that you will have to provide some kind of practice for your students. This practice will entail either analogous practice such as writing segments of the multiplication tables, equivalent practice such as actual recitation periods, or preferably, both. In any case, precisely stated objectives suggest appropriate materials and procedures by pinpointing exactly to what skills or information students will have to be exposed, and in what kinds of observable behaviors they will need analogous and equivalent practice.

Objectives help make the evaluation of materials, procedures, and student achievement more objective and precise. If it is known prior to instruction exactly what students should be able to do after instruction, the teacher can evaluate the materials and procedures used during instruction to see to what extent they helped students achieve the objective. If students are unable to accomplish the objectives after instruction, it may be (but not necessarily) that either the materials or the procedures, or both, need to be changed.

Students also benefit from precisely stated objectives because they can compare their abilities before instruction and study, with their abilities after, and see concrete gains. The fact that the means of evaluation is clearly stated reduces the chance that a student will feel that a biased evaluation has been made and will increase his faith in his own abilities.

Since parents and administrators have a right to know exactly what is going on in your classroom, precise instructional objectives can again assist you. After reading your precise instructional objectives, parents and/or administrators can assess the legitimacy of your goals as well as your effectiveness in helping students to achieve them. Since your instructional goals are stated specifically and objectively, their assessments of what you are doing and how well you are doing it will also tend to be specific and objective.

Precise objectives function as both a pretest and a morale builder. By including in your precise instructional objectives some which are really prerequisites to the course, you are not only able to ascertain exactly where each of your students is academically, but can, at the same time, make it possible for the majority of your students to achieve success early in the term by achieving those objectives.

Knowing exactly where each student stands academically also enables you to explain why some students are farther along in their work than others and thus protects you from charges of incompetence (if all of your students do not achieve the minimum objectives).

Precise instructional objectives increase your confidence and sense of purpose. Robert Mager has voiced the opinion that a teacher has no business in front of a class if he or she cannot state exactly what is to be accomplished.[3] This opinion is particularly valid if you consider the image conveyed to students, parents, administrators, associates, and even yourself, when you know exactly what you intend to accomplish as compared with the image conveyed when your goals are nebulous. The confidence and sense of purpose generated by a set of precise instructional objectives is easily communicated to others and tends to cause them to have more faith in you and your ability. Being able to generate a feeling of confidence is certainly helpful in facilitating the teaching-learning process, and precisely stated instructional objectives can help generate such a feeling. Precise instructional objectives can, in short, help make you more professional.

In summary then, some of the ways the utilization of precise instructional objectives can help improve the teaching-learning process are by:

1. Exposing educational goals to critical analysis.
2. Providing clear and definite goals for both the student and the teacher.
3. Facilitating the selection of appropriate instructional materials and procedures.
4. Making the evaluation of materials, procedures, and student achievement more objective and precise.
5. Functioning as both a pretest and a morale builder.
6. Increasing your confidence and sense of purpose.

4. What Are Some of the Disadvantages of Precise Instructional Objectives? A number of educators, including James Popham[4] and R. J. Kibler et al.,[5] have answered opponents of precise instructional objectives. Many of the arguments and counter arguments concerning the disadvantages of precise instructional objectives are presented below.

One disadvantage cited was that precise objectives seem to

concern trivial and unimportant educational goals. This disadvantage is directed more to the abuse of a tool than as an inherent weakness. Very often teachers are pressured into writing precise instructional objectives without first being given adequate instruction. The resulting objectives are often narrow, restrictive, and very low on the scale of cognitive levels (which range from mere memorization, through application and analysis, to synthesis and evaluation). When low cognitive-level objectives such as "recite" this, or "list, in writing," are allowed to dominate the teaching-learning process, the intellectual development of the students may be seriously hampered. Unfortunately, since low-level cognitive objectives are the easiest to write, many teachers simply produce lists of such objectives and assume they are helping their students. When *only* low-level cognitive objectives are used, their use does indeed weaken the teaching-learning process and opens educators to charges of being irrelevant and concerned with minutiae. The easiest way to avoid this criticism is to avoid using low-level cognitive objectives. Writing objectives for the higher cognitive levels is more difficult and requires more thought, but the rewards are greater.

You should be aware of the fact that precise instructional objectives are a part of a hierarchy of goals and objectives. One such hierarchy is described next.

At the very top of the scale are the broad kinds of goals suitable for use in a school's statement of philosophy. One such goal might be: "The student will be able to communicate with others both orally and in writing, in a manner that satisfies his need for expression and the requirements of those under whom he may become employed or receives further education."

A second level of goals reflects the objectives of specific programs, such as a Language Arts program within a school. A typical program goal might be: "The student is able to apply correctly the conventions of English grammar and usage in speaking and writing."

A third level of goals reflects the objectives of particular courses within a program. Typical goals at this level might be: "The student will know that special verb forms exist for use with singular and plural subjects; and the student is able to use appropriate singular and plural subjects."

A fourth level of objectives reflects a more refined view of how both you and your students will know when the course goals have been achieved. It is at this level that you would definitely use what we have described as precise instructional objectives. A typical objective at this level might be: "Given twenty sentences, ten with plural subjects and ten with singular subjects, the student will list, in writing, the correct number form of the verb (is, are) with at least 90 percent accuracy."[6]

A part of the problem concerning triviality in precise instructional objectives may be that teachers, thinking primarily in terms of objectives at the third and fourth, and sometimes only at the fourth level, fail to show the relationship of these objectives to the larger goals. It is possible, for example, to assume that the last goal shown above is trivial. It becomes a rather important goal, however, when it is seen in its proper relationship to each of the other goals listed.

The specification of particular texts, page numbers, stories, and/or sources is usually inappropriate at any of the above mentioned levels because the desired behavior should be applicable to more than just a single instance. Consider the following examples:

1. The student will be able to analyze, in writing, any short story by Edgar Allen Poe, in terms of plot, antagonist, and protagonist.

2. The student will be able to analyze, in writing, any short story, in terms of plot, antagonist, and protagonist.

The second objective includes a much greater range of experiences than does the first and is therefore a more desirable objective.

Another disadvantage cited for precise instructional objectives is that they can limit and restrict the teaching-learning process. Again we are dealing with an abuse of precise instructional objectives rather than with an inherent weakness. Only when a teacher allows them to do so can precise instructional objectives limit or restrict the teaching-learning process. Precise instructional objectives are a tool. They specify a *minimum* set of competencies to be acquired by students, but they constitute no holy writ or legal contract. There is no reason why these objectives cannot be changed or modified to meet changing needs, and no reason why they should limit what goes on in the classroom. Remember, they comprise a minimum set of competencies, not a maximum set. It is expected that students will acquire far more information and skill than is specified in the list of precise instructional objectives, and those teachers who go no further than their stated objectives are definitely misusing them. It would be foolish, for example, for a teacher to stifle the exploration of an idea that catches the interest of the class simply because there is no objective listed concerning that idea. If the teacher provides no objectives at all, however, the students will have little recourse other than to waste their time and energies bouncing from one disconnected idea to another. Research has shown that student performance very closely parallels teacher expectations. Remember this as you write your objectives.

Another disadvantage: some of the more intuitive and subjective elements of the teaching-learning process may either be eliminated entirely, or so changed by being forced into the precise instructional objective mold, as to be useless. Some educators feel that aspects of the teaching-learning process can no more be minutely dissected, labeled, and measured than can the surface of a bubble; the very act of examining it destroys it. To the extent that this claim is accurate, precise instructional objectives can definitely be harmful.

And finally, by their very attempt to impose order and precision on the teaching-learning process, precise instructional objectives crush the spontaneity and learn-for-the-sake-of-learning attitude essential for true education. Here again, if precise instructional objectives crush spontaneity, they do so because the teachers using them allow them to do so. It is the person, not the tool, that is causing the problem. The mechanization and dehumanization which some people attribute to precise instructional objectives exist only if one considers having a demonstrable goal mechanistic or dehumanizing. In a mass education system, attempting to operate without demonstrable goals invites chaos and dissatisfaction among all concerned.

In review then, some of the disadvantages associated with the utilization of precise instructional objectives are:

1. They seem to concern trivial and unimportant educational goals.

2. They can limit and restrict the teaching-learning process.

3. They can eliminate entirely some of the more subtle, intuitive, and subjective elements of the teaching-learning

process or force these elements into such an unnatural mold as to make them useless; and

4. By their very attempt to impose order and precision on the teaching-learning process, they can crush the spontaneity and learn-for-the-sake-of-learning attitude essential for true education.

It is hoped that the examination of these disadvantages makes clear the fact that rather than being real disadvantages, most of the points examined are really abuses. Precise instructional objectives are an educational tool. How that tool is used is crucial.

5. *Is the Use of Precise Instructional Objectives Increasing or Decreasing?* There is little doubt that the use of precise instructional objectives is increasing. Almost all professional education journals contain articles concerning precise instructional objectives and textbook publishers are turning out whole series of books containing not only specific precise instructional objectives, but also the instructions and content necessary for their accomplishment.

As a teacher, you will probably come into contact with precise instructional objectives in one of three ways. You may be asked to *select* a series of precise instructional objectives from a book of such objectives and to base your instruction on those objectives. Westinghouse Learning Corporation puts out four such volumes[7] and these can be examined in the teaching materials center of virtually any university library.

You may be asked to *rewrite,* in precise terms, nebulous objectives that were previously in a curriculum guide or a course syllabus. It is important that you recognize that to rewrite a general objective such as "understand the Bill of Rights," will require significant work. The objective first must be analyzed to determine just what is being sought, it must then be broken into manageable segments and finally each segment must be cast in precise terms. Converting general objectives into precise instructional objectives is seldom an easy task, and seldom is it possible to convert one general objective into just one precise instructional objective.

Another way in which you may come into contact with precise instructional objectives is simply being asked to write them for your own class. This method or option is by far the best for you because it allows you to capitalize upon the specific requirements of your students and your own academic abilities. When you have to use someone else's objectives, they may, or may not, take these factors into consideration.

There is at least one other way in which you may come into contact with precise instructional objectives and that is when a commercial company, such as Behavioral Research Laboratories, contracts with your school system, as BRL did with the Gary, Indiana, school system, to take over all or part of the education of the system's students. This "performance contracting" is based wholly on precise instructional objectives, but since the contracting company often brings in its own teachers or hires selected teachers from the contracting school system, you may or may not be a part of the program.

6. How Do I Go About Writing and Using Precise Instructional Objectives? The first step in writing precise instructional objectives is to sit down and list all the information and skills that you definitely want your students to acquire. It is your responsibility, by virtue of your position and training, to try to select the most meaningful and important goals of your academic area.

Some of the factors you will want to consider to formulate a list of objectives include: the needs and desires of your students, the expectations of the community and school administration, legal requirements, the structure of your subject area, and your own academic strengths and weaknesses.

Sources to which you can turn for ideas for appropriate objectives include: newer texts, compilations of objectives such as that published by Westinghouse Learning,[8] instructional objective exchanges such as that operated by Dr. James Popham,[9] other teachers, curriculum guides, and unit plans.

After the list is as complete as you can make it, phrase each objective in terms that make its accomplishment observable and measurable, add in any conditions that you feel are important, and state a minimum acceptable standard of performance. Tell the student and yourself exactly what has to be done to accomplish the objective. Writing precise instructional objectives is a time-consuming and exacting task, but the time is well-spent because the objectives you write will pave the way to effective and successful teaching-learning experiences.

Organize the precise instructional objectives in some logical order (easy-to-difficult, specific-to-general, etc.) so that students can make steady progress toward their accomplishment.

Add to the list any objectives suggested by students. This is an important step. The basic list of objectives will naturally be compiled by you since it is you who are the expert in your particular area. It would be grossly unfair to deny students the opportunity to include their own ideas also, however, because they and you both share an involvement in the teaching-learning process. Just be sure to phrase their suggested objectives in precise terms.

Test your objectives in a number of ways. Asking a friend, student, or associate to read them and then to tell you what he thinks he would have to do to accomplish them is one way. If his interpretation differs from yours, or if you find yourself saying, "What I really meant was . . .," then rewrite the misleading objective(s).

As another way of checking how well an objective is stated, Robert Mager suggests asking yourself whether another competent person could, on the basis of the objectives you wrote, agree with your identification of students who successfully achieved the objective.

The testing of your objectives is crucial because very frequently you will read into an objective more than you put down on paper. Someone who is less familiar with the objectives is less likely to read into them things that are not there. It is strongly recommended that a second person, preferably a student, double-check your instructional intent and the precision with which you express it.

A good rule of thumb is that each objective should be able to stand by itself. If, for example, you were to take one of the objectives out of the list of objectives, it should make sense all by itself. To assure this is so be sure to have a sampling of students read the objectives. Their reading abilities may be different from your perceptions of those abilities.

Prior to the beginning of actual instruction, hand the list of precise instructional objectives to the students and discuss them. Having the list will enable students to know exactly what will be expected of them and will help them see the relevance of the teaching-learning activities. As instruction proceeds, it is assumed that you will frequently point out the relevance of particular learning activities to the accomplishment of particular objectives.

Do not hesitate to add, delete, or modify precise instructional objectives or the teaching-learning activities associated with them simply because they are written down. Provided you use as much care in the addition, deletion, or modification of objectives as you should have used in their original writing, the changes can make the objectives fit the needs of you and your students more closely.

7. What Are Some of the Common Errors and How Might I Go About Correcting Them? One of the common errors made when writing precise instructional objectives is the *omission of an observable behavior*. Although a precise instructional objective without an observable behavior is a contradiction in terms, you will probably encounter such objectives. The following examples may help you recognize them and be able to rewrite them.

Lacking an observable terminal behavior

The student will be able to:

1. Know the difference between a debit and a credit.

2. Understand the power of mass media to influence public opinion.

3. Grasp the significance of the "rules of the road."

Rewritten in acceptable form

The student will be able to:

1. Define, in writing, the terms "debit" and "credit" and give an example of each.

2. Describe, in writing, at least two kinds of mass media and describe in no more than one page, why, in his or her opinion, one has a greater influence on public opinion than the other. Support answers with examples.

3. List, in writing, at least three "rules of the road," and state at least one probable consequence of violating each rule.

(These objectives are not intended to include all the knowledge, etc. implied by ambiguous terms such as "know" and "understand.")

Another common error made when writing precise instructional objectives is the *omission of a minimum acceptable standard*. This error is usually made because the writer of the objective knows just what he has in mind but neglects to put in on paper clearly. The following examples may help you to recognize such objectives and be able to rewrite them.

Lacking a minimum acceptable standard

The student will be able to:
1. Read and understand material written at a tenth-grade level.
2. Write a short paper dealing with his views of mandatory education.
3. Write a poem.

Rewritten in acceptable form

The student will be able to:
1. Given a page of material written at a tenth-grade level, read the material within ten minutes and achieve a score of at least 80 percent on a written comprehension test dealing with the material read.

(Note: Although a time limit is not usually a crucial minimum acceptable standard, in certain kinds of objectives, such as the one above, it is critical.)

2. In a paper of no more than three pages, state his or her position on the issue of mandatory education and substantiate this position by references to specific facts or examples.

3. Write a poem of at least four lines in iambic pentameter.

Still another common error made when writing precise instructional objectives is *having an objective imply one behavior but call for another.* This problem usually arises when the objective writer has a broad, general objective in mind but finds that to measure accomplishment of that objective he must ask for either a more specific, or a completely different behavior than the one implied. The following examples illustrate objectives in which the behaviors sought are not those to be demonstrated, and show how these objectives might be rewritten in acceptable form.

The behavior sought is not that which is to be demonstrated.

The student will be able to:
1. Demonstrate his or her knowledge of ice skating by executing a figure eight.
2. Show his or her understanding of the War of 1812 by naming two generals involved in it.
3. Demonstrate his or her ability to bake a cake by describing the ingredients to be used, how they are to be combined, and how long the cake should bake.

Each set of rewritten objectives reflects the two behaviors called for in each of the original objectives.

The student will be able to:

1. Demonstrate his or her knowledge of ice skating by listing, in writing, at least two current ice skating stars and by describing at least two evolutions of the modern ice skate; or

Demonstrate his or her figure-skating ability by executing a figure eight forwards and backwards.

2. Show his or her understanding of the War of 1812, in part, by describing, in writing, at least two causes and two effects of that war; or

Demonstrate his or her ability to memorize the names of generals involved in early American wars by listing, in writing, the names of two generals involved in the War of 1812.

3. Demonstrate his or her ability to bake a cake by selecting, combining, and baking the appropriate ingredients to produce a cake eight inches square and at least one inch high; or

Describe the procedure for baking a cake by indicating, in writing, the ingredients to be used, how they are to be combined, and how long the cake should bake.

(Note: The important point is that the behavior implied must be the behavior demonstrated. One does not demonstrate an ability to swim by talking about it—one swims.)

8. What Is the Relationship Between Objectives in the Cognitive and Affective Domains? Instructional objectives are usually divided into three taxonomic domains: the *Cognitive* (which concerns itself with "the recall or recognition of knowledge and the development of intellectual abilities and skills"[10]); the *Psychomotor* (which concerns itself with manipulative and motor skills); and the *Affective* (which concerns itself with "changes in interest, attitudes, and values, and the development of appreciations and adequate adjustment."[11])

Objectives written for the cognitive domain or the psychomotor domain (as are all of the objectives in this chapter) cause teachers relatively few problems. The task of writing objectives for the affective domain is somewhat more difficult. Here are some of the problems with the affective domain as described by Dr. Benjamin Bloom.

Objectives in this domain are not stated very precisely; and, in fact, teachers do not appear to be very clear about the learning experiences which are appropriate to these objectives. It is difficult to describe the behaviors appropriate to these objectives

since the internal or covert feelings and emotions are as significant for this domain as are the overt behavioral manifestations.
Then, too, our testing procedures for the affective domain are
still in the most primitive stages.[12]

Two difficulties, then, in writing objectives for the affective
domain are: (1) that it is not possible to observe the terminal behavior
directly, and (2) measurement of the terminal behavior, in order to
determine whether or not it has been achieved, is imprecise. Consider
the following affective-domain objective:

—The student will demonstrate respect for the flag by standing
during the Pledge of Allegiance.

Since it is impossible to see "respect" per se, the first step in
stating this objective was determining an observable behavior which
we could accept as reflecting the terminal behavior (respect) that we
were really after. It is immediately apparent that "standing during the
Pledge of Allegiance" may, or may not, truly reflect "respect."

A second logical step (which has not been taken) would be to
determine some minimum percentage of times the student would
have to demonstrate the behavior before we could assume the objective has been accomplished.

The utilization of affective-domain objectives also differs from
that of either cognitive- or psychomotor-domain objectives in
another respect. When you write cognitive- or psychomotor-domain
objectives, you give them to students prior to instruction so that they
will know exactly what is expected of them. If you were to follow this
procedure when dealing with an affective-domain objective, such as
one concerning an attitude, you could not be sure that the attitude
being displayed was real, or whether it was being temporarily
generated for your benefit.

Although the use of precise instructional objectives in the
affective domain is more difficult and less precise than their use in the
cognitive domain, you should not, and in reality cannot, ignore it. It
is a mistake, in fact, to even consider the two domains as separate or
distinct entities. Feelings and emotions affect our perceptions and our
actions whether we want them to or not. Regardless of how diligently
we may try to deal only with factual information or skills in the
classroom, for example, we will deal also with attitudes and values if
by no means other than by the examples we set. Since both domains

affect the student, you, as an educator, should be able to write objectives in both areas. You should be aware, however, that some educators seriously question whether or not the focusing of instruction purely to change attitudes is a legitimate educational endeavor. These educators maintain that the primary function of public education is to provide students with a sufficiently extensive background of factual information and cognitive skills to enable them to reach their own conclusions and develop their own attitudes.

In light of the difficulties involved with writing objectives in the affective domain, and the disagreement among educators as to the legitimacy of this endeavor, you would probably do well to explore more thoroughly the issues involved and to reach your own conclusions. At the current time more emphasis is being given to the cognitive domain than to the affective domain.

SUMMARY

A precise instructional objective is a statement of instructional intent. It contains an observable terminal behavior, conditions under which that behavior is expected to occur, and a minimum acceptable standard of performance.

Precise instructional objectives can help to improve the teaching-learning process by providing clear and definite goals for you and your students. They facilitate the selection of appropriate instructional materials and procedures and make evaluation of student achievement more objective and precise. Precise objectives function as pretests and morale builders, and will increase your sense of confidence and purpose. Abuses of precise instructional objectives, however, such as writing them only on a low cognitive level, having them concern trivial or unimportant goals, or allowing them to restrict or dominate the teaching-learning process, can seriously interfere with that process.

Since the use of precise instructional objectives is increasing rapidly, and since you may be asked to either select, rewrite, or write them for your own use, it is wise to have a procedure to follow. One procedure involves listing the information and skills you want your students to acquire, casting those desires into observable and measurable objectives, organizing the objectives, providing for student input, testing the objectives, handing them to students prior to instruction, making whatever modifications may be necessary to tailor the objectives to the exact needs of you and your students, and then frequently pointing out how particular learning activities help students accomplish particular objectives.

Some of the common errors made when writing precise instructional objectives include omitting an observable behavior, omitting a minimum acceptable standard, and implying one behavior but having the objective call for another. Care in writing the objectives can eliminate these errors.

There is a close relationship between the cognitive and the affective domain. At the present time, the observation and measurement of cognitive objectives (those dealing with the acquisition of information or skills) is more certain and precise than is the observation and measurement of affective objectives (those dealing with feelings, emotions, values, and attitudes). Even so, it is a grave error to ignore the affective domain or even think of it as a separate entity. The two domains are inextricably combined and although the cognitive domain is of primary concern to us now; as more precise measures become available for the affective domain, it may increase greatly in importance.

LEARNING ACTIVITY 2: The following are samples of precise instructional objectives that meet the criteria of acceptability described earlier; that is, each contains an observable terminal behavior, conditions under which the behavior is expected to occur, and a minimum acceptable standard of performance. Study them and identify each component.

History The student will be able to:

1. Write, in class, a paper of no more than two pages, describing two technological similarities between the Civil War and World War II.

2. Given graphs showing the supply of a product and the demand for that product, list, in writing, when the selling prices would be greatest and least.

English The student will be able to:

1. Given an editorial containing statements of fact and statements of opinion, underline at least 90 percent of the opinions.

2. Select three of Shakespeare's plays and list in writing, without the use of aids, the antagonist, protagonist, and type (comedy, tragedy, etc.) of each.

Science   The student will be able to:

1. Write, from memory, the names of five compounds, five mixtures, and five elements.

2. Given the appropriate equipment and one hour, determine and list, in writing, the amounts of each component of a given mixture.

Mathematics   The student will be able to:

1. Given a yardstick, determine and write down the number of square yards of carpeting needed to carpet a specified room.

2. Compute and write the amount due on a loan of a given amount, and held for a given length of time at a given rate of interest.

Note: All of the objectives begin "The student will be able to . . ." because under ideal conditions you would be able to tailor objectives to meet each student's individual needs. In reality, we assume students selected at random would be able to demonstrate achievement of any objective.

LEARNING ACTIVITY 3:   None of the following objectives is stated in acceptable form. Use the rating scale below to pinpoint the weakness(es) in each objective, rewrite the objective in acceptable form, and check your responses with those furnished.

> *Rating scale*
> 1. Lacks an observable behavior
> 2. Lacks a minimum acceptable standard
> 3. Both 1 and 2
> 4. The terminal behavior sought is not that which is to be demonstrated

The student will be able to:

1. Know the democratic principles upon which our country is founded.

2. Be an alert and an aware citizen.

3. Study and eventually understand the importance of the coda and cadenza to concertos.

4. Know the names of the U.S. senators from his or her home state.

5. Demonstrate comprehension of selected accounting practices

by correctly doing certain accounting forms selected by the teacher.

6. Verbally communicate effectively.

7. Demonstrate his medical diagnostic skill by prescribing appropriate medication for a surgery patient.

8. Be physically fit.

9. Take an active role in society.

10. Demonstrate typing skill by typing two letters.

11. Write a proper letter.

12. Understand the plight of the poor people in our country.

13. Demonstrate an understanding of democratic principles by stating the three branches of our federal government.

14. List, in writing, the strengths and weaknesses of the United Nations.

15. Demonstrate an ability to write precise instructional objectives by achieving a score of at least 80 percent on a forced-choice test dealing with behavioral objectives.

Answers

1. 3	4. 1	7. 4	10. 2	13. 4
2. 3	5. 3	8. 3	11. 2	14. 2
3. 3	6. 2	9. 3	12. 3	15. 4

Possible Rewrites   (Other variations may also be acceptable):

The student will be able, without aids and within one class period, to:

1. List in writing the requirements for elections, and length of terms, of U.S. congressmen.

2. Select a current legislative issue and write a letter to the appropriate congressman expressing his or her views on that issue and citing supporting examples and/or facts.

3. Describe, in a paper of no more than two pages, the function of the coda and cadenza in a concerto.

4. Write the names and political parties of the U.S. senators from his or her home state.

5. Given the appropriate ledger and journal entries, construct a balance sheet with no errors.

6. Using oral commands only, guide a blindfolded student around the room with sufficient accuracy to keep the student from bumping into no more than two objects.

7. Given four sets of symptoms, diagnose the correct disease in at least three of the cases.

8. Within medical restrictions, if any, meet or exceed the standards set by the President's Council on Physical Fitness, for his or her age group.

9. Write a letter to the editor of the local paper expressing his or her views of a current local problem and supporting the viewpoint with specific facts and/or examples.

10. Type two letters demonstrating two different business forms without errors.

11. Write a one-page letter consisting of a heading, salutation, body, and closing in block style without error.

12. Describe in a paper of no more than two pages at least three factors inhibiting the elimination of poverty within our country and cite supporting facts and/or examples.

13. Demonstrate an understanding of democratic principles, in part, by stating the three branches of our federal government and explaining, with the use of examples, how these interrelationships might safeguard any democratic process.

14. List, in writing and within thirty minutes, at least two strengths and two weaknesses of the United Nations as a decision-making body.

15. Demonstrate an ability to write precise instructional objectives by writing three such objectives, each of which contains all component parts.

LEARNING ACTIVITY 4:   For further discussion and/or other viewpoints, read any or all of the following:

1. D. Cecil Clark, *Using Instructional Objectives in Teaching* (Glenview, Ill.: Scott, Foresman, 1972).

2. Robert F. Mager, *Preparing Instructional Objectives* (Palo Alto, Calif.: Fearon Publishers, 1962).

3. Paul D. Plowman, *Behavioral Objectives* (Chicago: Science Research Associates, 1971).

4. James Popham and Eva L. Baker, *Systematic Instruction* (Englewood Cliffs, N.J.: Prentice-Hall, 1970).

EVALUATION

The objectives of this chapter will be demonstrated via both an objective and a written test. Take the following self-test as practice for the formal evaluation.

PART 1

Read each question carefully and then select the correct or most correct answer.

1. Of the following, which is the most desirable terminal behavior?

(1) orally state, (2) underline, (3) appreciate, (4) understand, (5) know.

2. The use of precise instructional objectives guarantees that all students will learn effectively.

(1) true, (2) false.

3. Before precise instructional objectives are used, at least two people should have worked with them (including the writer).

(1) true, (2) false.

PART 2

Use the following rating scale to pinpoint the weakness(es), if any, in each of the following objectives:

Rating Scale

1. Lacks an observable behavior.

2. Lacks a minimum acceptable standard.

3. Both 1 and 2.

4. The terminal behavior sought is not that which is to be demonstrated.

5. The objective is acceptable.

The student will be able to:

4. Write a critical reaction to *Moby Dick*.

5. Write the names of two great men.

6. Recite the Pledge of Allegiance without error.

7. Demonstrate his or her knowledge of forest growth by correctly selecting the proper power saw with which to cut plywood.

8. Understand quadratic equations well enough to correctly solve, on paper, any three that are given, without the use of aids and within thirty minutes.

9. Demonstrate easy mathematical skills with at least 80 percent accuracy.

10. Fully understand the terms volt, ohm, and alternating current.

11. Demonstrate good physical condition by running the mile in less than six minutes.

12. Given a series of names, list them correctly, in writing.

13. Demonstrate knowledge of meat preparation by stating at least two ways to prepare each of the following: beef, veal, and lamb.

14. Translate written French into written English.

15. Be proud to be an American 85 percent of the time.

ANSWERS

Part 1	Part 2			
1. 2	4. 2	7. 4	10. 1	13. 5
2. 2	5. 2	8. 5	11. 5	14. 2
3. 1	6. 5	9. 1	12. 2	15. 1

PART 3

Rewrite each of the following objectives so that each contains an observable terminal behavior, conditions under which that behavior will occur, and a minimum acceptable standard.

16. The student will be able to develop good instructional objectives.

17. The student will know why precise instructional objectives are important.

PART 4

Write three precise instructional objectives dealing with your special field of knowledge. Each of these objectives must contain an observable terminal behavior, conditions under which that behavior will occur, and a minimum acceptable standard.

PART 5

18. You will be able to write, without aids and within ten minutes, two precise instructional objectives each of which contains an observable terminal behavior, any necessary conditions, and a minimum acceptable standard.

19. You will be able to list, in writing, at least two reasons for the wide acceptance of precise instructional objectives.

PART 6

Since the ultimate objective of this chapter is to develop your ability to write acceptable precise instructional objectives, take this opportunity to write three or four (or more) precise instructional objectives and have them checked by a friend, an associate, or your instructor. As with anything else, writing good precise instructional objectives requires some practice. Take your time, and write good objectives.

NOTES

1. Robert F. Mager, *Preparing Instructional Objectives,* (Palo Alto, Calif.: Fearon, 1962).

2. Ibid.

3. Robert F. Mager, Behavioral Objective Workshop, Illinois State University, August 10, 1971.

4. James Popham, "Probing the Validity of Arguments Against Behavioral Goals." Paper presented at the February 9-10, 1968, American Education Research Association Meeting in Chicago, Illinois.

5. R. J. Kibler, L. B. Barker, and D. T. Miles, *Behavioral Objectives and Instruction,* (Boston: Allyn and Bacon, 1970).

6. Victor Doherty and Walter Hathaway, "Goals and Objectives in Planning Evaluation: A Second Generation," in National Council on Measurement in Education, *Measurement in Education,* Vol. 4, No. 1 Fall 1972, p. 3-4.

7. John Flanagan, William Shanner, and Robert Mager, *Behavior Objectives: Volume 1—Language Arts; Volume 2—Social Studies; Volume 3—Science; Volume 4—Mathematics,* (Palo Alto, Calif.: Westinghouse Learning Press, 1971).

8. Ibid.

9. James Popham, The Instructional Objectives Exchange, P.O. Box 24095, Los Angeles, Calif. 90024.

10. Benjamin S. Bloom, ed., *Taxonomy of Educational Objectives, Handbook 1: Cognitive Domain,* (New York; David McKay, 1965), p. 7.

11. Ibid.

12. Ibid.

chapter 3

Taxonomy of Instructional Objectives

OBJECTIVES

1. Given a list of objectives, you will be able to discriminate by selecting among affective, cognitive, and psychomotor objectives with at least 80 percent accuracy.

2. Given a list of objectives at various levels of the cognitive domain, you will be able to discriminate between those that are at the lowest cognitive level (knowledge) and those that are higher with at least 80 percent accuracy.

3. Given a set of cognitive objectives, you will be able to select the general level represented—knowledge, comprehension, application, analysis, synthesis, and evaluation—with at least 80 percent accuracy.

4. Given a set of affective objectives, you will be able to select the general level represented—receiving, responding, valuing, organizing, and characterizing—with at least 80 percent accuracy.

5. Given subject matter from your major area of study, write one instructional objective for each major level of the cognitive domain—knowledge, comprehension, application, analysis, synthesis, and evaluation—which includes the three basic criteria for acceptably written objectives.

6. Given the specified format for writing affective objectives, you will be able to write one instructional objective at each level of the affective domain.

PREASSESSMENT

Make use of the questions below as you proceed with this chapter. Each question is followed by a number that links it to the *Instructional Procedures* included in this chapter.

1. What are the three domains in which objectives are written? *(1)*

2. What type of skills fall within the cognitive domain? *(2)*

3. Is the cognitive domain limited to simple recall of information, or are more complex skills required? *(2)*

4. What areas do the affective domain encompass? *(3)*

5. Which do schools emphasize more (as reflected by their evaluation procedures), the cognitive domain or the affective domain? *(3)*

6. What kinds of skills make up the psychomotor domain? *(4)*

7. What are the four major areas of the psychomotor domain? *(4)*

8. In what courses is more emphasis placed on the psychomotor domain? *(4)*

9. In what courses is more emphasis placed on the cognitive domain? *(5)*

10. In what courses is more emphasis placed on the affective domain? *(5)*

11. Do objectives always fall within only one of the three domains? If not, could you give an example of an objective that would involve two domains? Three domains? *(5)*

12. Why are so many objectives written at the lowest cognitive level? *(6)*

13. When tests are prepared for the cognitive domain, do you think the questions generally fall at the lowest cognitive level? *(6)*

14. When objectives are divided into the lowest cognitive level and those higher than this lowest level, which of the six levels of the cognitive domain (is, are) the same as the lowest cognitive level? *(6)*

15. Which of the six levels of the cognitive domain (is, are) the same as those higher than the lowest level? *(6)*

16. What is the reason for an intermediate step in the classifying of objectives? *(6)*

17. What kinds of skills are required at the lowest cognitive level? *(6)*

18. What kinds of skills are required at levels higher than the lowest cognitive level? *(6)*

19. Give two examples of objectives at the lowest cognitive level. *(6)*

20. Give at least two examples of objectives at levels higher than the lowest cognitive level. *(6)*

21. What are the six levels of the cognitive domain? *(7)*

22. Are the lower levels of the cognitive domain always inherent in a higher cognitive objective? *(7)*

23. Give a higher cognitive objective that would include processes from lower cognitive levels. *(7)*

24. What are the three different behaviors involved at the comprehension level? *(9)*

25. Write an objective in your subject area at the comprehension level. *(9)*

26. What is the difference between the comprehension level and the application level? *(9, 10)*

27. Why is the application level so closely related to the later life of the student? *(10)*

28. Give an example within your subject area of a school situation that the student could apply to later life. *(10)*

29. Write an objective in your subject area at the application level. *(10)*

30. What is the basic definition of the analysis level? *(11)*

31. Write an objective in your subject area at the analysis level. *(11)*

32. Explain how synthesis is different from application in relation to the expectations of student products. *(12)*

33. Explain the relationship between synthesis and analysis. *(11, 12)*

34. What is the relationship of synthesis to convergent and divergent thinking? *(12)*

35. What types of class projects would be best suited for synthesis objectives? *(12)*

36. After writing three application objectives and three synthesis objectives, explain the difference between these objectives. *(12)*

37. What part may analysis procedures play in evaluation objectives? *(13)*

38. What part may synthesis procedures play in evaluation objectives? *(13)*

39. Write an objective in your subject matter area at the evaluation level. *(13)*

40. Why are so few affective objectives included in the typical course? *(14)*

41. Why can cognitive objectives be known to the student while the affective objectives should not? *(14)*

42. What are some methods of evaluating students for the affective domain? *(14)*

43. What are the five levels of the affective domain? *(14)*

44. What are the main parts to an affective objective? *(14)*

45. How do affective objectives differ from cognitive objectives? *(14)*

46. What is the relationship of the receiving level of the affective domain to the cognitive domain? *(15)*

47. Write an objective in your subject area at the receiving level. *(15)*

48. How does the responding level differ from the receiving level of the affective domain? *(16)*

49. Write an objective in your subject matter area at the responding level. *(16)*

50. What new element is required at the valuing level that was not required at the lower two levels of this domain? *(17)*

51. Write an objective in your subject area at the valuing level. *(17)*

52. What is the difference between organizing a value system and organizing subject matter? *(18)*

53. Why is the organization level so important among school-oriented procedures? *(18)*

54. Write an objective in your subject matter area at the organization level. *(18)*

55. Why would the characterization level generally not apply to school situations? *(19)*

56. What is the nature of the progression from the lowest level of the affective domain to the highest level? *(19)*

57. Explain the meaning of the following: "Organization of the affective domain is hierarchical by nature." *(19)*

INSTRUCTIONAL PROCEDURES

INTRODUCTION

As you learned while working through the previous chapter, there are many advantages to the precise statement of instructional objectives. The teacher benefits in that objectives help him or her to focus more accurately on the immediate task. The student gains in a number of ways, but perhaps most important to him, is that for once he knows exactly what is expected of him and can proceed immediately toward the completion of that expectation.

While the procedures mentioned are very useful to the prospective teacher, further work on objectives is necessary. In most schools, a majority of the questions asked students are of the simple recall type. Admittedly, there are many facts that we must expect students to learn. In addition, these facts form a basis for manipulation using higher-order mental operations. For example, many tests in social studies classes ask for the recall of dates, names, and places in regard to historical data. Unfortunately, too few tests in this area ask for the application, analysis, or evaluation of these facts. In other words, the test ends with the regurgitation of material. Yet teachers cannot be expected to provide test questions and objectives for higher-order skills in this area called the cognitive domain unless they have been provided with an informational base from which to proceed. This chapter should provide such a base.

The cognitive domain dominates the subject matter areas of the school (with the exception of the skill areas—physical education, art, typing, shorthand, industrial arts, etc.—where psychomotor skills also become quite important). In recent years, however, numerous educators have stressed the need for more emphasis on the affective domain. Many teachers realize the importance of dealing with the affective domain (attitudes, feelings, values, interests, etc.), but they rarely engage in systematic instruction in this area. This chapter should provide teachers with an adequate base so that they can effectively include several levels of the affective domain.

The purpose of this material, then, is to provide you with the necessary information so that you will be able to identify objectives from all three domains (cognitive, affective, and psychomotor). You should be able to write and identify objectives at all major levels of the cognitive and affective domain.

LEARNING ACTIVITY 1:   *1. Three Domains*   The previous chapter dealt with learning to recognize and to write precise instructional objectives. No attempt was made to separate the infinite number of possible objectives into the three major classifications of objectives—cognitive, affective, and psychomotor. Unless teachers are aware of these, they are likely to place undue emphasis on any one to the exclusion of the others. Admittedly, classes or areas of study often emphasize one of the three domains. For example, art, physical education, and industrial education focus primarily on neuromuscular skills—the psychomotor domain—with less time devoted to the teaching of facts, ideas, concepts, or values. Conversely, mathematics and science deal basically with facts, ideas, propositions, and the manipulation of this material, giving less attention to the development of neuromuscular skills or values.

2. The Cognitive Domain   The teaching of intellectual skills falls within the cognitive domain—the teaching of acts, ideas, propositions or concepts and further manipulation of these facts, ideas, propositions, or concepts. As will be discussed later, objectives rarely fall totally within one domain, but their primary emphasis, in the case of the cognitive domain, includes all of the "knowing," "thinking," or "problem-solving" processes. The largest percentage of instructional objectives in the schools would fall within this category.

The cognitive domain includes objectives that range from the simple recall of information to the more complex skills of analyzing or evaluating information on the basis of known criteria. Because it includes such a wide range of intellectual skills, a classification scheme for the cognitive domain will be presented in a later portion of this chapter.

Examples of objectives that fall within this domain include the following:

The student will be able to:

1. List the first three presidents of the United States.

2. Given a list of five types of milling machine cutters, describe the shape and use of at least four.

3. Given two equations, identify the one which represents a circle.

4. Given a textbook and a list of words found within its glossary, locate the glossary and list the definition it gives for each word.

5. Given a list of plural nouns, write the singular form of each one.

6. Using the basic principles of the Dewey and Library of Congress classification systems, devise his or her own logical classification system.

7. Name at least five generals who fought in World War II.

3. The Affective Domain   While the cognitive domain contains the intellectual skills, the affective domain encompasses attitudes, interests, appreciation, and values. Although every educator wants his students to leave that particular course or grade with increased knowledge and intellectual abilities, the educator also wants to instill within the learners certain values and attitudes. This, of course, involves the affective domain. The following objectives, often listed by schools, fall within this domain.

The student will:

1. Appreciate the democratic process
2. Become a better citizen
3. Take pride in his or her citizenship
4. Show evidence of good sportsmanship
5. Appreciate good music
6. Value good workmanship
7. Enjoy mathematics
8. Develop a taste for art
9. Show concern for his fellow man
10. Appreciate good books

Each of the above, while containing an affective intent, lacks the necessary behavior that can be accepted as evidence that a particular value or attitude is held by the student. The following affective objectives better reflect good objective writing. Notice that each is composed of two components, a statement of the attitude or value, followed by the specific behavior which can be accepted as an indication of the value or attitude.

The student will:

1. Show his or her growing interest in good music by attending at least three of five concerts during the school year.

2. Demonstrate his or her belief in good sportsmanship by congratulating his or her opponent at the conclusion of each match.

3. Value good workmanship as evidenced by spending time outside of class to improve his or her industrial arts project after having already received a grade for the project.

4. The Psychomotor Domain The psychomotor domain encompasses those skills which require neuromuscular control and coordination. These motor skills receive major emphasis in such courses as art, physical education, typing, music, industrial education, and home economics. This does not mean, however, that these courses limit themselves to the development of psychomotor skills, or that other courses exclude all psychomotor skills.

While several classifications of psychomotor skills exist, at least one classification system divides this domain into four major areas: (1) gross bodily movements, (2) finely coordinated movements, (3) nonverbal communication behaviors, and (4) speech behaviors.[1] Included in the many possible instructional behaviors desired for the psychomotor domain are shooting a basket, typing a letter, passing a football, producing a certain vocal sound, making a cut with a band saw, sewing on a button, drawing a map, etc.

Objectives in this domain also follow the procedure of precise instructional objectives noted in the previous chapter. Examples follow:

The student will be able to:

1. Make three out of five baskets from the free-throw line.

2. Type a letter of three paragraphs and 150 words in ten minutes with all errors corrected.

3. Swim twenty-five yards without resting or receiving any form of aid.

4. Focus a microscope so that the bacteria can be counted.

5. Play a simple melody of three measures on the piano with no errors.

5. Interrelationship of the Three Domains The illustrative objectives presented in this chapter have, up to this point, fallen within one of the three domains with practically no overlap into the other domains. In actual teaching-learning situations, however, desirable experiences may often include any two of the three domains or conceivably all three. Most writing exercises except copying include the actual motor skill of moving the pen (psychomotor) as well as the cognitive process the student uses to place the proper thoughts on paper (cognitive). Similarly, all speech involves the actual use of mouth-throat muscles to produce the sounds (psychomotor) and the cognitive processes to use words in a meaningful way. In an art class, the teacher may first have a student practice how to draw lines to produce depth (psychomotor), then teach him the relation of lines and other methods of producing depth (cognitive), and finally elicit his beliefs regarding the aesthetic value of these procedures in certain paintings provided for the student (affective).

Throughout this chapter, categorization of objectives into certain domains or into the various levels of a domain is not intended to restrict the learner from writing objectives that cross domains. Nor does it imply that a particular subject or area must focus on objectives within a particular domain. Rather, this categorization should help the learner clarify the various domains and the levels within them for writing effective instructional objectives.

The following exercise will provide practice in identifying objectives in the cognitive, affective, and psychomotor domains. Classify each objective below as affective (A), psychomotor (B), or cognitive (C).

    _____ 1. Given specific criteria and twenty-five sets of alternative solutions, the student will determine which of two possible solutions for each problem of social unrest is most likely to eliminate the problem.

    _____ 2. The student will be able to recite the Emancipation Proclamation from memory with no more than two errors.

    _____ 3. The student will be able to thread a movie projector properly so that when the projector is turned on, the film will not flicker.

_____ 4. The student will show his or her increased interest in band music by attending eight out of ten band concerts offered during the year.

_____ 5. Given thirty quadratic equations, the student will be able to write the correct solutions to at least 80 percent of these problems.

_____ 6. The student will demonstrate his or her concern for the democratic principles of free enterprise by articulating at least one principle verbally during an ungraded class discussion.

_____ 7. The student will show his or her growing awareness of art by participating at least twice in art club discussions.

_____ 8. The student will be able to transfer bacteria from a culture to a petri dish in a manner that produces properly spread colonies. No contamination is permitted.

_____ 9. The student will show his or her interest in world leaders by associating the name of at least three leaders with their countries out of five given in an ungraded inventory.

_____ 10. After reading an article on small engine application, the student will summarize the article in no more than 100 words.

_____ 11. The student will be able to throw a softball no less than thirty yards in a level area.

_____ 12. The student will form the past tense of ten verbs with 80 percent accuracy.

_____ 13. After a study of chord progression, the student will write a twelve-measure composition.

_____ 14. After watching a badminton match, the student will be able to criticize in writing at least three faults which were committed during play.

_____ 15. The student will show appreciation and enjoyment in the foods lab by willingly helping to put the equipment back into its proper place at least three times per week and without threat of his grade being lowered.

Answers are given at the end of the chapter.

LEARNING ACTIVITY 2: *6. Lower and Higher Cognitive Objectives* The first portion of this chapter alluded to the classification of objectives within the cognitive domain using Bloom and others[2] as a base. This classification is necessary if you want your students to reach all or at least most levels of cognition. Since the easiest objectives to write are frequently the most simplistic, a surfeit of objectives and evaluation items have generally been prepared at the lowest cognitive level. Objectives at this level probably outnumber the objectives written at all other levels of the cognitive domain. Therefore, if educators can be taught to discriminate between objectives at the lowest level and those above it, they will have taken a major step toward maximizing their students' abilities.

Before moving to classification at each of the levels, therefore, a transitory step might be taken by dividing the cognitive domain objective into two sections: 1. Those objectives that fall at the lowest level (L); 2. And those objectives that are higher than the lowest cognitive level (H). Using the six major levels of the cognitive domain that will be developed later, this intermediate procedure would classify the six levels as follows:

(L)	Lowest cognitive level	=	Knowledge
			Comprehension
(H)	Higher than the lowest		Application
	cognitive level	=	Analysis
			Synthesis
			Evaluation

The lowest cognitive level, knowledge, includes situations and conditions in which the student is expected to remember, memorize, recall, or otherwise bring to bear information he had previously seen, learned, or been exposed to. Within this level, objectives may range from the recall of specific and isolated material to the knowledge of criteria by which these specifics should be judged.

Examples of objectives at the lowest cognitive level (L) follow:
The student will:
1. Recall eight of the ten major exports of the United States.
2. Given twelve vice-presidents, match at least seven with the correct president.

3. List at least four of the six safety rules presented in the text. It should be noted in the above objectives that remembering is the essential element rather than the more complex mental processes.

Objectives that are higher than the lowest cognitive level (H) include all of the cognitive processes above memorization or specific recall of information. If an objective does *not* specifically call for recall, memorization, or a regurgitation of material, it falls within this higher cognitive level.

Examples of objectives that are higher than the lowest level (H) include:

The student will:

1. Given a method for solving quadratic equations, solve eight out of ten equations.

2. Given a thirty-minute speech, restate within two minutes the four major points presented.

3. Given a complex poem new to the student, relate at least five major poetic elements utilized.

4. Given a topic and two possible sources, prepare a three-minute speech containing the basic speech elements already outlined in class.

5. Given five paintings and criteria for judging paintings, rank without error these paintings in order from best to poorest.

The exercise which follows will provide practice in identifying objectives at the lowest cognitive level (L) and those that are higher than the lowest cognitive level (H).

Identify whether the following objectives are at the lowest cognitive level (Knowledge) or whether they are higher than the lowest level. Place an *L* in the column before those objectives that are at the lowest cognitive level; place an *H* before those objectives that are higher than the lowest level.

———— 1. Given the class to which vertebrates belong, the student will recite the kingdom, phylum, and class characteristics of five vertebrates with at least 80 percent accuracy.

———— 2. Given the age, weight, and height of a child, plan a diet for one day that includes the minimum acceptable vitamins, minerals, and calories.

———— 3. Given a list of ten ordinary, everyday acts performed by animals and human beings, the student will recall those actions that are learned from those that are not learned (reflex) with at least 80 percent accuracy.

_____ 4. Given an outline map of Asia, complete the map by filling in the names in the proper locations of at least fifteen countries.

_____ 5. Given a table or graph of the results of an experiment, (1) interpret the results; (2) determine whether the results support, refute, or have no bearing upon the hypothesis tested.

_____ 6. Given an unfamiliar graph on population trends, correctly list at least three points that can be drawn from this graph.

_____ 7. When given a description of each, the student will match the following four kinds of weather fronts; (1) warm, (2) cold, (3) stationary, (4) occluded.

_____ 8. Define from memory all of the following words as they are used in regard to minorities: bigotry, persecution, prejudice, intolerance.

_____ 9. After viewing four TV programs over a two-week span, evaluate them by producing a guide that indicates (1) the nature of each program; (2) the audience for whom it is intended; and (3) your critique of the program, the latter being approximately 100 words.

_____ 10. Given three current economic controversies in the United States, evaluate the arguments used, select which position you support on each issue, and defend that position by stating specific facts and/or examples, in a paper of no more than one page.

_____ 11. The student must list eight out of ten archeological dating techniques.

_____ 12. After viewing an incident in a traffic safety film, the student will list seven out of ten potential accident hazards.

_____ 13. The student will name five American novelists from the Realistic Period between 1870 and 1920.

_____ 14. Given a twelve-word sentence in Spanish not pre-

viously studied, the student will translate correctly
at least ten of these words.

Answers are at the end of the chapter.

LEARNING ACTIVITY 3: *7. Instructional Objectives at Each Level of
the Cognitive Domain* For the most part, where objectives have
been used in secondary school systems, most of these have been
written at a low level of cognition. Although many educational
practitioners and philosophers agreed that there were many levels of
thinking, none of the lists of thinking levels gained general acceptance until a committee of the American Psychological Association
addressed itself to the problem. This group, under the direction of
Benjamin S. Bloom, developed a taxonomy or classification basis for
educational objectives.[3] The resultant taxonomy or classification was
composed of six major classes:

1.00   Knowledge
2.00   Comprehension
3.00   Application
4.00   Analysis
5.00   Synthesis
6.00   Evaluation

While the above group has been further subdivided into
subclasses, for our purposes only the major classifications listed above
will be emphasized. As will be realized later, these major classes are
arranged in a hierarchy—that is, they are ranked with knowledge
(1.00) being the lowest, and evaluation (6.00), the highest. In addition, for the most part, the lower levels of the cognitive domain are
inherent in objectives written at higher levels. For example, an
objective at the comprehension level often implies that recall (knowledge level) of specific information is present before comprehension
takes place. Similarly, when an objective is written at the evaluation
level (6.00), the teacher could logically expect the student to recall
specific information (knowledge—1.00), to demonstrate an understanding of this particular information by changing the form of the
information (comprehension—2.00), then use this information to
break down a new situation into its component parts (analysis—
4.00), and finally, apply this analysis as a base with which to evaluate
the new situation according to known criteria (evaluation—6.00).

For example, one objective at the evaluation level is as follows:

Given ten new articles about the Civil War, the student will rank these with 80 percent accuracy from highest to lowest according to their agreement with the Northern cause.

Presumably the student would be required to go through the following cognitive processes in completing the objective: (1) memorize the basic precepts involved with the Northern cause and the Southern cause (knowledge); (2) glean these precepts from others' writings (comprehension); (3) analyze which of these precepts most clearly conform to Northern views, Southern views, or unbiased views (analysis); and finally (4) rank these from highest to lowest according to their agreement with the Northern cause and support this ranking with defensible criteria (evaluation). Of course these brief examples are only a few of an infinite number which could be used to demonstrate how objectives at any but the lowest step of the cognitive domain could contain elements of levels below them. With this brief overview of the background and interrelationship of cognitive levels in mind, we now move to a brief description of each level of the cognitive domain.

8. *1.00 Knowledge*[4] Knowledge, the lowest level of the cognitive domain, includes situations and conditions in which the student is expected to remember, memorize, recall information he or she has previously seen, learned, or been exposed to. Within this level, objectives may range from the recall of specific and isolated material to the knowledge of criteria by which these specifics could be judged.

Examples of knowledge-level objectives follow:

1. The student will write the names of forty of the fifty states.

2. The student will, shown six international road signs, write the meanings of any five.

3. The student will recall in chronological order eight of the ten events that helped lead to Britain's entry into World War II.

It should be noted in the above objectives that remembering is the essential element rather than the more complex mental processes.

9. *2.00 Comprehension* Comprehension, the level that is perhaps most often emphasized in secondary schools, is the ability to know the meaning of material or ideas and make some use of the knowledge. This is involved primarily with three different behaviors— *translation, interpretation,* and *extrapolation* (the ability of estimation or conjecture). Translation means changing material from one

form to another. For example, changing technical language to less complex terminology; changing a lengthy discussion into a very brief one; being able to read a musical score or an architect's drawing; or to translate poetic language into ordinary English. Interpretation goes beyond translation in that it takes a much broader view. For instance, while translation changes from one form to another, interpretation might require a generalization based on the changes that were discovered. Interpretation includes gleaning the more essential data from certain material. In extrapolation, the learner would not only state what something means but also the possible consequences of what is learned. Of the three basic behaviors, the first two—translation and interpretation—are most often found in instructional objectives.

Examples of *comprehension* objectives follow:

1. The student will write the names of twelve of the first fifteen notes in the musical composition. (translation)

2. Given a graph of economic cycles for the past fifty years, the student will make a written prediction of the economic trend for the next four years. (extrapolation)

3. Given a technical paragraph from a specialized journal containing four main ideas, the student will paraphrase the material, retaining the meaning in at least three of the paraphrased statements. (interpretation)

10. 3.00 Application   Application refers to using material (that is learned or comprehended) in new and different situations. The primary difference between this level and the comprehension level is that at the comprehension level a student must know material well enough to use it in a typical situation. At the application level, the student is given a problem that is *new* to him, and he must bring the comprehended material (rules, methods, concepts, principles, laws, and theories) to bear upon this new problem. Students are taught many abstractions in the situations they face in life. Examples of school situations applied to later life include unlimited possibilities, yet a few might clarify the situation:

1. A student learns basic bookkeeping in school; later keeps his own books for a small company he starts.

2. Student learns basic components to a letter; needs letter-

writing ability to explain an involved credit mix-up at a chain store.

3. Student learns area of triangle; uses this to figure cost per square foot of small irregularly shaped lot.

4. Student learns fundamentals of psychological behavior; uses this as basis for judging reactions of fellow workers toward him.

5. Student learns basic speech principles; needs this ability when suddenly called on to be spokesman for his fellow employees.

In terms of the school situation itself, finding "new" situations or problems is not always easily done. Teachers may often be forced to offer contrived or fictional situations, find material with which the student has not had contact, or try to bring a new slant to a static situation.

Sample objectives for the application-level follow:

1. Given the assets and liabilities of a corporation, the student will construct a simple balance sheet with no errors.

2. Given the budget of the student council for the past ten years, the student will prepare a chart showing the relative status of this year's budget to the other nine years.

3. Given the principles for "breaking" a zone defense, the student will apply these principles in diagramming passes on a 2-1-2 zone, using no more than five passes.

4. Given the principles of the law of supply and demand, the student will use these principles to indicate in writing the probable success of a candy sale in January.

5. Given the grades of thirty-two students on a test, the student will calculate and write the standard deviation for these scores within .3 of the correct answer.

11.4.00 Analysis While higher on the taxonomic scale, analysis may be easier to understand than some of the previous levels. In its most basic form, analysis involves breaking down material into its component parts and finding the relationships among them. In many cases this breaking down of materials or communications may be the final purpose in an objective, while in other instances, it is an essential step prior to the final evaluation (6.00) of material. Using a simplistic analogy, analysis is what one would do when he wanted to distinguish the various instruments and thus the characters in Tchaikovsky's *Peter and the Wolf.* From an educational point of view more would undoubtedly be required, such as the separation of important from unimportant material, fact from fiction, logical from illogical, relevant statements from irrelevant, etc.; the division of a larger entity into its organizational parts.

Examples of analysis-level objectives include:

1. Given three sentences that clearly explain a difficult philosophical statement, the student will circle at least seven verbs, descriptive adjectives, and adverbs that add clarity to the statement.

2. Given a new sixteen-line poem, the student will separate those similes and metaphors which promote the general theme as compared to those that are neutral or merely descriptive to the theme with at least 75 percent accuracy.

3. Given an explanation of C-14 and potassium-argon dating techniques, the student will describe in writing the effectiveness of each in determining the age of a human bone found on a given site.

4. Given eight species of wood, the student will write the names of each as determined from wood density, grain pattern, and smell with 75 percent accuracy.

5. In class the student will be able to identify in writing at least four of the significant points which have bearing upon the outcomes of a given case of contractual dispute.

12. *5.00 Synthesis*   While analysis is involved in breaking down materials into their component parts, synthesis is the ability to put known parts, principles, etc., together to make a new entity or new whole. Using a musical analogy again, when a composer attempts to develop a new composition, he or she may well begin with basic chords and, using music theory principles, develop these logically into a melody. Moving from this simplistic analogy, synthesis is involved in each of the following examples:

—using learned techniques of writing to produce a new essay.

—developing an overall game strategy in facing a particular team.

—choreographing a creative dance movement.

—drawing up a proposal for a math or music experiment.

In developing a synthesis lesson, it is important to make sure you are asking divergent questions—those that would allow each individual, using his knowledge, to come up with his own unique creation. Thus, if twenty members in a class were assigned to work on a so-called synthesis objective and all responses were exactly the same, this could *not* be considered synthesis. In synthesis, each objective calls for uniqueness, creativity, and/or originality.

Following are synthesis-level objectives:

1. Given up to ten board feet of lumber, the student will design and make his or her own corner shelf, to be judged by the criteria established in class for finished products.

2. Given five required movements and other alternative movements, the student will work these into a ten-minute exercise session in which he moves without break from movement to movement.

3. Given forty vocabulary words, the student will use each of these to construct a three-person dialogue taking a maximum of four minutes.

4. Given a budget of $25 or less, the student will plan menus for two days for a family of two that meet required nutritional standards and caloric intake requirements.

13. 6.00 Evaluation Evaluation, the highest level of the cognitive domain, includes making judgments about the value of material for a given purpose according to specific criteria. As stated in the analysis section, after material is analyzed, then students can successfully evaluate them as to which is best, how they should be placed in rank order, or which have not measured up to a specific criterion level. We are forced to instantly appraise, judge, evaluate, or decide on the value of certain material. And, in fact, the evaluating of student material is one of the larger tasks facing the preservice teacher.

Care must be taken in writing evaluation objectives so as to exclude those dealing with values, opinions, or feelings which more properly are a part of the affective domain. As a reminder, be sure your required evaluations are based on known criteria.

Examples of evaluation-level objectives are below:

1. Given ten advertising layouts, the student will decide which two most closely agree with the criteria developed in class and write a paragraph explaining how these layouts meet the criteria.

2. Given ten new articles about the Civil War, the student will rank these with 80 percent accuracy from highest to lowest according to their agreement with the Northern cause.

3. Given criteria for judging chord compositions, the student will determine if his or her peer is correct in the use of chord progression with two chords being the maximum number allowed incorrect.

The following exercise will provide practice in identifying objectives at each level of the cognitive domain. The second exercise should be used as practice in writing objectives at each level of this domain. Be sure to include all three components of a precise instructional objective as detailed in the previous chapter.

Identify the level from the cognitive domain where each of the following falls. For example, number 1 falls at the 1.00 level—knowledge.

1—Knowledge   3—Application   5—Synthesis
2—Comprehension   4—Analysis   6—Evaluation

_____ 1. The student will be able to list eight of the criteria of normal and neurotic adjustment without reference to outside materials.

_____ 2. Given a lecture on American society at the turn of the century, the student will list the trends affecting the structure and functions of the family and the role of women and children.

_____ 3. After studying the four basic ways to ask a question in French, the student will apply these principles to a given sentence by converting this sentence to four different questions.

_____ 4. Given a metric pattern, the student will write with 90 percent accuracy a ten-line poem using that meter.

_____ 5. Given government safety standards, the student will determine the adequacy of safety practices in a specific housing project to see if they measure up to the standards.

_____ 6. After watching a TV drama involving social conflict, the student will write a two-page paper in which he or she explains the ways in which social or group pressure affects the behavior of characters in the play, citing examples from the drama.

_____ 7. After a study of democratic group action, the student will apply at least one principle learned in a simulated town meeting.

_____ 8. Given three highly complex passages that describe a tragic event; the student will distinguish the passage that best understates the event and support his or her decision by underlining the understatement.

_____ 9. Given information on metaphors, the student will write an extended metaphor of approximately 200 words interpreting the experience of winning.

_____ 10. Given ten major generalizations about American Indian culture, the student will recall eight of these.

_____ 11. The student will be able to verbalize to the teacher's satisfaction an explanation of Huxley's theory of evolution as taken from his first lecture to the working man. The verbalization must include reference to the anatomical structures involved.

_____ 12. The student will be able to interpret in writing the meaning of eight out of ten notations on a musical score.

_____ 13. Given basic architectural limitations and present-day prices, the student will design a municipal building for a city of one million inhabitants which would cost no more than $3 million.

_____ 14. The student will be able to underline illogical conclusions in four out of five statements.

Answers appear at the end of the chapter.

Write an objective for each level of the cognitive domain. Each objective should satisfy the conditions of appropriately written cognitive objectives. For the best practice, relate all objectives to one subject area.

Knowledge

Comprehension

Application

Analysis

Synthesis

Evaluation

Learning Activity 4:   *14. Instructional Objectives at Each Level of the Affective Domain*   Of the three domains—cognitive, affective, and psychomotor—the affective domain is used the least and talked about the most. The affective domain is made up of attitudes, interests, appreciation, and values.

Most teachers want students to appreciate and enjoy certain areas of learning and have these become a prominent part of students' value systems. Yet few teachers work diligently toward instruction designed for the affective domain. In addition, where course objectives are written, only a few affective objectives are generally included in the course framework. There are undoubtedly many reasons for the exclusion of this domain, yet a few are obvious to the experienced teacher:

1. In most courses teachers are expected to give a certain number

of grades, and the affective domain does not readily lend itself to grades and grading procedures.

2. Where grades are given in the affective domain, teachers cannot justify these specific grades as readily as they can grades given in areas where more objective measures are possible. Therefore, teachers feel less able to defend themselves against irate students and parents complaining about low grades in this area. It should be noted that in most cases, teachers would not want to give grades in the affective domain. Instead, evaluation measures are used to indicate whether a change in this area has indeed taken place.

3. How does a teacher *know* a student now possesses a certain value? In many cases the evaluation of this value is accomplished by indirect means and, therefore, lacks validity as well as the objectivity so often required. Also, some of a student's most important values are those he is reluctant to discuss freely with others.

Most teachers fully intend to emphasize at least some aspects of the affective domain; and in such areas as English, physical education, art, and music, the affective domain may involve much of the teacher's intended outcomes for the course. Unfortunately, in too many cases where the affective domain has been emphasized strongly, the evaluation reverts back to an innocuous objective test, often at the lowest cognitive level. The English teacher was undoubtedly sincere when he told his students' parents during the school visitation that his main intent was to help the students develop a sincere appreciation for literature. The four objective tests over American literature which made up over 80 percent of their course grade only proved this teacher's lack of ability in objectively evaluating the attainment of affective objectives.

While these and other problems exist, a thrust in education to move again toward the instruction of beliefs, values, interests, etc., indicates the necessity for prospective teachers to become competent in providing instruction in this area as well as finding ways to evaluate student progress toward achievement of affective objectives.

As has been mentioned in the previous paragraphs, evaluation of affective objectives is one of the larger problems we face. First, there is the question of how to do it. When a teacher tries to gauge when improvement has been made in the areas of interests, feelings, or attitudes, he has to be careful the student is *not* aware of what is being expected. If a student discovered that a teacher's objective was for the student to read more books as a result of the class, he would, in most cases, try to please the teacher, perhaps hoping that the side effects might result in a higher grade. Therefore, while in the cognitive domain students should be allowed to see the objectives so that they know what to expect; in the affective domain students should *not* be allowed to see the objectives so that they do not contaminate their reactions as a result of trying to please the teacher or raise their grade. If an attitude inventory is used, the student will probably be able to ascertain the behavior desired, but he still should not be told the objective and thus remove all doubt.

Second, how do we evaluate students? The methods used in the cognitive domain do not work for the affective domain; therefore, other evaluation techniques must be found. Since some affective behaviors (e.g., reading a book, talking about a particular subject, listening to music, playing tennis) can be readily observed, some teachers measure the student's advancement by carefully looking for the desired actions or the absence of these actions. Another possibility is for the teacher to score the students on a general observational scale; this scale must often be revised to fit the needs of a particular value or interest. In an English class where the teacher's objective is "for the student to show an increased interest in reading as evidenced by his reading novels and short stories during an unassigned portion of the class," the teacher would, over several such periods, observe which students used the free time for reading and compare this with the past experiences of these particular students. Undoubtedly, only a few students would show improvement during this particular period.

Another method for evaluating the affective domain is the self-evaluation inventory. This inventory may reflect how a student feels about himself or how competent he considers himself in relation to specific courses or abilities. In most cases inventories like this should be provided at both the beginning and end of a course or series of courses so that possible changes can be noted. Since the teacher wants an honest assessment of the student's reactions, he should make the student aware that no grades will be given. Likert scales (statements either decidedly favorable or unfavorable with an opportunity to respond on a scale from strongly agree to strongly disagree), semantic differential scales (similar to Likert scales except using polar adjectives rather than statements), or even conversation with the student, are other ways of measuring behavior.

Yet another problem in evaluating the affective domain is that change in this area is often times slow. Students may show only limited improvement over a period of time covered by the teacher's observations, and then, years later, emerge with seemingly great improvement in a particular area. Since affective objectives could readily apply to lifelong interests, this slow but steady progress may on occasion be more desirable than an attitude or interest that blooms quickly and fades away at the same rapid pace.

Like the cognitive domain, the affective domain has a hierarchical structure with the following levels:

1.00   Receiving
2.00   Responding
3.00   Valuing
4.00   Organization
5.00   Characterization by a Value or a Value Complex

All five of these areas have been subdivided into levels by David R. Krathwohl et al.[5]; but this package will be concerned with only the five major divisions.

Writing objectives in the affective domain causes some concern among educators since affective objectives do not readily fit the criteria of acceptability. *The procedure which must be used in writing affective objectives is the following:* (1) Think of an affective area you, as a teacher, would like to see altered in students. For instance, "to increase the student's appreciation of the history of the Civil War era." (2) Find an appropriate level in the affective domain that indicates this increase in appreciation. For instance, at level 3— valuing—"The student will voluntarily check out and read books on Civil War history." (3) Link the affective area you would like changed to the level described. For example, "The student's appreciation of Civil War history will increase as evidenced by an increase in the number of books on Civil War history that he voluntarily checks out and reads." (Note: As can be seen in the above objective, a minimum acceptable standard is included. The behavior, "increase in number of books in Civil War history," can be logically accepted as evidence that the individual has an increased appreciation of Civil War history.) This level is involved with learning about a value while the next level (responding) refers to acting out the behavior indicated by the value.

15. 1.00 Receiving   Receiving is the level at which the student is provided with certain phenomena or stimuli and he or she shows his or her awareness or consciousness of actively receiving information by making appropriate responses. This level is more than just sitting and listening to what the teacher is doing or saying. In other words, the student shows in class discussion that he or she is aware of what the teacher is doing, or if listening, he or she listens with respect or listens carefully to what is said. Of course, this first step is essential if the teacher is to proceed toward instruction that will help the student to develop further his interests or to value something.

This lowest level is somewhat similar to the cognitive domain is that while not required to memorize or recall information, students are expected to show their consciousness of a phenomenon, object, or state of affairs in some overt means. For example, suppose the teacher's objective was for the student to show his awareness of the importance of the theme in a musical selection. The student would probably be expected to: (1) listen to a minute or two of the musical number which represents the theme, and then (2) listen to the teacher playing the theme on the piano, and finally, (3) tell the teacher in a later part of the selection where the theme was reintroduced.

Sample objectives of the receiving level are as follows:

1. The student will show his or her awareness of the theme of the cat in *Peter and the Wolf* as evidenced by telling the teacher when that musical theme is introduced and when repeated.

2. The student will show his or her recognition that all points of view must be discussed in a democratic setting by letting classmates who hold opposing views about a controversial issue give these views.

3. The student will show his or her interest in current affairs by reading the newspaper and by indicating on an ungraded survey which sections or columnists he or she prefers.

16. 2.00 Responding   The responding level is that point when the student is not just attending to a situation but instead is acting out a particular value. At this level, he or she reacts and actively participates in accordance with that particular value. This participation could be the result of an assignment, the student's own willingness to respond, or even some satisfaction the student received from participating. For this level to be achieved, the teacher can often set up a situation that would lead toward student participation and enjoyment. Many educational objectives are written at the responding level and many relate to standards that both students and teachers find desirable.

Objectives at the responding level could include:

1. The student will complete his laboratory work as evidenced by turning in his or her workbook exercises at the end of each laboratory session.

2. The student will show his or her interest in shop safety by observing all safety rules.

3. The student will show his or her interest in class-related materials by checking out books on the subject from the library other than those needed for classroom assignments.

4. The student will show evidence of appreciation of a videotape replay of *Hamlet* by voluntarily discussing the play during a free-response situation.

17. 3.00 Valuing   The valuing level is when the student, through a slow internalization process, has attached some particular worth to an object, an interest, or some other phenomenon. Further, the student must display this on a consistent enough basis so that it becomes the student's belief or attitude. He or she must show a commitment to something. This commitment must not only endure over an extended period of time, but also must require an investment of energy in the object or phenomenon that the student values. For example, he or she will give active support to some project and/or get others to share these values. Clues to what a student considers valuable are evidenced by overt behavior. At this level, for example, a student is more than just thrilled by having seen a particularly good drama on TV. He or she goes beyond this by browsing in book stores for more plays by the same or similar playwrights, by making up a program of reading plays, by watching the TV guides carefully so as not to miss good plays, and/or by even reading critical responses to these plays or by influencing others to do the same.

Valuing-level objectives might include:

1. The student shows his appreciation for a particular author's work by reading the author's biography in the school library.

2. The student consistently shows his or her concern for new students by walking with new students to class and sitting with them in the cafeteria until they have developed friendships of their own.

3. The student shows his or her concern for the improvement of help for the aged by volunteering to spend one evening a week, without pay, working with the aged in a local shelter care home.

18. 4.00 Organization   As students are faced with successive values and acceptance or rejection of them, they soon face situations in which more than one value is encountered. They are then forced to organize various values into a value system, find the relationships of values to each other, and finally decide which are the more important. The problem is *not* one of organizing but rather of conceptualizing a number of values that might apply to a certain conflict to resolve it. This then is the level at which cognition, at the higher levels, enters into the affective domain. In a school atmosphere where value conflicts arise, the teacher would try to provide the student with a rational base for resolving the conflicts. In testing whether this level has occurred, the teacher would try to determine if a comparative evaluation between or among values has taken place.

Organization-level objectives might include:

1. The student will regulate his or her body's demand for rest and exercise during trying activity periods (for which he or she has volunteered) by setting up a scheduled program of rest and activity that meets his or her body's demands, and allows him or her to perform credibly.

2. The student will resolve his or her strong feelings about the need for privacy with a belief that there is strength in group action by aiding the student council in completing group projects.

3. The student will form judgments on the life-style he or she would like to pursue by filling out a self-analysis form involving reactions to possible life situations as they are affected by money, family responsibility, and desire for recognition.

19. 5.00 Characterization by a Value or Value Complex   This, the highest level of the affective domain, illustrates an individual with a value or value system that has controlled his or her behavior for a long period of time. He or she is recognized and characterized by this value complex. He or she can thus be expected to react in a certain way as a result of it. Generally, this level is not reached until some years after students have finished their formal education. However, this does not keep teachers from working toward achieving this particular level.

Objectives at the characterization level might include:

1. The student will indicate complete confidence in his or her ability to succeed by demonstrating this self-confidence in public speaking.

2. The student will show he or she has integrated the value of being truthful and honest with the value of maintaining good interpersonal relationships by consistently reacting to situations in a way that does not compromise honesty but sustains good interpersonal relationships.

3. The student shows the integration of music into his or her life by not only practicing the piano whenever he or she has free time, but also by being an active member of the appropriate community musical groups over an extended period.

Three exercises follow: The first will provide practice in identifying objectives at each level of the affective domain. The second should be used as practice in writing objectives at each level of this domain. Be sure to include the two major components of an affective objective as detailed in the introduction to this section of the chapter.

The final exercise will provide a review of both the cognitive and affective domains and will give added practice in classifying objectives similar to that provided in previous exercises.

Identify the level from the affective domain at which each of the following objectives falls. For example, number 1 falls at the characterization level (5).

1—Receiving   3—Valuing   5—Characterization
2—Responding   4—Organization

_____ 1. Students show their strong feelings regarding the rights of all individuals by giving equal time, courtesy, and attention to everyone regardless of differing viewpoints, and by insisting on these rights when they are in danger of being abridged.

_____ 2. The student will show his interest in a movie on genetics by responding positively towards genetics on an ungraded interest survey given several days after the movie.

_____ 3. The student will demonstrate concern for others by sharing his or her work materials during class.

_____ 4. The student will show commitment to artistically appropriate choices and arrangements by decorating his or her room in relation to these choices.

_____ 5. The student will demonstrate maturity by being able to revise judgments and to change behavior in light of new evidence.

_____ 6. The student will show that he or she understands the relationship between physical needs and physical limitations by prescribing a physical fitness program in line with these limitations.

_____ 7. The student will show interest in art by visiting museums when not assigned to do so.

_____ 8. The student shows an interest in differing cultural patterns by participating in a discussion of these patterns.

_____ 9. The student will show an appreciation of classical music by listening to classical records whenever he or she has free time, and by encouraging others to listen.

_____ 10. The student will demonstrate a stronger concern for individual rights than for majority rule as shown by his responses to a nongraded questionnaire which properly differentiates these two values.

_____ 11. The student will indicate a commitment to a certain area óf science by checking out and reading many scientific books, conducting experiments on his own, and reporting voluntarily on these activities to the teacher.

_____ 12. The student will exhibit a high degree of support for chess by helping to form a school chess club and then volunteering to serve as an officer in order to give the club adequate impetus.

_____ 13. The student will demonstrate a belief in self-control as demonstrated by his or her ability to speak calmly, rationally, and to the point when confronted by high-stress situations involving conflict developed by the teacher.

_____ 14. The student will demonstrate interest in poetry by reading poetry during the free reading periods.

_____ 15. The student will show interest in Hawthorne's short stories and their locale by entering into a discussion of the geography involved and the effect it must have had on the characters of the stories.

Answers are at the end of the chapter.

Write an objective for each level of the affective domain. Each objective should satisfy the conditions of appropriately written affective objectives. For the best practice, relate all objectives to one subject area.

Receiving

Responding

Valuing

Organization

Characterization of a Value

LEARNING ACTIVITY 5: _Optional_

1. Read pages 44-110 and 125-155 in Robert J. Kibler et al., _Behavioral Objectives and Instruction._ Read the portions of pages 125-155 that relate to your teaching fields. In pages 117-187 note the examples of infinitives for each taxonomic classification for use in your writing of objectives. The rest of this book provides further background in instructional objectives.

2. Read Chapter 3 and pages 99-109 in Chapter 4 in John B.

Hough and James K. Duncan, *Teaching, Description and Analysis.*
Compare this with the treatment of the taxonomies by Kibler.

3. For examples of objectives from the various levels of the
cognitive domain, examine the appropriate volume of *Behavioral
Objectives* by John Flanagan et al. There are four volumes, one each
for social studies, science, math, and language arts.

4. From a high school textbook in your teaching field, identify
content which permits students to perform each of the six cognitive
skills in the taxonomy.

EVALUATION

The following self-test is similar to the one which will be
provided by the instructor to determine your proficiency in using the
concepts included in this chapter. You should use it for equivalent
practice.

PART I

Attempt to classify each of the following objectives into the
correct domain and taxonomic level according to the following
scheme:

C—Cognitive	*A—Affective*	*P—Psychomotor*
1—Knowledge	1—Receiving	
2—Comprehension	2—Responding	
3—Application	3—Valuing	
4—Analysis	4—Organization	
5—Synthesis	5—Characterization	
6—Evaluation		

For instance, the objective "The student will be able to list all the
presidents of the United States before Lincoln without error" would
be labeled "C-1."

_____ 1. Given a chapter describing a particular political
situation, the student should be able to construct a
three-part diagram of that system which accurately
reflects the structure of the situation.

_____ 2. The student will show more interest in home
economics by joining Future Homemakers of
America and attending most of the meetings.

_____ 3. The student will write from memory the basic ideas
expressed in at least five of the first ten Amendments to the Constitution.

_____ 4. The student will evaluate in writing the living conditions of the black man in the South from 1820–1860 and 1900–1920, by telling in which (if either) of these historic periods it was better to have lived and why, using primarily economic criteria.

_____ 5. The student will demonstrate an understanding of the battle of Gettysburg by drawing a map with legend showing the directions from which Union and Confederate troops came, the main lines of each side on a given day, and the major points of attack—all with at least 75 percent accuracy.

_____ 6. On a straight track, the student will be able to run 300 yards in 1½ minutes.

_____ 7. The student will show an understanding of the five Amendments discussed in class by rephrasing each of them in his or her own words, from memory, on a test during class.

_____ 8. Following a lecture on the subject, the student will be able to list six out of nine factors that led up to the Spanish-American War.

_____ 9. The pupils will show tolerance for each other by being attentive when others speak in direct conversation and not interrupting them.

_____ 10. In a three-page essay, written during class, the student will compare and contrast the five ideas of Hamilton and Jefferson concerning governmental power. The student will conclude which of these two men's ideas they would have supported if they had lived in those times and tell why.

_____ 11. Given a chapter of material, the student should be able to summarize it into a paragraph in which the major points are accurately presented.

_____ 12. The student will show more concern for children as evidenced by listening attentively to children when visiting a nursery school or other place.

_____ 13. Given five pieces of material and an analysis of the five fiber reactions to an acid test, alkali test, and flame test done in class, the student will be able to describe an ideal fabric.

_____ 14. After being given a demonstration on sawing silver, the student will be able to saw a piece for a ring without wasting any material.

_____ 15. Following a lecture on the subject, the student will be able to list at least seven reasons why the Puritans left England for the New World.

_____ 16. Given the necessary material, the student should be able to develop a plan for urban renewal of one area of a hypothetical city that would result in the least possible number of families that are to be moved.

_____ 17. The student will demonstrate more responsibility toward society by volunteering to help with a drug prevention program and ignoring his or her peer group's pressure to experiment with drugs.

_____ 18. When called upon in class, the student will be able to recite Newton's Law of Motion word for word.

_____ 19. After reading the material, the student should be able to determine and report the reasons behind the Red Scare of the 1920s in the United States.

_____ 20. Given the sculptures done by the class, each student will choose the one he or she thinks is best using the criteria provided in class.

_____ 21. The student will show an interest in the story assigned to be read, as demonstrated by his willingness to read it during the free time at the end of the period.

_____ 22. The student will demonstrate the value of a nutritional diet by eating three well-balanced meals a day.

_____ 23. Given three garments of varying prices, the student will choose the garment he or she considers to be the best buy, and give three reasons for the decision based on the construction of the garment and the criteria for this developed in class.

_____ 24. The student will verbally list from memory five styles of oil painting without error.

_____ 25. The student will obey the bus rules, as demonstrated by not being corrected in the bus line for one month.

_____ 26. Given a film on how to paint to produce certain colors, the student will apply what he or she learned by mixing six combinations of his own colors, with at least five matching the desired colors.

_____ 27. Given only a description of ingredients and resulting texture, and then given ten pictures of cakes, the student will be able to classify all ten as either butter cake, angel food cake, or chiffon cake.

_____ 28. Given comprehensive material on the waste of natural resources and legislative pointers to include, the student will be able to write a legislative bill calling for conservation.

_____ 29. The student will exhibit good habits in completing his or her homework, as demonstrated by his refusing to play with his friends until his homework is done.

_____ 30. After reading the novel *Grapes of Wrath*, the student should be able to explain why the people moved to the West during the Depression, using at least five examples.

_____ 31. After lessons on finding the area of rectangles and triangles, the student will be able to apply the formulas he learned by solving 90 percent of the problems on a test that requires him to find the areas of rectangles and triangles.

_____ 32. When the student is given the necessary material, he should be able to draw at least five similarities between the Illinois and California state welfare programs.

_____ 33. The student will be able to state from memory the four main ingredients in pastry.

_____ 34. Given pencil, crayon, and ink, the student will produce a drawing using all three media in one drawing.

_____ 35. Given five examples of electrical design, the student will choose the best one for the motor to be used and verbally explain why it is good, using criteria developed in class.

_____ 36. Given ten slides of contemporary sculptures, the student will be able to explain in writing at least five similarities and differences about each one.

_____ 37. Given the slab, pinch, and coil methods of making a hand-built pot, the student will make one using all three methods.

_____ 38. The student will develop in one class period a sequentially written outline for alleviating the black housing problems in America today.

_____ 39. The student shows his commitment to football, as demonstrated by his keeping records of every home game.

_____ 40. The student will be able to recite orally without error the Preamble to the Constitution.

_____ 41. The student will demonstrate an interest in math by working extra problems not assigned and turning them in to the teacher.

_____ 42. On an in-class test, the student will compare and contrast the three causes of the Civil War discussed in class to those three causes discussed concerning World War II.

_____ 43. The student will be able to compare the Bill of Rights and the Emancipation Proclamation by listing at least three similarities between the two.

_____ 44. The student will be able to solve 90 percent of the problems on a written math exam of two-digit multiplication problems.

_____ 45. The student will show his awareness of the need to develop good study and reading habits as shown by his positive responses on an ungraded survey.

_____ 46. Given a patterned garment during class, the student will be able to describe a possible meaning of at least three of the pattern symbols.

_____ 47. The student should be able to compare and contrast

the executive branches of a democratic and a
communistic government.

_____ 48. The student will demonstrate his belief in fair play
by refusing to join his friends in baiting the new
student teacher who just took over the class.

_____ 49. After reading a chapter, the student will be able to
recall at least three results of the Industrial
Revolution.

_____ 50. Given necessary materials, the student should be
able to develop a ten-year plan for agriculture in a
hypothetical country, which integrates the concerns of finance, demands, scientific developments,
manpower potential, and cultivation of new
lands.

PART 2

Write a precise instructional objective for each of the following
levels of the affective and cognitive domains:

Knowledge:

Comprehension:

Application:

Analysis:

Synthesis:

Evaluation:

Receiving:

Responding:

Valuing:

Organization:

Characterization:

ANSWERS

LA 1	LA 2	LA 3	LA 4
1. C	1. L	1. 1	1. 5
2. C	2. H	2. 1	2. 1
3. B	3. L	3. 3	3. 2
4. A	4. L	4. 5	4. 3
5. C	5. H	5. 6	5. 5
6. A	6. H	6. 4	6. 4
7. A	7. L	7. 3	7. 2
8. B	8. L	8. 6	8. 1
9. A	9. H	9. 5	9. 3
10. C	10. H	10. 1	10. 4

11. B	11. L	11. 2	11. 3
12. C	12. H	12. 2	12. 3
13. C	13. L	13. 5	13. 5
14. C	14. H	14. 4	14. 2
15. A			15. 1

<u>LA 5</u>

1. C-2	11. C-2	21. A-2	31. C-3	41. A-3
2. A-3	12. A-1	22. A-2	32. C-4	42. C-4
3. C-1	13. C-5	23. C-6	33. C-1	43. C-4
4. C-6	14. P	24. C-1	34. P	44. C-3
5. C-2	15. C-1	25. A-2	35. C-6	45. A-1
6. P	16. C-5	26. C-3	36. C-4	46. C-2
7. C-2	17. A-4	27. C-4	37. P	47. C-4
8. C-1	18. C-1	28. C-5	38. C-5	48. A-4
9. A-2	19. C-2	29. A-4	39. A-3	49. C-1
10. C-6	20. C-6	30. C-2	40. C-1	50. C-5

NOTES

1. Robert J. Kibler, Larry L. Barker, and David T. Miles, *Behavioral Objectives and Instruction*, (Boston: Allyn and Bacon, 1970).

2. Benjamin S. Bloom, ed., *Taxonomy of Educational Objectives: Handbook 1, Cognitive Domain*, (New York: David McKay, 1956).

3. Ibid.

4. For the sake of continuity, this level is repeated from the previous section except that different objectives are used.

5. David R. Krathwohl, Benjamin S. Bloom, and Bertram B. Masia, *Taxonomy of Educational Objectives: Handbook II, Affective Domain*, (New York: David McKay, 1964).

chapter 4

Preassessment

OBJECTIVES

1. You will be able to demonstrate comprehension of the role of preassessment in the GMI by answering a set of objective questions with at least 80 percent accuracy. *(Knowledge, Comprehension)*

2. When given a series of ten behavioral objectives with three preassessment procedures described for each, you will be able to select the most appropriate preassessment procedure from the three provided for at least eight out of the ten objectives. *(Analysis)*

3. When given a behavioral objective and a hypothetical situation, you will be able to design a preassessment procedure that conforms with the principles described in this chapter. *(Synthesis)*

PREASSESSMENT

To determine how you stand in relation to the objectives and content in this chapter, make use of the following questions to guide your study. Each question is followed by a number that links it to the Instructional Procedures included in this chapter. If you can now answer a high percentage of the questions, you may wish to go on to the evaluation at the end of the chapter without further study.

1. What is a comprehensive definition of preassessment? *(1)*

2. Which type of preassessment is more important? *(1)*

3. What is a definition of adolescence? *(2)*

4. What is a common reaction among college students returning to the high school? *(2)*

5. Describe the psychological-sociological position of the adolescent. *(2)*

6. What are the basic needs of the adolescent? *(3)*

7. Why haven't the physical needs of all adolescents been fulfilled? *(3)*

8. What reinforcement principles can be linked to the self-concept? *(3)*

9. What effect has the breakup of the American home had upon the school? *(4)*

10. Describe the adolescent dilemma. *(4)*

11. Why and when should teachers use the cumulative record of students? *(5)*

12. Where are cumulative records kept? *(5)*

13. What cautions are in order with regard to the dissemination of information in cumulative records? *(5)*

14. What effect can preassessment have on objectives? *(6)*

15. How can classification of objectives into taxonomic levels assist in determining preassessment procedures? *(7)*

16. When is preassessment unnecessary? *(7)*

17. List at least six possible preassessment procedures. *(6, 7, and 8;* Learning Activity 1 and 2)

18. What is meant by "equivalent preassessment?" *(8)*

19. When is equivalent preassessment not the best assessment procedure? *(8)*

20. Describe the problems which may be incurred if preassessment is counted on grades. *(9)*

21. When may preassessment test items be used as content? *(10)*

22. What is meant by "collected" versus "grouped" preassessment? *(11)*

23. When may preassessment cause student frustration? *(9, 11)*

24. When given an objective and possible preassessment procedures, how do you select the best preassessment for that objective? (Learning Activity 1)

25. When given a hypothetical teaching situation and an objective, how do you describe a preassessment procedure that does not violate any of the basic principles of preassessment? (Learning Activity 2)

INSTRUCTIONAL PROCEDURES

LEARNING ACTIVITY 1: *Introduction* The first part of this section is designed to give you the necessary background to achieve your objective. It is filled with information, definitions, and relationships that you will need to understand in order to demonstrate competency.

1. The Larger Definition of Preassessment Many teachers who understand objectives, learning procedures, and evaluation sections of the GMI have still not maximized its potential for student learning because they have not instituted good preassessment procedures. In the strictest sense, preassessment of pupils within the GMI framework attempts to pinpoint the exact relationship between the objectives and the capabilities of the pupil. It seems obvious that any prescriptions for learning designed by you, as the instructor, will be enhanced if you know precisely where the student is in relation to the objective. In a larger sense, however, preassessment involves more than an attempt to see this relationship in terms of the intellectual position of the learner in regard to a cognitive objective. It must be viewed as an attempt to include the psychological-physical status of the pupil as well. Therefore, there will be two areas of emphasis in this section. The first exploration will be of some of the basic psychological principles that help teachers to understand and gather data to adjust learning activities for pupils. In the second part, principles will be presented which are helpful in structuring formal procedures for assessing the student's current intellectual or psychomotor readiness to achieve particular objectives.

2. The Adolescent Dilemma In order to gain some overall perspective of the adolescent, it is necessary to achieve insight into basic characteristics of the typical teen-ager. When he begins the secondary-school stage, he is about twelve years old. A twelve-year-old child is considered by most people to be just that, a child. During the next six years, he or she will experience the trauma of the transition to adulthood, while still maintaining status as a child. Suddenly, at eighteen he or she is thrust into the adult world with its adult responsibilities. He or she can fight in wars, vote, marry, and engage in other adult courses of action. During these years of adjustment, the student is in a state of awkwardness. He is too old to be treated completely as a child and resents it if he or she is, and is not old enough to be treated as an adult, and has difficulty reacting positively to adult status. Thus, the dilemma of the adolescent emerges. They are pulled toward the adult world and at the same time frightened by it. They are preoccupied with self-identity and often appear unable to focus attention upon the complexities of life. Peer approval is an overpowering urge that seems necessary to help overcome the nagging self-doubts. Gaining approval of the adult world seems important, but if he or she becomes too dependent upon it, he or she feels compromised.

The result is the teen-agers of today. They have no more power over their own destiny than their environment will give them. By and large, adolescent reaction such as engaging in the fads of dress and moderate anti-social behaviors must be viewed as being within the range of acceptability for that age group.

Preservice teachers returning to the high school environment are often very much surprised at the apparent change that has taken place during the few years that they have been away. However, it is not so much the change in the school which has occurred, but the change in the preservice teacher that causes the momentary shock.

3. Adolescent Needs   Before examining aspects of the psychological needs of youngsters, let's look at physical needs. One often assumes, erroneously, that the physical needs of almost all youngsters in school have been relatively well taken care of. M. D. Alcorn et al.[1] have compiled statistics which challenge this assumption:

> High school teachers instruct approximately 150 to 200 students each day. Research-based estimates indicate that in an average group of that number:
> 1. Five to ten will have speech defects requiring attention if therapy has not been provided in the elementary school.
> 2. Three to six are afflicted with sufficient hearing loss to require medical attention.
> 3. Twenty to fifty require corrective lenses to achieve "normal" vision.

4. Ten to fifteen suffer from known allergies, such as eczema, asthma, hay fever, and hives.

5. One to ten have epilepsy, diabetes, or cardiac disability.

Add to this list the students who come to school hungry perhaps not because there wasn't food, but because the available food was not prepared.

It should not be implied from this that the teacher should be able to diagnose instantly any impediment to student success, but merely that teachers should be much more alert to the physical condition of their students than they sometimes are. The physical aspect of preassessment must be taken into account when designing instructional strategies. One wonders at teacher naivete in such instances as when a student with thick glasses is assigned to a seat in the rear of the room.

The psychological needs of students are even more difficult to deal with. Many educational psychologists have attempted to pinpoint the psychological needs that the adolescent must satisfy in order to function in the learning environment effectively. L. Cronbach[2] refers to the two basic needs of "approval" and "affection" as being paramount. Abraham Maslow[3] establishes the categories of "safety needs," "belonging and love needs," "esteem needs," and "self-actualizing needs" as key factors.

Because the teacher is not and should not consider himself an amateur psychologist, it is usually best if a single principle, such as self-concept, guides most of the thinking in assessing what will help to maximize learning in relation to the psychological needs of youngsters. C. M. Lowe[4] points out that there are widely differing ideas about "self-concept," but among them is a widely accepted premise that students who have a good self-concept can function more effectively in the teaching-learning situation than others. Teachers may view psychological assessment of student needs as a determination of the self-concept of the pupil. The classroom procedures used by teachers should be designed to maintain positive self-concepts in their pupils. There is some evidence that the student with a positive self-concept can learn even within a negative environment, while the student with a weak self-concept requires a supportive environment with much positive reinforcement.

4. Adolescent Home Relationship Assessment   Maslow[3] points out
that one place where the adolescent has in the past been able to fulfill
many of his or her needs has been within the family. With the gradual
breakup of this unit in the United States, the school is being charged
with more of the responsibility for helping pupils fulfill their needs.
In addition, the school is required to compensate for the lack of
motivation for learning found in many homes.

Sometimes the teacher will have opportunities for family
contacts, and, as an observer, may be able to pick up helpful data for
assessing the home relationships and their effects on the student. At
any rate, the teacher can gain insight into the conflicts that exist
between parent and offspring during this period, and use this basic
knowledge as a background framework in psychological assessment.

The adolescent period is characterized by a series of experiments
in which both the parent and the child begin to experience periods of
severance. There is an unstated agreement that these severances are
temporary. But there is an increased possibility of permanent disasso-
ciation at this time as the maturing youngster reaches the culmina-
tion of his adolescence. There must be a recognition by both parties
that each has a stake in the other and yet the adolescent must feel that
he is a worthy and responsible individual away from home.

As the youngster increases the length of these severance periods,
he or she is likely to be engaged in certain activities that seem exciting
and adult-like but which parents do not approve of. When the
adolescent exceeds parents' definition of "tolerable," the teacher can
be faced with a projection of that problem in school. In assessing the
potential success of any learning situation, the teacher *must* take into
account the possibility that a youngster may be undergoing temporary stress because he or she is at odds with parents regarding the state
of asserted independence.

5. Psychological Assessment Data Sources   There are a number of
excuses used by teachers to avoid the responsibility of psychological
assessment. One of these is that they are "afraid they might prejudice
themselves against the student." This is like saying that a doctor
should not use medical records because he doesn't want to be
influenced by prior diagnoses. Another excuse is that the teacher
"should deal with intellectual skills only, that we don't know
anything about the affective domain anyway." This ignores all the

studies that indicate that psychological barriers inhibit learning more than intellectual incapacity.

There are a variety of records in schools which may be used for preassessment purposes. Cumulative records can supply much valuable information. In larger schools, the cumulative records are usually available in the counseling office. In smaller schools, they may be found in the principal's office. In a few secondary schools and elementary schools, they may be in the hands of the homeroom teacher.

There is a wide variety of information in cumulative records that can assist the teacher in assessment. Data will range from academic marks and intelligence and other test scores to medical records and teacher anecdotes. Especially valuable are student autobiographies and reports on problems by specialists. Needless to say, information in the cumulative records is highly confidential and must be treated as privileged information.

A second source of information is the student himself. In addition to being able to communicate directly with students, assessment clues can also be gathered from written responses to open-ended questions.

6. Preassessment for Intellectual or Psychomotor Status   After the teacher has obtained basic information regarding the psychological status of the pupil, he or she is ready to make a preassessment of the student's relative cognitive and/or psychomotor readiness to achieve specific objectives. The direction that preassessment must take is usually dictated by the content of the courses of study. However, if instruction is based on a set of precise instructional objectives, the goals provide the direction. It is appropriate in terms of the general model of instruction to orient preassessment toward specific instructional objectives, but when they are unavailable, it is difficult to obtain specific preassessment information.

7. Guidelines for Linking Cognitive Objectives to Preassessment   In Chapter 3, you learned how to classify objectives into cognitive levels. It is easier to determine preassessment procedures for objectives that have already been classified. Objectives in the knowledge and comprehension levels can often be preassessed with short paper-and-pencil tests. Responses can be checked quickly to determine each student's understanding of basic facts and concepts.

At the application level, the skill described in an objective may be preassessed in one of the following ways: (1) the objective logically follows a preliminary lesson at the knowledge and comprehension levels, and the teacher already knows the status of the pupils; (2) the teacher may ask students to demonstrate certain concepts in such a way as to ensure that they can make appropriate applications; (3) the students may be asked various questions about how to apply some area of knowledge, and sufficient response is generated to determine their present status.

As an example, suppose the students had memorized parts of Roberts' *Rules of Order* at the knowledge level and showed understanding of it through questioning at the comprehension level. If you, as the teacher, are now ready for election of class officers, any of the three procedures may be applicable. You may have received enough input, from the activities undertaken during the course of accomplishing the objectives at the knowledge and comprehension levels, to determine the status of the class's background in actual election procedures. You may actually hold a brief "practice" session to preassess readiness, learn about possible roles, what to review, or other adjustments. Or you may be able to ask the students verbally if they have engaged in student elections before and how they would react to specific hypothetical situations.

Analysis objectives are designed to increase analytical skill in a particular content area. You, as the instructor, may also want to encourage analytic skill that is not dependent upon the content—for example, being able to discern fact from opinion in editorials and essays does not depend upon the topic of the writing. It may be about politics, history, education, ecology, or whatever. In these instances, preassessment is the process of determining the extent to which students can successfully perform analytical operations. Consequently, their knowledge of specific content is of less importance.

When the preassessment is made regarding student's present skill in subjects such as chemistry and math where there is an interrelated structure of increasingly difficult concepts, the preassessment procedure may be necessary only at the beginning of the course of study. After the status has been determined for each student, you may dispense with most further preassessment since all subsequent content will be new to the student.

8. Two Basic Preassessment Principles There are two principles that are basic to preassessment. First, the accuracy of the preassessment depends upon the extent to which it is able to measure validly the terminal behavior called for in the objective. For example, if you have a knowledge or comprehension level objective that you intend to check through the administration of an objective test, preassessment could take the form of an oral quiz or essay-type questions in which students were asked to explain concepts, etc. However, the assessment procedure that would be most effective would be to administer a parallel form of the final evaluation itself. If the terminal behavior called for in the objective is for the student to distinguish between fact and opinion in editorials by underlining key words, leading a discussion after a TV editorial and attempting to assess that ability of each student from his or her discussion is much less effective than assessment from underlining.

Occasionally, the terminal behavior cannot be demonstrated during preassessment. In these instances, you cannot insist upon equivalent preassessment. For instance, a behavior may depend upon such special conditions as those available only during particular times. Field trips and viewing an eclipse are examples of this. In this instance, you may structure a hypothetical situation, similar in nature to the final evaluation situation, and use it for preassessment.

The second basic principle is to approach preassessment in the most direct way possible. In some instances, preassessment of each pupil in an equivalent situation may necessitate detaining the whole class while the skills of one student are being considered. If, for example, the skill being preassessed is that of being able to give a five-minute extemporaneous speech, it would certainly be unwise to have each student deliver a five-minute speech. Not only is this a waste of class time, but it is also likely to produce a good deal of student disinterest.

9. Testing and Student Response When preassessment is in the form of a test, you will have to provide special instructions for students. By the time students reach the secondary school, they have become test-wary. They have been exposed to literally hundreds of tests. Tension automatically builds as a conditioned response to tests and may bias the results obtained. Consequently, students should be informed that scores obtained on preassessment instruments are not used as a basis for marking. Students should also be told that they may be required to respond to items which they know nothing about. If they understand that the purpose of the testing is preassessment rather than evaluation, less difficulty should be experienced.

That motivation can have significant effect on raw scores has been convincingly shown in such studies as Roger Farr et al. did in which "junior high school students in a control group, when the time between pre- and post-testing was only one week, gained an average of 10.2 raw score points on the *Nelson Reading Test* even though no specific instruction in reading intervened."[5] However, an equivalent experimental group's average gain was 14.7 raw score points with the only difference being extrinsic motivation in the form of prizes at the time of the post-test.

Since providing students with prizes for completing preassessment tests seems to be an unacceptable procedure, how can you help to insure accurate test assessments? The answer seems to be in creating an atmosphere in which the students realize that making a sincere effort will save themselves time and problems later. They should understand that their responses will help you to provide the kind of information that will expedite the designing of appropriate learning activities.

10. Preassessment Tests as an Instructional Tool   Ideally, you will have built an item pool large enough so that preassessment test items will not have to be repeated on the final evaluation. In addition to the obvious advantage of more accurate final assessment because of no prior exposure to individual items, you may be able to use the preassessment items themselves as the specific topic of class discussion. Students who have made a serious effort to answer questions are interested in learning information related to their responses. Consequently, preassessment procedures may motivate students and provide a basis for involving them in the instructional process.

11. Spaced Versus Collected Assessment   James Popham and Eva Baker have also pointed out that the student "will come to feel frustrated if he scores poorly on the test. This is a factor to consider, and may suggest that pretesting be conducted in small pieces rather than in one overwhelming course-covering session."[6]

In addition to considering possible student frustration when preassessing, it is also necessary for you to consider the possibility that the student's relative knowledge and skill level will change during the course of study. When working on the material, prior background plus new insight may make a student's early pretest a less reliable indication of present status. Therefore, it is recommended that you preassess many times during the course of the semester, rather than in one huge initial test.

LEARNING ACTIVITY 2: In this exercise, appropriate practice will be provided for Objective 2. You will be required to tell which of the preassessment procedures described is best for a particular cognitive objective.

For each of the following three objectives, pick the more appropriate preassessment procedure and tell why the alternative procedure is less acceptable.

Objective—Given three garments with varying prices, the student will be able to choose the garment he or she judges to be the best buy as determined by its construction, and give three reasons for the decision.

Preassessment Choices—(1) Take a field trip to a local department store and let students pick out garments they like; (2) give a paper-and-pencil test on the qualities of good garment construction.

Your Choice (Circle 1 or 2) *Why?*

Answer: Although the behavior described for the field trip seems to be the act of selecting dresses, the key to the objective is being able to make selections which can be defended in terms of the qualities of good construction. The teacher would be hard-pressed to discern a student's ability to make appropriate selections and formulate logical reasons for his or her choices in the field-trip situation.

Objective—The student will be able to list at least five factors that led to the Spanish-American War.

Preassessment Choices—(1) Ask students to write down as many factors that led to the Spanish-American War as they can; (2) Lead a discussion over the factors leading to the Spanish-American War and note each student's responses.

Your Choice (Circle 1 or 2) *Why?*

Answer: Pressessment choice 1 is best because it provides the teacher with information regarding each student's current knowledge of the factors in the most direct way.

Objective—Students will be able to differentiate between specimens of the following tapeworms: *Taenia solium, Taenia saginata, Dipyli-dium caninum, Multiceps mulliceps, Echinococcus granulosus,* and *Hymenolepis nana.*

Note: This objective is for an advanced science course covering a unit in parasites.

Preassessment Choices—(1) Have students take the test at the beginning of the unit; (2) Preassessment is not needed.

Your Choice (Circle 1 or 2) *Why?*

Answer: It is unlikely that any of the students can already perform the behavior in the objective because of the uniqueness of the material.

LEARNING ACTIVITY 3: In each of the following, check the most appropriate preassessment procedure from the three alternatives presented.

1. The student will be able to recite the four main ingredients in pastry in front of the class.

a. Have each student stand in turn and attempt to state the four main ingredients of pastry.

b. Have each student jot down the four main ingredients of pastry on a piece of paper.

c. Preassessment would probably not be helpful.

2. Given the necessary material, the student should be able to develop a workable plan for urban renewal in a hypothetical city.

a. Have students attempt to outline a workable plan for urban renewal in a hypothetical city.

b. Give a test on the information that would be needed for anyone to build such a plan.

c. Ask each student if he or she feels prepared to develop a plan for urban renewal in a hypothetical city.

3. Given the executive branches of two different forms of government, the student will be able to identify and explain at least three similarities and four differences between them.

a. During a discussion on the topic of comparing executive branches of governments in a democracy and an autocracy, have an observer note the responses of each student.

b. Give an essay test in which the students compare the two governments.

c. Give a test over the organization and functions of the executive branch of each of the two governments.

4. Given a series of ten pictures of shop safety violations, the student will be able to explain the violation in each picture.

a. As students make minor safety violations, the teacher notes each as he or she corrects it.

b. No preassessment is necessary.

c. Give students copies of the ten pictures and ask them to identify the safety violation.

5. The student will be able to lay out a pattern as determined by correctly positioning the pattern according to its size and the width of material, appropriately selecting patterns of the material, and placing the pins with the proper seam allowances.

a. Show slides of laid-out patterns on a screen and have students respond on paper to questions about each.

b. Pass out patterns and material and assess each student's layouts.

c. Ask each student if he or she has laid out a pattern before.

6. The student will be able to explain the mores of the Drib Indian Tribe, a hypothetical tribe constructed by the teacher.

a. No preassessment is necessary.

b. Ask each student to make up the mores of an imaginary tribe.

c. Lead a discussion about the use of hypothetical models and observe the behavior of the class members.

7. The student will be able to demonstrate a fundamental

comprehension and interest in a monetary system by explaining how the monetary system works in this country and by participating actively in a group discussion regarding this subject.

    a. No preassessment is necessary.

    b. Give a test on our monetary system.

    c. Break the class into small groups with group leaders and secretaries, and have each group attempt to discuss one interesting aspect of the monetary system.

8. The student will be able use the five basic hand tools used in making jewelry as demonstrated by constructing an assigned piece of jewelry that conforms to a six-point checklist.

    a. Give a paper-and-pencil test which covers the use of the five tools.

    b. Have each student describe how to use each tool.

    c. Set up a simple operation for each tool and observe student competency with each tool.

9. Given ten slides of previously unseen contemporary sculptures, the student will be able to classify each into one of three basic categories.

    a. Have students attempt to classify three slides of sculptures into three categories.

    b. Have students explain in writing the characteristics of each category.

    c. No preassessment is needed.

10. The student will be able to solve 90 percent of the two-digit multiplication problems on a written math test.

    a. Have the students verbally respond to the question, "Do you know how to solve two-digit multiplication problems?"

    b. Have each student attempt to solve five representative two-digit multiplication problems.

    c. No preassessment is necessary.

Answers

1.	b	6.	a
2.	b	7.	c
3.	c	8.	c
4.	c	9.	a
5.	b	10.	b

LEARNING ACTIVITY 4:   In this activity, you will perform equivalent practice for Objective 3. Brief descriptions of two hypothetical situations are given, along with a behavioral objective. Construct a preassessment is possible and practical. One story problem for each provided. Since there is no right or wrong answer for this exercise, the model is one of a number of possible preassessment procedures.

Hypothetical Situation—You are teaching ninth-grade remedial mathematics. You have completed a review of the simple operations of addition, subtraction, multiplication, and division, and the students can perform them reasonably well. You are now ready to start applying these skills to word problems.

Objective—When given a series of twenty one-operation story problems that can be solved by either addition, subtraction, multiplication, or division, the student answers with 90 percent accuracy and will be able to group the problems according to which operation is needed to solve them.

Your Preassessment Procedure

Model Preassessment Procedure—In this case, equivalent preassessment is possible and practical. One story-problem for each of the four operations should be enough to give an indication of the ability of each student. These four problems should be classified by each student under test conditions.

Hypothetical Situation—You are teaching a class in agricultural methods. The students have a small plot on the school grounds, but also take three field trips each year to local farms and agriculture-products manufacturing and outlet firms.

Objective—Given a choice of three types of fertilizer stocked by an agricultural outlet firm, the student will be able to compare price and quality of the products as applicable to the school plot, select the one he or she considers to be the best buy, and justify that selection by giving at least three reasons.

Your Preassessment Procedure

Model Preassessment Procedure—Equivalent preassessment is not possible since the objective will be evaluated while on a field trip. However, we can ascertain the extent to which the students have each of the prerequisite skills to perform the objective ultimately. Therefore, the best we can do is to construct a hypothetical situation on paper and have each student respond to it. From their responses, the necessary learning activities can be designed.

EVALUATION

OBJECTIVE ONE

The following true-false test is similar to the one which will be used by the instructor to evaluate your comprehension of the material presented on preassessment. Determine if each statement is true or false. The numbers following each question refer to the *Instructional Procedures* of this chapter. You should expect to get 20 out of 25 correct to demonstrate competence.

TRUE-FALSE

_____ 1. Preassessment attempts to pinpoint the relationship between instructional objectives and the competence of the pupil. *(1)*

_____ 2. The cognitive status of the pupil in relationship to an objective is more important than his psychological status. *(1)*

_____ 3. Adolescence is a term that covers a developmental period in life that many psychologists consider more traumatic than most other life periods. *(2)*

_____ 4. College students returning to their former high school are usually close enough in age to the students so that the high school student behavior is not surprising to them. *(2)*

_____ 5. In today's school almost all physical needs of youngsters have been taken care of. *(3)*

_____ 6. The psychological needs of students have been determined by psychologists to stem from the two categories of self-concept and affection. *(3)*

_____ 7. When preassessing psychological needs in terms of student self-concept, teachers can use their findings to determine the type of reinforcement for each individual. *(3)*

_____ 8. In general Maslow and others feel that the breakup of the home relationship has forced the school to accept responsibility for more student need-fulfillment. *(4)*

_____ 9. Students are generally able to leave home problems at home and not let them become manifested in deviant behavior patterns at school. *(4)*

_____ 10. The authors of this package would condone the position that it is acceptable not to use data found in the cumulative records because of the potential bias it can cause in the mind of the teacher. *(5)*

_____ 11. The cumulative record must be kept in the central office of a school as mandated by law. *(5)*

_____ 12. Information in cumulative files is confidential and should be treated as privileged information. *(5)*

_____ 13. After preassessment, teachers may find that they are not completely free to change objectives because of course requirements. *(6)*

_____ 14. Classification of an objective into intellectual levels can assist in pointing the way to a preassessment procedure for the objective. *(7)*

_____ 15. In some ongoing situations a preassessment procedure for a new objective may be unnecessary because of the information already in the possession of the teacher. *(7)*

_____ 16. Simply asking students if they have had experience with the skill described in an objective would not be an acceptable preassessment for any objective. *(7)*

_____ 17. When sharpening analytic skills, preassessment is confined to assessing student analytic ability. *(7)*

_____ 18. The closer preassessment is to being equivalent to the skill described in the objective, the more accurate the preassessment will become. *(8)*

_____ 19. If the skill described in the objective is one in which preassessment is only possible on a one-to-one basis, equivalent preassessment may be unwise. *(8)*

_____ 20. Students should be told that preassessment tests count on grades to insure adequate effort on their part. *(9)*

_____ 21. Preassessment over untaught material may cause frustration in pupils because of low success rates. *(9)*

_____ 22. It is unwise to use specific items from a preassessment test as objects of later instructional activities. *(10)*

_____ 23. Use of the same items on preassessment test instruments and later evaluation instruments is never acceptable. *(10)*

_____ 24. Preassessment is ideally better when spaced throughout a course than given entirely at the beginning. *(11)*

_____ 25. Students' skills and knowledge are changing constantly, but not at a rate that would affect the rate of preassessment administration. *(11)*

OBJECTIVE TWO

Along with the following ten objectives are given three possible preassessment procedures. One has been deemed superior to the other two. You are to select the preassessment procedure which is better even though all may be considered poor. You should get eight out of ten correct.

1. The student will be able to explain the four-step procedure for artificial respiration as given in class.

    a. Have each student rise in turn and attempt to explain the four-step procedure for artificial respiration.

    b. Have each student attempt to jot down a procedure for artificial respiration on a piece of paper.

    c. Preassessment would probably not be helpful.

2. After study of the problem of river ecology, the student will be able to develop a plan for returning a specific river to its natural state. The plan must have a projected cost of less than $35 million and be implementable over a five-year period.

    a. Have students attempt to outline such a plan.

b. Give a test on the information that would be needed to produce such a plan.

c. Ask each student if he feels he is prepared for such an objective.

3. Given the election procedures of two different countries, the student will be able to compare and contrast them, explaining at least four similarities and three differences between them.

a. Give an essay test in which the student compares the two countries.

b. During a discussion on the topic, have an observer note the responses of each student.

c. Give an objective test over the election procedures of the two countries.

4. In a set of 15 slides of automobile-driving procedures, the student will be able to identify at least one safety violation in each slide.

a. As students drive, the driving instructor notes each safety violation as he corrects it.

b. No preassessment is necessary.

c. Show the slides and have students attempt to identify safety violations in each.

5. In making a pot, the student will be able to blend ingredients to get a proper clay consistency, and throw it on the turntable, as demonstrated by being able to produce any round-shaped object within a six-minute time interval.

a. Have students attempt to blend, and throw clay on turntables.

b. Ask each student if he has used a turntable before.

c. Show a film on proper clay-bending and -throwing and ask questions about it.

6. The student will be able to describe what he thinks life will be like in America in 200 years.

a. No preassessment necessary.

b. Ask each student if he has thought about the future.

c. Lead a discussion about the importance of thinking about the future and observe the behavior of the class members.

7. The student will be able to add at least one pertinent remark during a small group project to show his ability to participate in a democratic action.

a. No preassessment necessary.

b. Give a test on democratic actions.

c. Break the class into groups each with a simple project and observe behavior.

8. Given ten hypothetical descriptions of chemical compounds, the student will be able to classify at least eight of the compounds into one of four categories.

a. Have students attempt to classify four descriptions into the four categories.

b. Have students explain in writing the characteristics of each of the four categories.

c. No preassessment is needed.

9. Given the necessary ingredients and an advanced recipe, the student will be able to cook the prescribed food so that the product meets the standards described on a six-point chart.

a. Give a test on the meaning of each term used in the advanced recipe.

b. Have students try to cook, using advanced recipes.

c. Ask students if they have ever cooked using advanced recipes.

10. On a written test, the student will be able to solve at least six out of seven calculus problems dealing with the maximum and minimum of volume of containers.

a. No preassessment necessary.

b. Have students attempt to solve two such problems without any explanation.

c. Ask students if they have solved maximum and minimum volume-of-container problems before.

OBJECTIVE THREE

In this evaluation, you will be given a hypothetical teaching situation and an objective for which you must construct a preassessment procedure. Your answer should not violate any principles advocated in the chapter.

Hypothetical Situation   You are teaching a geography class for tenth-graders. The class is composed of a heterogeneous mixture of races, backgrounds and abilities. The class has spent the first few weeks in a self-instructional package program dealing with the geographical phenomena of Canada. You are now ready to use the content the students have learned as a tool in developing their analytic skills.

Objective Given three geographical phenomena each for Canada and the U.S., the student will be able to give at least four similarities and three differences in the effect of those phenomena on the two countries.

Preassessment Procedure

ANSWERS

OBJECTIVE ONE

1. T	6. F	11. F	16. F	21. T
2. F	7. T	12. T	17. F	22. F
3. T	8. T	13. T	18. T	23. F
4. F	9. F	14. T	19. T	24. T
5. F	10. F	15. T	20. F	25. F

OBJECTIVE TWO

1. b	3. c	5. a	7. c	9. a
2. b	4. c	6. a	8. a	10. a

OBJECTIVE THREE

Since the teacher's intention is to sharpen analytical ability, the key to accomplishment of the objective is to have a body of content to use as a vehicle to manipulate. Since the class has just completed a geographic unit on Canada, preassessment could take the form of a test to determine what analogous information is already known by the students about the United States.

NOTES

1. M. D. Alcorn, J. S. Winder, and J. P. Schunert, *Better Teaching in Secondary Schools,* (New York: Holt, Rinehart and Winston. 1970), p. 21.

2. L. Cronbach, *Educational Psychology,* 2nd ed. (New York: Harcourt, Brace, 1963).

3. Abraham Maslow, *Motivation and Personality,* (New York: Harper and Row, 1954).

4. C. M. Lowe, "The Self-Concept: Fact or Artifact?", *Psychological Bulletin,* Vol. 58, 1961, pp. 325-336.

5. Roger Farr, J. Tuinman, and E. Blanton, "How to Make a Pile in Contrasting," *Phi Delta Kappan,* Vol. LIII, No. 6 (February 1972), pp. 367–369.

6. James Popham and Eva Baker, *Systematic Instruction,* (Englewood Cliffs, N.J.: Prentice-Hall, 1970), p. 74.

chapter 5

Instructional Methods

OBJECTIVES

You will be able:

1. given a precise instructional objective or a hypothetical classroom situation, to select the most appropriate instructional method and state, in less than two pages, at least two reasons why the selected method is the most appropriate; and

2. given a particular instructional method, to describe, in less than two pages, the kind of goals for which the method is most appropriate, at least two elements concerning its utilization, and at least one possible weakness associated with that method.

PREASSESSMENT

The following questions reflect the information presented. Each question is followed by a number that links it to a particular subtopic in this chapter. If after looking through this section you are sure that you already possess this information, you may want to try demonstrating the above objectives immediately. If so, go directly to the evaluation section at the end of this chapter. If you find that you are not sure of some of the information you may either refer to the particular subtopic indicated or, preferably, read the entire chapter.

1. What three things should guide your selection of an instructional method? *(Introduction)*

2. When are lectures most appropriate? *(1)*

3. What kind of lecture guide is easiest to use? *(2)*

4. Should students be encouraged to recopy their notes? *(2)*

5. Should student participation be part of a lecture, and if so, how? *(2)*

6. Who usually profits more from a lecture, younger or older students? *(3)*

7. What are two situations in which the questioning method would be most appropriate? *(4)*

8. What is meant by the overhead questioning technique? *(5)*

9. If a student fails to hear a question because of inattention, what should you do? *(5)*

10. What is the single greatest problem with the questioning method? *(6)*

11. How can demonstrations be particularly helpful to students who are not verbally adept? *(7)*

12. What is the first step in conducting a demonstration? *(8)*

13. What should you do if there is not enough time to enable all students to practice what was demonstrated? *(8)*

14. What is the major weakness associated with demonstrations? *(9)*

15. What are the three rules that should be followed during a general discussion? *(11)*

16. How can digressions be limited? *(11)*

17. What kind of thinking is developed by use of guided discussions? *(13)*

18. What is a major problem associated with the use of guided discussions? *(15)*

19. What are the steps of the inquiry method? *(16)*

20. Can the inquiry method be used effectively during a single class period? *(18)*

21. What are three things you can do to encourage participation during an exploratory discussion? *(20)*

22. What are two advantages to brainstorming? *(22)*

23. How should a brainstorming topic be stated? *(23)*

24. What kind of topics are most appropriate for an open debate? *(25)*

25. When is a panel discussion most appropriate? *(28)*

26. How can brighter students be prevented from dominating a panel discussion? *(30)*

27. When would a sociodrama be most appropriate? *(31)*

28. What are three steps in conducting a sociodrama? *(32)*

29. What is the single greatest danger in using sociodramas? *(33)*

30. How can individual presentations be encouraged? *(35)*

31. What is the usual class reaction to a peer's report? *(36)*

32. Who should make the initial contact when arranging for an outside speaker? *(38)*

33. Should a speaker be limited to a particular topic? *(38)*

34. Why are follow-up activities important when an outside speaker is used? *(39)*

35. Who has the final legal responsibility for students when they are on a field trip? *(41)*

36. What legal protection is carried by "waiver of responsibility" forms? *(42)*

37. What is the minimum number of days necessary for a field trip? *(42)*

38. What should be the main point of concern when evaluating any instructional method? *(Conclusion)*

INSTRUCTIONAL PROCEDURES

Read the following information using the previous questions as a guide. You will note that the discussion of each instructional method is divided into three main parts: purposes, utilization factors, and weaknesses. You are encouraged to compare the various methods on the basis of the divisions, thereby clarifying for yourself in which situations each method might be most advantageously employed.

INTRODUCTION

Knowing how and when to vary instructional methods—how and when to deliver a lecture, conduct a general discussion, or utilize a question-and-answer period—is part of the knowledge that can help you become a dynamic and interesting educator rather than just another teacher. Your choice of instructional methods will, of course, be dictated by the particular instructional objectives being sought and by the particular needs and abilities of your students. Nevertheless, being familiar with the strengths and weaknesses of a wide variety of instructional methods will enable you to choose and use the most appropriate for any given situation, thereby maximizing the benefits of the time and effort you put into planning the lessons and gathering together the materials. This chapter is designed to provide you with that kind of information.

LEARNING ACTIVITY 1: *1. Lectures—Purposes* Lectures are most appropriate when you want to convey a lot of information quickly. For example, if you wanted to point out the similarities in the causes of wars throughout history you would be well advised to use a lecture. A broad topic such as this would require the incorporation of many facts with which students would probably not be familiar. In such a situation the burden of carrying the class falls mostly on the teacher, and relatively little student participation can be expected.

Lectures are also appropriate when you want to explain a process such as that by which a bill becomes a law, or when you want to summarize a large block of information such as the main points in a unit dealing with the legislative process.

2. Utilization Factors Lectures are, undoubtedly, one of the two or three most commonly used instructional methods. Although you are probably familiar with a number of lecture techniques by virtue of having been exposed to many (perhaps too many) lectures, here is a review of some of the more important points which can help make your lectures interesting and informative to your students.

1. *Be sure that students know how to take notes efficiently.* Remind them that it is generally useful to:

a. Use an outline form to list the main points of a lecture;

b. Write down or paraphrase only the most important points;

c. Listen for numerical clues such as "There are *two* key points here. . . ."

d. Write neatly enough that recopying the notes will not be necessary; and

e. Leave sufficient room in their notes to add their own thoughts and questions.

2. *Use only a word or phrase outline as a lecture guide,* (anything more complex will tend to either confuse you or cause you to read from your notes). Also, typewritten sheets of paper

are usually easier to use than note cards since there are fewer items to get out of sequence.

3. *Use language of appropriate formality and complexity* and if new words are introduced, make it possible for students to understand their meanings from the context in which they are used.

4. *Help students see the logic in how the information is organized* (cause-effect relationships, chronological order, easy to difficult, etc.) by stating at the beginning of the lecture what you intend to talk about and how you intend to proceed. Be sure also, that the lecture has a definite beginning, middle, and end.

5. *Provide variation by using an overhead projector or a chalkboard* to outline main points and to spell out difficult or unusual words. It is also helpful to use charts, graphs, and pictures whenever possible, and to change your position in the room from time to time.

6. *Vary the pitch and volume of your voice* both to emphasize important points and to avoid talking in a monotone.

7. *Use numerous examples in your lectures* and, whenever possible, personalize them by using a student's name, for example, "If David bought six books. . . ."

8. *Provide for frequent student participation* throughout the lecture by asking questions, but remember that a lecture is primarily a "telling" process and that the bulk of the questions, both student- and teacher-generated, should come at the end of the lecture.

9. *Provide moments of silence* during which students can get caught up with their note-taking or can ask questions. Look for nonverbal behaviors of students which might indicate confusion or questions, and respond to those students.

10. *Differentiate between facts and opinions in the lecture,* and emphasize key points by slowing down as you state them, rephrasing them, or writing them on the overhead projector or the chalkboard. Your behavior should communicate to students what the most important points are.

3. Weaknesses Partly because lectures are relatively easy to direct and control, and partly because standing before a group of students and telling them something fits easily into many people's conception of what teaching is, lectures tend to be overused. It is therefore important to keep in mind certain potential weaknesses of the lecture method. It is important to remember, for example, that because lecturing is a "telling" process, it encourages passive, rather than active, student participation. In many instances a dittoed handout would do as well as a lecture. It is equally important to remember that lectures do not provide much of the student-teacher interaction that is necessary to evelute the instructional process fully; that they can, and do, foster a blind acceptance (especially by younger or slower students) of the information presented; that they do not capitalize upon student interest or creativity; and that they tend to center more upon the information itself than upon the learner or what he is to do with the information.

Because the degree to which students can profit from lectures is usually directly related to the degree to which they can listen attentively, take good notes, deal with abstractions, and assimilate and categorize new information; and because these skills are usually more highly developed in older and/or more advanced students, it would be wise to limit the bulk of your lectures to students of this type. Lectures for younger or less advanced students should be relatively infrequent and of relatively short duration. If the points described previously are taken into consideration along with the kind of students in the class, the use of lectures should pose no problem. The lecture *is* still one of the most efficient ways to convey information.

4. *Questioning*   Questioning consists primarily of having students answer questions posed by the teacher. Questioning is particularly appropriate when your instructional goals require that you determine the extent to which students can give oral answers to questions concerning specific information (such as information included in a reading assignment); when you want to increase retention of important points by isolating and emphasizing them (such as the steps of the scientific method); and when you want to provide students with practice in answering questions orally, so that written practice or performance can be facilitated.

5. *Utilization Factors*   Since the main emphasis of the questioning method is upon asking questions, here are a few points which can help you ask questions effectively.

1. *Use the "overhead" questioning technique:*
   a. State the question clearly.
   b. Pause. This leave the question "hanging overhead" so that all students are likely to consider it. If the question is complex or lengthy, you may want to repeat it at this point.
   c. At random call upon a student (by name preferably, or by pointing) to answer the question.
   d. Give the student who answered the question immediate feedback concerning the accuracy and completeness of his response.

2. *Stand while asking the questions.* This helps students focus their attention upon you and upon what you are saying. Moving about the room is also a good idea.

3. *Do not punish wrong answers* by embarrassing a student. When possible use the part of the response that is correct or state the right question to the answer provided. Ask for other ideas from other students. Providing clues is a good idea, but care must be taken not to make the clues too obvious or students may feel that you are trying to belittle them.

4. *Do not reward inattention* by continually repeating questions. If a student does not hear a question because he or she was not paying attention, go on to another student.

5. *Whenever possible use student responses* or comments as springboards for further questions. This not only gives you an opportunity to restate the correct response or point, but enables you also to mention the student's name as the source of the correct answer or point, thereby providing that student with additional, high-level, positive reinforcement.

6. *Try to reinforce every student positively* but take care that your reinforcements do not begin to sound phony or condescending.

6. *Weaknesses* Probably the greatest weakness of the questioning method is the tension that it tends to produce. Under the best of circumstances, asking students a series of questions will cause some tension because students will be worried about making incorrect responses. If the questioning deteriorates into an interrogation

process, if the teacher assumes the role of inquisitor, or if the students have reason to fear embarrassment at the hands of the teacher, the tension can increase to the point that learning is inhibited.

To help reduce student tensions during a question-and-answer period, it is important to have genuine respect for students and individuals, and to remember that successes (especially public successes) facilitate learning much more than failures do. Try to find something good in every response and positively reinforce every effort, but do both honestly.

Other potential weaknesses of the questioning method include the basic competitive nature of the method, the fact that it does not capitalize upon student interests or creativity, and the fact that student-to-student interaction is minimized.

7. *Demonstration—Purpose* Demonstrations are usually welcome and beneficial additions to what is often a verbally oriented, teaching-learning process. Demonstrations are most appropriate when it is possible to show students a skill or process, rather than trying to provide a verbal description. A demonstration of artificial respiration techniques or flame test techniques, for example, would be much more meaningful than lectures or even diagrams of the same things. Demonstrations are also useful in providing opportunities for less verbally adept students to experience success. A student might be able to apply artificial respiration quite well even though he cannot verbally describe the process smoothly.

8. *Utilization Factors* The first step in conducting a demonstration is trying it out in private to be sure you know exactly what you are doing. While it is not usually detrimental to "learn along with your students," when the learning can possibly result in bodily harm (and most demonstrations have this potential), it is wisest to practice first.

Once you are ready to conduct the demonstration for the class, there are a few points which, if followed, can increase the value of your efforts.

1. *Be sure that all necessary equipment and material is available*, in operable condition, and that some spares are also available.
2. *Provide students with a short verbal description* of what they are going to see and of how each piece of equipment will be used. It is a good idea to emphasize safety rules at this time.
3. *Make sure all students can see* what is going on.

4. *Go through the demonstration verbally describing each step.* Use the overhead projector or the chalkboard to list appropriate steps, spell difficult or unusual words, and to generally facilitate notetaking. Prepared transparencies would be useful here.

5. *Have the students practice what was demonstrated* as soon as the demonstration is completed and any questions have been answered. Student practice is an integral part of demonstrations and should not be omitted. If it is impractical to have each student engage in the practice, have a small group of students practice while the others observe.

6. *Observe the students as they practice* and provide corrective feedback. Do not try to correct individual idiosyncrasies unless they threaten to be detrimental to the student's performance.

7. *Have both good and poor examples available,* if the demonstration or subsequent student practice is going to result in some tangible product. This will aid students in assessing their own performances.

9. Weaknesses The major potential weakness of the demonstration method is the tendency on the part of both students and teachers to concentrate solely on the demonstration itself, rather than spending time on both the theory behind the demonstration or the later applicability of the skill or knowledge. To guard against this tendency, it is wise to ask questions, particularly divergent and probing questions, throughout both the demonstration and the later practice. This will help students to generalize their knowledge.

10. General Discussion—Purpose A general discussion is a very common and very useful instructional method. Its primary purposes are to give students practice in on-the-spot thinking, clear oral expression, and both posing and responding to specific and general questions. General discussions are also useful for the diversification of views and the exploration of ideas. A typical keynote question for a general discussion concerning sex education might be "What is meant by sex education?"

11. Utilization Factors Conducting a good discussion requires a bit more preparation and skill than is apparent at first. Some of the more important points are as follows.

1. *Gather together information, sources, and materials,* and make them available to students. A large part of the success of a

discussion depends upon the degree to which students are prepared. Without some knowledge of the topic students will be unlikely to make meaningful contributions to a discussion.

2. *Make sure all students know and follow some simple operating rules:*

    a. Comments should be tolerant and impersonal;

    b. Ideas, not individuals, should be the main focus of attention; and

    c. Only one person should speak at a time.

3. *Whenever possible, arrange chairs in a circle* or semicircle so that face-to-face communication is possible.

4. *Write down a series of key questions* or points for use in stimulating or guiding the direction of the discussion.

5. *Encourage students to do the talking* and keep the discussion going from student to student rather than from student to teacher.

6. *Prevent monopolization of the discussion* by one or two students (or by yourself) by asking for comments by some of the nonparticipants. Do not, however, force a student to participate. If a student is reluctant to participate, you can try asking him or her simply for an opinion from time to time, but if he or she still chooses not to participate, go on to another student. Some students prefer to hold their comments until they are sure of what they want to say and thus feel safe.

7. *Limit digressions* by asking students how their comments pertain to the discussion or by direct statements such as, "We seem to be getting off the topic."

12. *Weaknesses* Discussions, although widely used, have a number of drawbacks. The amount of new material that can be "covered," for example, is severely limited. In addition, evaluation of student participation is difficult although the use of checklists (number of contributions, quality: good, fair, poor, irrelevant, original) are possible criteria for evaluation. Finally, some academic areas are not well suited to the general discussion method of instruction. Algebra and chemistry are two such areas.

13. *Guided Discussion—Purpose* Guided discussions are most helpful with younger or less advanced students and can help them develop skill in convergent and inductive thinking. A typical keynote

question for a guided discussion concerning problem-solving might be, "What would be the very first step in solving a problem?"

14. Utilization Factors   Since your main purpose in using a guided discussion is to help students "discover" some idea, principle, etc., it is important that you generate a list of questions that anticipate student responses (both correct and incorrect) and can be used to lead student, step by step, to the discovery.

Since it soon becomes apparent to students that you are seeking specific answers to your questions, answers which are already known and predetermined, make it clear to students why you are taking them through this slow process (to give them practice in inductive thinking), and keep the discussion short (no longer than twenty minutes). In most instances it is advisable to tell students that the questions are designed to lead to some discovery and that they are to figure it out as quickly as possible.

15. Weaknesses   Aside from being very time-consuming, if the guided discussion is used with the wrong group of students (too old or too advanced), they might feel that the teacher has little or no respect for their abilities. In addition, guided discussions are highly controlled and manipulated by the teacher so divergent responses are discouraged. As a means of showing how an orderly, step-by-step process can result in a clear and logical conclusion, guided discussions are fine. For any other purpose other kinds of discussions will probably serve better.

16. Inquiry Method—Purpose   The inquiry method helps students further develop the analytical skills they began developing in the guided discussions. The main thrust of the inquiry method is the utilization of the scientific method of inquiry to gain new information with a minimum of help from the teacher. This method gives students practice in critical thinking, gathering and analyzing data, and reaching conclusions.

17. Utilization Factors   Since the inquiry method will require that students acquire a good deal of information on their own, it is a good idea either to gather together appropriate materials or to put them on reserve in the library.

Although the term "scientific method" has been in existence for centuries, it means different things to different people. It would be wise to agree with your students on a workable definition and use that as a guide for your discussions. One commonly accepted definition of the scientific method consists of the following steps:

1. State the problem.
2. State the hypothesis (possible solutions).
3. Gather, evaluate, and categorize all available data.
4. On the basis of the data, reach a conclusion.
5. Publicize results (to facilitate replication), make predictions, or take action appropriate to the conclusions reached.

To maximize the benefits of the inquiry method, you should act as a resource person and encourage students to do their own research for data and answers. To the extent that you provide direct answers, the experience is weakened.

Finally, you will find it helpful to establish a timetable and to follow it. Without such a guide the experience may bog down, conclusions may not be reached, or the overall value of the experience will be decreased or lost altogether.

18. Weaknesses Because the inquiry method requires that students do independent research and because the teacher refrains from simply telling students answers, this method (when used for a single class period) tends to be slow and limits the amount of new material that can be explored. In addition, slower students may have difficulty working on their own and may therefore need special help and encouragement before they will feel confident enough to participate. One alternative is to simply use the "scientific method" format in a one-day discussion.

19. Exploratory Discussion—Purpose Exploratory discussions provide students with an opportunity to explore basic issues from a number of different standpoints. Since part of this purpose is achieved by having students voice their opinions and ideas, the method is also useful for encouraging reluctant participants to join in the discussion. This method is particularly good for stimulating interest in a new unit or topic and finding out where students are in terms of their background and general knowledge about a topic. A typical keynote question for an exploratory discussion concerning political corruption might be "Are the majority of politicians corrupt?"

20. Utilization Factors Since this method depends upon wide student participation for its effectiveness, you must do all you can to encourage such participation. Here are some of the things you can do.

1. *Broadly define the topic area* so that the discussion does not ramble on aimlessly.

2. *Do not make judgments* as to whether a particular contribution is good or poor.

3. *When you inject your own ideas, try to do so as an equal.* Sitting in a chair at the same physical level as the students helps to convey the idea that all contributions to the discussion will receive a fair, impartial hearing.

21. Weaknesses One of the strengths of the exploratory discussion method is its relatively free-wheeling nature and the absence of critical evaluations of student contributions. These same strengths, however, also contribute heavily to the method's weaknesses. Because of the general nature of the discussion and the lack of evaluation, many students will feel that they have wasted their time. In addition, covert evaluation of student participation is even more difficult here than with other kinds of discussions.

22. Brainstorming—Purpose Brainstorming is a problem-solving technique which increases the probability of reasonable decisions as a result of consideration by a number of people. The technique is particularly useful in the classroom because it brings out ideas which might not otherwise be expressed and because it limits the degree to which brighter students can dominate the activity. Brainstorming would be appropriate if students were trying to come up with ways to earn money for a field trip or if they were attempting to solve some hypothetical problem such as what the ruler of country X should do if country Y launches an attack.

23. Utilization Factors The structure of a brainstorming session is more rigid than the structures of most other instructional procedures and any deviation from the plan can seriously weaken the whole experience. Here are the steps of a brainstorming plan, in the order they should occur.

1. *State the problem as a simple question.* Brainstorming does not lend itself well to the solution of broad and complex questions. When faced with such problems, break them into sub-problems and deal with them separately. A brainstorming session centered on the question of "What things can we do to help ourselves speak more clearly and precisely," for example, will be more effective than one centered on the more complex problem of "How to communicate better."

2. *Explain the rules.*

a. A chairman will be appointed for each group of between six and twelve students. His function will be to get things started and to see to it that no discussion or evaluation of ideas takes place.

b. A recorder will be appointed for each group. His function will be to write down each idea as it is presented, trying to group them into logical arrangements with appropriate headings.

c. All ideas will be accepted and none will be discussed.

d. "Hitch-hiking" on previously stated ideas is encouraged.

e. Quantity, not quality, is the most immediate goal.

3. *Divide the students* into groups of between six and twelve students and appoint a chairman and recorder for each group. Physically separate the groups as much as possible to encourage independent thinking among groups.

4. *Allow about fifteen minutes for students to generate ideas.*

5. *Bring the class together as a whole,* appoint a recorder, and list on the board the ideas that have been generated. Be sure to get one idea from each sub-group recorder before allowing the next recorder to report an idea from his group. This will prevent any one group from finding that all of its ideas have already been mentioned.

6. *Ask for any additional solutions* that may not have evolved from the group discussion. This will provide an opportunity for students who feel the procedure has cut them short to contribute.

7. *Discuss with the entire class* the suggested solutions and/or assign some or all of the solutions to study groups for further investigation.

24. *Weaknesses*   Because this method results in so many suggestions, it often provides the basis for rather lengthy discussions. Sometimes it is hard to allow sufficient time for all of the resulting ideas to be fully discussed by the whole class. To help alleviate the time constraints, it is imperative that the step-by-step procedure be followed and that all of the rules be understood.

All of the instructional methods described so far have placed the major responsibility for providing actual instruction upon the teacher. The next four methods place the students in position of providing the instruction and therefore have as a common condition that the students have been exposed to some instruction or have done some research which provided them with the requisite knowledge.

25. *Open Debates—Purpose* Open debates are useful when you want to explore a significant amount of new material, while at the same time encourage voluntary participation. The method is particularly useful when two sides of an issue are to be explored (such as the arguments for and against building an atomic power plant in a nearby area) but when you do not want to have the whole class engage in research necessary to acquire the basic facts to be discussed. This method is well suited to summary kinds of activities.

26. *Utilization Factors* As with any kind of debate, the first order of business is the selection of a topic. It is suggested that topic grow out of on-going student work and that it capture the interest of the class.

Once a suitable topic or problem has been identified, the next step is to select small groups of students to do the necessary research and to present their sides of the issue.

The actual debate is conducted as follows:

1. A speaker from each side makes a short (less than ten minutes) formal presentation.

2. A second member of each team makes a shorter (less than five minutes) presentation as a rebuttal.

3. The debate is open to the whole class with questions and/or comments being directed either to a team, a team member, or a previous contributor from the class.

4. The teacher should act as moderator and should take care that questions and comments follow in pro-con sequence so that neither position receives undue emphasis.

5. A speaker from each side should make a brief (less than five minutes) summary presentation.

6. Spend sufficient time at the end of the debate to summarize and categorize the new information presented and discussed.

27. *Weaknesses* Probably the greatest potential weakness in this and other methods that depend upon the students for the bulk of the actual instruction is that the brighter students tend to dominate the proceedings. As moderator, you will want to elicit comments from as

many students as possible. Your efforts in this respect will be facilitated if you make continual references to the information presented by the teams.

It must also be realized that although new information can be, and is, presented and explored in an open debate, the amount of new material that can be dealt with is much smaller than would be appropriate with a lecture or with individual reports.

28. Panel Discussion—Purpose The main purpose of a panel discussion is to enable a small group of students to explore a particular topic in depth and then to act as a source of information for the rest of the students. This method is also valuable for giving students practice in organizing information and providing instruction to their peers. As with most kinds of discussion and debates, panel discussions are best used during the developmental or culminating phases of instruction rather than during the initiatory phase. This is so because students need to have some orientation concerning both the topic to be explored and how the method itself works.

29. Utilization Factors The first step in using the panel discussion is to decide upon a suitable topic for exploration with the class. Once this is done the teacher should assign a small group of students (about six) to act as a panel, do the necessary research and prepare the presentation. The actual discussion can be conducted in a number of ways, one of which is described below.

1. *The moderator or panel chairman should briefly describe the topic* the panel is prepared to discuss and should identify each member of the panel along with the special area of interest of each.

2. *The panel members then accept questions from the class* and respond to them using notes or an outline, but not prepared presentations.

3. *The moderator should see to it that all panel members participate* and that there is time at the end of the discussion for a brief summation to highlight the main points presented or conclusions reached.

4. *Sometimes it is more desirable to have each member of the panel give a brief explanation* of what he or she has covered in relation to the overall topic. This procedure enables the rest of the students in the class to acquire base data and therefore to be more able and willing to participate intelligently.

30. Weaknesses Here again the teacher must guard against the likelihood that the brighter students will tend to dominate both the panel and the overall discussion. To help encourage all panel members to participate, you may want to consider using option number four described above. This guarantees full participation. You can also make it a point to ask for the opinions of any student, panel member or not, who is not participating. (By asking only for an opinion you are minimizing student fears of making an incorrect response. This, in turn, makes it more likely that the student will participate.)

Panel discussions are, of course, not well suited for use as an introductory activity. Students will benefit much more if they are somewhat familiar with the general topic of the panel discussion.

31. Sociodramas—Purpose Sociodramas can be used when your instructional goals include the exploration and dramatization of social problems in order to increase students' insight into the feelings, viewpoints, and problems of other members of society. Because sociodramas deal more with the affective domain than with the cognitive domain, they also have value with regard to enabling slower students to participate on a more equal basis. The exploration of topics such as management-labor relations and conservative-liberal politics would be fertile ground for sociodramas.

32. Utilization Factors When using a sociodrama, it is imperative that you remember that you are not a trained psychiatrist and that you are not engaging in psychodramas (a therapeutic technique) to help students work out personal problems.

Keeping the above facts in mind, the first step in conducting a sociodrama is to identify a situation in which two or more people can interact, and define the specific roles and positions of each of the participants.

Once this is done the remaining steps of the sociodrama are as follows:

1. Ask students to volunteer to play particular roles. If there are no volunteers, select students to play various roles but do not force any student to do so against his will.

2. Give the participants two or three minutes to discuss how they will act out the given situation but make clear the fact that they are not to rehearse.

3. Have students act out their roles as they feel they should.

4. Have a second set of participants act out the same situation before any discussion takes place by the class.

5. Stop the sociodrama immediately if a student steps out of role or begins to get emotionally involved, or if he or she freezes. In such situations, you can explain to the class the effect that controversial issues have on peoples' actions and how sometimes emotions actually override strictly logical actions and responses.

6. At the conclusion of the second sociodrama a general discussion should be held during which students should compare and contrast pertinent points in the two dramatizations.

33. Weaknesses The principle weaknesses of a sociodrama revolve about the fact that in playing a role, a student may uncover personal problems which the teacher is unprepared and unqualified to handle. Serious psychological damage can result if a teacher attempts to act as a psychiatrist and in such a case the teacher would be both ethically and legally liable.

Assuming that the teacher is aware of this primary danger, other problems which will have to be dealt with involve the facts that students will be reluctant to participate (at least at first) for fear of appearing foolish; and that it is virtually impossible to evaluate either the sociodrama as a whole, or individual participation. As with other manifestations of the affective domain, one would plan to use a sociodrama more because of a belief that such an experience would be beneficial than from empirical evidence that such was the case.

34. Individual Presentation—Purpose Individual presentations afford the teacher an ideal opportunity to capitalize upon the particular interests and hobbies of individual students for the benefit of the entire class. Individual presentations are also valuable because they clearly convey to students the fact that the teacher respects their particular abilities and views their achievements as valuable. Even though only a few students may choose to make individual reports, the democratic feeling that is generated goes far in establishing rapport with the entire class.

35. Utilization Factors Before students can be expected to volunteer to make a presentation, they will have to be encouraged to do so and will have to be assured (by the way each lesson is conducted) that they will not be embarrassed by either the teacher or by their peers.

When students do volunteer to make a presentation, carefully assess its relevance to what is going on in the class at the time, and to general student interest. If the planned presentation sounds appropriate, begin making plans with the student for its implementation. Among the factors you should discuss with the student are the following:

1. *Approximately how long will the presentation take?*
2. *Will any special equipment be needed?* (If so, plan to have it on hand.)
3. *Be sure the student understands at least the basic points* of whatever instructional method he or she intends to use. For example, if it is to lecture, be sure to tell the student not to read from notes or move through the presentation like an automaton. Tell the student that the presentation will be better received if he or she can involve other students than if he ignores them, but that he or she should not expect them to have the same degree of expertise in the topic.

36. Weaknesses Individual presentations represent a unique problem to the teacher. While students are used to receiving instruction from an adult teacher, they are often unsure of how to react to information from a peer. Many times they act as if the information is of little interest to them and offer neither questions nor comments. You can help offset this reaction by asking some questions yourself and by soliciting comments from students. Be sure to remember also that unless you help the student presenting the report or demonstration to learn the basics of that presentation method, it will probably not be very successful, and students will be discouraged from volunteering.

We have already seen how students can gain information through your efforts (via lectures, demonstrations, and various kinds of discussion), and how they can gain information largely through their own effort (again via discussions and also via debates, sociodramas, and individual presentations). In addition to these two sources of information, there is an important third source; the community. By involving members of the community you can not only improve school-community relations, but more important, show your students the relevance of what they are studying.

37. Outside Speakers—Purpose The primary purpose of using an outside speaker is to expose your students to a person who is relatively expert in a particular area and/or who may have different ideas than those explored in class, and to do so in a situation in which learning can take place. It would be appropriate, for example, to ask a banker to speak to the class about acquiring various kinds of loans, or to ask a policeman to speak about participation in crime prevention.

38. Utilization Factors   Arranging to have a speaker come to your class is not difficult, but it does require more than a chance meeting with a potential speaker and an off-the-cuff agreement for a next-day appearance. Listed below are some of the steps which can help maximize the potential inherent in an outside speaker's presentation.

1. *Isolate a topic* about which a speaker could provide valuable information.

2. *After discussing possible speakers* with your students, agree on one.

3. *Obtain permission from the school administration* to bring the speaker into your classroom. It is wise to put your request in writing and to ask that it be signed by the person giving permission. (This avoids any confusion later should the question ever be raised whether permission was granted.)

4. *Contact the speaker* and explain:

   a. Who you are and where you teach.

   b. The age and grade-level of your students.

   c. What it is the class is studying.

   d. How you feel he or she could make a valuable contribution.

5. *Agree upon a specific date, time, and topic*, if the speaker is willing to speak to your students.

6. *Tell the speaker the kinds of questions* the students could not satisfactorily answer for themselves.

7. *Have your students read whatever material is relevant and available* if the speaker is going to discuss a relatively new topic. This will enable them to ask more intelligent questions and will tend to increase their overall attentiveness.

8. *Discuss with students proper behavior* and stress that they are not to monopolize the speaker's time trying to show off their own knowledge.

9. *Have a student meet the speaker* on the appointed day at the school entrance and escort him or her to the room.

10. *After briefly introducing the speaker,* allow him or her to conduct the presentation in any way desired as long as time for a summary and for questions at the end is provided.

11. *With the speaker's permission make a tape recording* of the presentation to use with other students, to reuse in your own classes, and for later analysis.

12. *In your follow-up activities, be sure that a thank-you note is sent* to the speaker and be sure that you integrate the information he presented with the information you have already presented and intend to present.

39. Weaknesses One of the potential weaknesses in the use of outside speakers is that they may leave your students with incorrect information and/or highly biased views. It is therefore important not only that you pay close attention to what the speaker is saying, but also to the way your students seem to be interpreting it. Unless the nature of the presentation was such that you anticipated a biased viewpoint, be sure to ask appropriate questions during the question-and-answer period to exposed incorrect data and/or biased views. If you did anticipate a biased viewpoint, be sure to provide counteracting data on the following day. The ultimate responsibility for what your students learn while in your class is yours—not a speaker's. If you fail to compensate for incorrect data or biased views, your students may remain misinformed.

40. Field Trips—Purpose Sometimes it is more valuable to bring your students to the place, thing, or person being studied than to try to describe it in your classroom. Once it is decided that the most appropriate way to achieve a particular objective or set of objectives is to take a field trip, the actual planning can get under way. Here are some of the more important steps.

41. Utilization Factors

1. *Formulate with students specific objectives* and/or questions.

2. *Have students take responsibility* for obtaining information about the trip.

3. *Get written permission for the trip* from the school administration and get all details regarding school policy concerning field trips (such as excusing student absences from other classes, obtaining parental permission, and acquiring necessary finances, transportation, etc.).

4. *If the field trip requires that any money be handled,* be sure

that accurate and *public* records are kept of all funds collected and disbursed. If a special bank account is opened, two signatures should be required for the withdrawal of funds. Two or more persons should check *all* financial matters.

5. *Consider proper safety precautions.* Bring a first-aid kit along and be sure that all students are aware of appropriate dress (for safety and social reasons) and if extensive walking is anticipated, emphasize that comfortable walking shoes should be worn.

6. *Make provisions for financially handicapped students*, students with special needs (physical, religious, dietary, etc.), and students who are unwilling or unable to go.

7. *Secure sufficient chaperonage* (about a one to six ratio) in the form of fellow teachers or known and trusted parents.

8. *Evaluate the trip* after returning to the classroom in terms of its meeting the prespecified objectives. Students should actively participate in the evaluation.

42. Weaknesses There are a number of potential weaknesses of which you should be aware. One of the most important potential dangers resides in the fact that you alone will have full legal responsibility for every student. The Waiver of Responsibility forms that most schools require parents to sign before their child can go on a field trip are *not* legal documents and do not protect the teacher. Although you can be sued as a consequence of some mishap, conviction on the basis of negligence or incompetence is unlikely if it can be shown that your actions were those which a reasonable and prudent parent (as defined by the court) would have taken.

Remember also that field trips require, at an absolute minimum, at least three class days (at least one each for planning, the trip itself, and follow-up activities). It is therefore important that the value of the trip be weighed against what could be accomplished in the same amount of time in the classroom.

Evaluation of a field trip must be done on the basis of how well the specified objectives were achieved. Do not evaluate a field trip merely on the basis of global and ambiguous feelings such as "It was worth it," or "We had a good time." If time was taken during the field trip to focus students' attention on the objectives of the trip, it is likely that not only will objectives be achieved, but that students will enjoy themselves as well.

CONCLUSION

In this chapter we have explored the purposes, utilization factors, and weaknesses of a number of instructional methods. The methods described are not meant to be all-inclusive. Not only are there many other instructional methods, but teachers frequently modify those included in this chapter so that they better fit their own particular needs.

As was pointed out at the beginning of the chapter, the selection of an instructional method does not take place until after the instructional objectives and the needs and abilities of the students have been considered. Once a method has been selected and used, evaluation of the lesson should be based first on whether or not students were, in fact, able to demonstrate the lesson's objective(s), and to what degree students were interested and involved. Feedback from students and from audio and/or video tape recordings can help make your evaluations more accurate and revealing.

LEARNING ACTIVITY 2: The following books contain additional information concerning instructional methods. If you would like to acquire data about other instructional methods, or other viewpoints concerning those methods described in this chapter, it is suggested that you turn to these sources.

1. Nathan S. Blount and Herbert J. Klausmeier, *Teaching in the Secondary School,* 3rd ed. (New York: Harper and Row, 1968), Chapter 8.

2. Leonard H. Clark, ed., *Strategies and Tactics in Secondary School Teaching,* (London: The Macmillan Co., 1968). Articles beginning on pp. 171, 188, 197, 201, 202, 205, 207, 209, 233, 308, 316, and 322.

3. Kenneth H. Hoover, *Learning and Teaching in the Secondary School,* 3rd ed. (Boston: Allyn and Bacon, 1971), Chapters 9, 10, and 13.

4. James B. McDonald, "Gamesmanship in the Classroom," in *Teaching: Vantage Points for Study,* Ronald Hyman, ed. (Philadelphia: Lippincott, 1968), pp. 308-314.

EVALUATION

You will demonstrate achievement of the objectives of this chapter via a written test. It would be wise at this point to review again the objectives listed on the first page of this chapter, and to go through the various instructional methods again, concentrating this time on comparing them on the basis of their purposes, utilization factors, and weaknesses. With this kind of preparation you should experience no difficulty demonstrating the required competencies.

For equivalent practice, formulate a hypothetical objective (or borrow one from some other chapter of this book) and select and defend an instructional method as described in the first objective. Also select an instructional method at random and attempt to achieve the second objective.

chapter 6

Lesson Planning

OBJECTIVES

1. You will be able to type a one-page lesson plan format and defend that format in a typed paper of no more than three pages in which it is explained how each of the included components contributes to student learning and why the format, as a whole, is sufficiently complete.

2. Using a self-prepared lesson plan format, type a lesson plan for a fifty-minute lesson in your teaching field and, in a one-page strategy statement, explain why the learning activities selected are best suited to both the objective of the lesson and the content.

PREASSESSMENT

The following questions reflect the information presented. Each question is followed by a number that links it to the *Instructional Procedures* included in this chapter.

1. What is a lesson plan? *(1)*

2. Must a teacher have a separate lesson plan for each class period? *(2)*

3. What is the main reason for writing a lesson plan? *(2)*

4. How long should a lesson plan be? *(3)*

5. What components should a lesson plan contain? *(4)*

6. What are the three most important lesson plan components? *(4)*

7. What are two ways of planning around a complex objective? *(4)*

8. Is it necessary to list materials for each lesson taught? *(4)*

9. How closely, if at all, should parts of a lesson be taught? *(4)*

10. How do I know which components I need, or how to arrange them in a logical lesson plan format? *(5)*

INSTRUCTIONAL PROCEDURES

LEARNING ACTIVITY 1: The first learning activity is to read this chapter. It is organized around a series of questions, the answers to which are intended to provide information concerning the definition, rationale, construction, and utilization of lesson plans.

1. What Is a Lesson Plan? Most educators would agree that a lesson plan is an outline of content and/or teaching-learning activities designed to enable students to achieve a stated objective.

2. Must a Teacher Have a Separate Lesson Plan for Each Class Period? No. The main reason for writing a lesson plan is to assure that a particular instructional objective is achieved. If it is impossible or impractical to achieve a given objective within a single class period, then the same lesson plan can and should be used until the objective is achieved. It should be noted, however, that most schools divide the day into class periods of set lengths of time. To the extent that teachers can select instructional objectives suitable to achievement within single class periods, they are more able to plan cohesive lessons. This is so because they are able to allocate blocks of time for specific learning activities (thus being sure to provide appropriate changes of pace), to organize these activities so that they build upon and contribute to one another (thus capitalizing upon whatever enthusiasm and learning momentum is generated), and to culminate each period with a strong lesson closure that leaves students with a definite sense of achievement.

When a teacher selects a complex objective as a basis of a lesson, the planning of that lesson becomes similarly complex. When a lesson is expected to be completed within a single class period, it is relatively simple to divide the time so that a variety of activities culminate with students actually demonstrating the objective of the lesson. With a complex lesson, achieving this end is not as simple. Whenever you, as a teacher, plan a lesson that will not be completed within a single class period, you must make sure to include in the plan a number of points at which the lesson can logically be brought to a close. This is imperative if sufficient time is to be allowed to review main points, to show interrelationships between pieces of new information, and to consolidate learning achievements generally. If students are forced to leave a class before a lesson is properly closed, as might happen if the lesson is interrupted by the dismissal bell, much of what has transpired may be lost. Planning for lesson closure in lessons that carry over to a second day is sometimes difficult, but it is always essential.

It should also be remembered that when lessons are not completed within a single class period, the teacher must be prepared not only to complete the lesson on the following day, but also to profitably utilize whatever time remains in that second class period. Since it is difficult to know just how much time will be needed to complete the previous lesson, it is a good idea to have a variety of learning activities planned so that none of the time will be wasted.

3. How Long Should a Lesson Plan Be?   It is seldom necessary for a lesson plan to exceed one page in length. Although there are some teachers who put down on paper virtually every word they intend to say in class and others who refuse to write down anything at all, most teachers have found that if they limit their lesson plans to what are, for them, the essential components, one page is sufficient.

4. What Components Should a Lesson Plan Contain?   At the very least, a lesson plan should contain a precise instructional objective and the content and/or teaching-learning activities which will enable students to achieve that objective. Once these components are included, a teacher may add whatever additional components he or she feels are necessary.

The precise instructional objective is, by far, the most important component of a lesson plan. The objective specifies what students will be able to do at the end of the lesson and, in addition, suggests appropriate teaching-learning activities. Some objectives, such as those written at very low levels of the cognitive domain, are often too simple and easily achieved to be used as the sole objectives for whole class periods. For example, an objective such as, "The student will be able to list, in writing, at least three components of an internal conbustion engine," would require little instruction on the part of the teacher and very little effort on the part of the students. It is likely that such an objective would be achieved very early in the class period, thus leaving the teacher with a large block of time for which no activities had been planned, and leaving students with the feeling that they had wasted much, if not all, of their time. Such situations are prime breeding grounds for discipline problems. A slightly more complex (and more suitable) objective might be, "The student will be able to describe in two or three written paragraphs how any three internal combustion engine components directly interrelate to produce power."

An opposite kind of problem comes into existence when teachers select a complex instructional objective, but fail to make their lesson plan reflect the fact that more than one class period will be needed to achieve the objective. For example, an objective such as, "The student will be able to describe at least three characteristics of a short story and, in less than three pages, defend a position that a given short story does or does not include these characteristics," would probably be too involved for students to do a really good job within a fifty-minute class period. In order to avoid student frustration (caused by being too rushed to do a good job), the teacher would either have to plan the lesson so that students could work on part of the objective during one class and complete it during the following class (being sure to provide a means for students to achieve a sense of accomplishment during both lessons), or simply divide the objective into two smaller objectives such as, (1) The student will be able to describe, in writing, at least three characteristics typical of short stories; and (2) The student will be able to, in a paper of less than four pages, defend a position that a given story does or does not include at least three characteristics typical of short stories.

It is generally more convenient, from a planning standpoint, either to select or divide instructional objectives so that they can be achieved within a single class period. When this is impractical, be sure to build into the lesson plan multiple closure points so that students are able to leave the class feeling that they achieved something definite.

A second important lesson plan component is the content. The form of the content will depend upon both the instructional objective and the teaching-learning activities selected. For example, if you, as the teacher, intend to spend a portion of a lesson giving a lecture, than at least a portion of the lesson plan should consist of a word or phrase outline of the information to be covered. If you intend to engage students in a discussion, then a suitable content component might consist of a series of questions by which students can be led to certain discoveries. Some teachers find it useful to include possible answers with the questions to serve as reminders and to help avoid needless digressions. A lesson based on a demonstration might require, as content, a brief step-by-step description of the procedure to be followed.

At times, the content of a lesson plan is only a vehicle by which an indirectly related objective is achieved. For example, if you had been building within students the ability to differentiate between statements of fact and statements of opinion, you might have a lesson with an objective such as, "Given an editorial from a newspaper, the student will be able to underline all statements of opinion." In a lesson plan for such an objective, it would be logical to include a content component consisting of one or more newspaper editorials. The editorials, however, would only be vehicles by which students were able to achieve an indirectly related objective.

Keep in mind the fact that for most lessons a variety of content forms will be utilized because few lessons are all lecture, or all discussion, or all demonstration. Regardless of the form(s) of the content, most teachers will find that this particular component constitutes the bulk of any given lesson plan. A good rule of thumb concerning the quantity of content needed is that, where appropriate, the content should contain all the data students need to achieve the objective, and in other cases, the content should be complete enough for another competent person to conduct the lesson and have students achieve the objective.

Just as the content component of a lesson plan follows logically from the instructional objective, so do the teaching-learning activities. It is in this component that you describe how students will go about acquiring the skills and/or information necessary to demonstrate the objective. If, for example, an instructional objective was, "The student will be able to list, in writing, four characteristics of a socialistic regime and cite at least one example of each characteristic as it exists in a noncommunist country," the teaching-learning activities might include a short lecture (to provide basic information), a discussion during which students could identify examples of some of the characteristics named (analogous practice), a short recitation during which students could orally review the main points covered and perhaps cite further examples (analogous practice), a short time for students to write out the characteristics, and examples (thus demonstrating the objective), and finally, a short time during which a few randomly selected papers were examined with the class (thus providing students with some feedback concerning their learning progress).

You will note that five different teaching-learning activites were included in the above example. Providing a variety of learning experiences not only minimizes the possibility of students getting bored (and perhaps causing discipline problems), but also provides students with a number of different opportunities to participate and to experience success.

Another common lesson plan component is the materials. Materials are used to specify what particular aids, if any, are needed to teach a given lesson. It is not necessary to include in a material section aids which are usually found in a classroom (such as paper or a chalkboard), but it is useful to include any materials for which special arrangements must be made (such as projectors or special maps or models).

Many teachers find it useful to include in their lesson plans a component labeled, "evaluation." An evaluation component has at least two uses. In cases where a lesson will carry over to a second class, you will want to include an evaluation section in which there is a description of how learning progress (or the lack of it) will be determined up to the point at which the first class ends. This is essential if students are to leave the class with a sense of achievement. It is the description of what they will have achieved.

In cases where the objective of the lesson is achieved within a single class period, evaluation consists, in part, of having students demonstrate the objective. It should be remembered that in order to be sure that each student has achieved the objective, each student must not only be given the opportunity to demonstrate the objective, but must also be given feedback on his individual performance. For this reason, final demonstration of objectives is sometimes put off to a later date, and students are simply provided with feedback concerning how well the class, as a whole, seemed to demonstrate the objective.

A second use of the evaluation component is to provide teachers with space in which to write down notes concerning how well specific teaching-learning activities seemed to work. A compilation of such notes can be used as a basis for modifying future lessons and improving overall teaching skills. Typical comments in an evaluation section might include, "The assignment was unclear and consequently few students were able to participate in the discussion," or "After students got used to the sociodrama, it seemed to be very well accepted and quite useful."

Some teachers, particularly those just beginning their careers, find it very useful to include a time component in their lesson plans. This component is nothing more than an estimation of how many minutes will be devoted to each of the various activities planned. By scheduling activities in this manner, a teacher is less apt unwittingly to allow one particular activity to dominate a whole class period and is less apt to find that the dismissal bell is ringing while he or she is in the middle of a demonstration or discussion. The inclusion of a time component does *not* mean that a teacher must spend exactly the number of minutes on a given activity as were planned, nor does it mean that a teacher should plan four minutes for this and eighteeen mintues for that. Approximations of needed time are all that are necessary to help keep the lesson moving at a well-planned pace.

Another important lesson plan component are the assignments. Assignments are learning activities that take place out of class. For this reason, some teachers simply include assignments as the last teaching-learning activity, but it is more common to provide a separate component for this element. One reason supporting a separate component for assignments is that with such a component, teachers will be more likely to remember to make the assignment known to students.

It should be noted that many educators look with disfavor upon the utilization of out-of-class assignments. These educators point out that the school has absolutely no control over the kinds of study facilities available to students once they leave the school building.

This being the case, assignments which may appear to be perfectly reasonable may prove to be impossible for some students to accomplish because of a need to work after school, no place to study, or similar reasons. Teachers should consider this danger before making out-of-class assignments.

There are a number of other possible lesson plan components. Those that follow are included for your perusal and require no further explanation: special announcements, the date, preliminary or routine tasks, the title of the course and/or unit, and the grade level.

In review, some of the most common lesson plan components include: a precise instructional objective (tells what students will be able to do after the lesson); content (consists of the actual information, questions, descriptions, etc., which will enable students to achieve the objective); teaching-learning activities (lists, in order, the specific activities which will be utilized to help students achieve the objective, sometimes divided into teacher activities and student activities); materials (includes those instructional aids which will be needed for a particular lesson and which are not usually found in the room); evaluation (a statement of how learning achievement is to be ascertained, and/or space for notes concerning the effectiveness of specific teaching-learning activities); and assignments (out-of-class learning activities). Other possible components include special announcements, the date, routine tasks, the title of the course and/or unit, and the grade level.

5. *How Do I Know Which Components I Need, or How to Arrange Them in a Logical Lesson Plan Format?* Beginning teachers would be well-advised to make their lesson plan formats as complete as possible. This is so not only because analysis of the lessons and of one's teaching is facilitated by complete lesson plans, but also because should another person need to take over the class (because the regular teacher is ill), less time will be wasted trying to determine just what it was students were supposed to be doing. As teachers gain more experience, fewer lesson plan components are necessary.

The arrangement of lesson plan components into a logical format is most easily accomplished by listing each of the components in the order it will be used in the lesson.

LEARNING ACTIVITY 2: Study the lesson plan formats following. Each of the components making up the two formats has been filled in to enable you be see better how it could be used in an actual lesson. Note particularly the contribution to successful teaching and learning made by each of the various components included and try to decide which components you would want to include in your own lesson plan format.

SAMPLE 1—ALL COMPONENTS
Class: Computer Science 101
Grade Level: Eleven
Unit: Computers and the Job Market
Date: Feb. 9, 1979
Routine Tasks: Take attendance, collect homework.
Announcements: All library books must be returned by next Friday.
Assignments: None

Objective: Each student will describe, in writing, at least two ways computers are affecting man's vocational and avocational activities.

Content:
   I. Nature of jobs is changing.
         A. Computers are taking over unskilled jobs.
         B. More complex jobs call for better educated workers.
         C. More industrial, in-house training programs are being started.
         D. More technical and vocational teachers are needed.
   II. Nature of workers is changing.
         A. More highly educated workers demand more autonomy.
         B. Nature of work enables workers to take better advantage of free time.
         C. Interest is growing in recreational and adult education.
         D. New needs of workers are creating new jobs.
Activities:
   1. Begin by asking, "What kinds of work do computers do?"
   2. Discuss various answers and build discussion around points included in the content section. (30 min.)
   3. Use overhead projector to outline main points as they are raised.

4. After all points have been discussed, turn off projector and review by asking students direct questions. (5 min.)

5. Pass out lined paper and have students demonstrate the objective. (5 min.)

6. Collect papers and orally go over three or four at random and anonymously to reemphasize main points and provide feedback. (5 min.)

Materials: Overhead projector, grease pencil, posters showing computerized machinery and popular recreational activites.

Evaluation: (This would be filled in after class, but might read something like:) Students were able to achieve the objective, but more visual aids would have stimulated the discussion by providing more clues.

SAMPLE 2—SUGGESTED COMPONENTS

Objective: Each student will describe, in writing, at least two ways computers are affecting man's vocational and avocational activities.

Content:
   I. Nature of jobs is changing.
      A. Computers are taking over unskilled jobs.
      B. More complex jobs call for better educated workers.
      C. More industrial, in-house training programs are being started.
      D. More technical and vocational teachers are needed.
   II. Nature of workers is changing.
      A. More highly educated workers demand more autonomy.
      B. Nature of work enables workers to take better advantage of free time.
      C. Interest is growing in recreation and adult education.
      D. New needs of workers are creating new jobs.

Activities:
   1. Begin by asking, "What kinds of work do computers do?"
   2. Discuss various answers and build discussion around points included in the content section.
   3. Use overhead projector to outline main points as they are raised.

4. After all points have been discussed, turn off projector and review by asking students direct questions.

5. About ten minutes before the end of the lesson pass out lined paper and allow students about five minutes to demonstrate the objective.

6. Collect papers and orally go over three or four at random and anonymously to reemphasize main points and provide feedback.

Materials: Overhead projector, grease pencil, posters showing computerized machinery and popular recreational activities.

Evaluation: (This would be filled in after class, but might read something like:) Students were able to achieve the objective, but more visual aids would have stimulated the discussion by providing more clues.

EVALUATION

1. Type, and hand to your instructor, a one-page lesson plan format and a typed defense of that format no longer than three pages that explains how each of the included components contributes to student learning and why the format, as a whole, is sufficiently complete.

2. Use a self-prepared lesson plan format to type a lesson plan for a fifty-minute lesson in your subject area. Type a strategy statement of no more than one page explaining why the learning activities you selected are best suited to both the objective of the lesson and the content.

chapter 7

Self-Instructional Packages

OBJECTIVE

Using specified models and a set of instructions, the pre-service teacher will be able to build a self-paced instructional package which contains a minimum of the basic four prescribed elements: (1) objectives, (2) preassessment, (3) learning activities, and (4) evaluation. (Application, Analysis, Synthesis)

PREASSESSMENT

If you have previously designed and constructed a self-instructional package, and if it exhibits the characteristics that are necessary, as stated in the evaluation section of this chapter, you may wish to submit it to your instructor to demonstrate your competence in this area. Since the objective describes the ability to build a product, assessment of that ability can be made only by examining a self-instructional package which you have constructed.

INSTRUCTIONAL PROCEDURES

INTRODUCTION

Throughout the educational community, teachers are turning to procedures that allow students to work at their own pace. One often-used technique is the self-instructional package.

Self-instructional packages differ from lesson plans in that they contain specific information for the student, not the instructor. They direct him in a way that allows him to learn at his own pace, with a minimum of guidance from the teacher. All of the chapters in this text can serve as models for self-instructional packages. In that sense, this chapter is a self-instructional package on building self-instructional packages.

Read the following material carefully and follow the step-by-step procedure as you construct your package.

LEARNING ACTIVITY 1:   *1. Selection of Content*   As a beginner in building self-instructional packages, it is wise to make a careful selection of the content you use. You will be sufficiently involved in the arrangement, design, and construction of your package without wanting to concern yourself with unfamiliar subject matter. Therefore, you should select an area that you are well-acquainted with.

2. Parts of a Self-Paced Package   A self-instructional package is composed minimally of the same four parts as the General Model of Instruction (Chapter 1).

1. The first part of a package is the statement of instructional intent in the form of *behavioral objectives.*

2. The second part of the package is the *preassessment* which is designed to aid students in determining the extent to which they are able already to exhibit the behaviors called for in the objective.

3. Next is a series of *learning activities* designed to provide appropriate practice that will enable students to demonstrate the competency described in the objective.

4. Finally, there is an *evaluation* section which explains how the student will demonstrate competency.

The four steps described above are the *minimum* elements that are necessary for a complete package. In many packages, supplementary material is contained in a separate section. However, these materials may be included in the learning activities or the evaluation sections. The following items are sometimes given equal status with the basic four parts.

5. A description of all the material needed to complete the package.

6. An enrichment section that will guide interested students to additional material and activities.

7. Tips on the estimated amount of time required to complete the entire, or portions, of the package.

8. A rationale (usually at the beginning of the package) that explains its importance to students.

9. Optional learning activities designed as alternative or supplementary experiences to the prescribed learning activities.

10. Self-evaluations that are engaged in prior to final evaluation, to provide feedback and insure readiness.

11. A section containing special instructions which explain unique features of the package, such as a warning to schedule a room, special material, or a group session, etc.

STEP 1—STARTING THE PACKAGE

If things were ideal, all parts of the curriculum (including self-instructional packages) would have evolved from a mutually perceived need on the part of students and teachers. Unfortunately, this is not often the case. The reason for including a particular item in the curriculum may vary from a mandate by the state to pressure applied by parents or a minority group of students.

As we have stated previously, your selection of an area of content to use in building your package should be based upon your familiarity with the material. After you have made this decision, you are ready for the relatively difficult task of *translating the content into behavioral objectives.*

The material learned and skills developed in Chapters 2 and 3 will be helpful in formulating your objectives. Understanding the taxonomies is essential in deciding upon the cognitive levels which are applicable to the content you have selected. Low cognitive objectives are usually easier to write than higher level objectives and therefore more often used. When the subject matter will lend itself to the development of such skills as analysis, synthesis, and evaluation, you should formulate appropriate objectives at these levels at every opportunity.

Examine Chapter 4 in this text as a model of a self-instructional package. On the first page of Chapter 4 notice that the first objective for the package is a low-level objective: "You will be able to demonstrate comprehension of the role of preassessment in the GMI by answering a set of objective questions with at least 80 percent accuracy." This asks the student to recall and comprehend information and concepts as demonstrated by passing a test. The second objective is an analysis-level objective: "When given a series of ten behavioral objectives with three preassessment procedures described for each, you will be able to select the most appropriate preassessment procedure from the three provided for at least eight out of the ten objectives." The student must be able to identify similarities and differences between his or her conceptual model of appropriate preassessment activities for supplied samples, and to identify the preassessment procedure that most closely agrees with the model assessment. It is obvious that this skill is of higher intellectual activity than the first.

The third objective requires an even higher level of intellectual activity: "when given a behavioral objective and a hypothetical situation, you will be able to design a preassessment procedure that conforms to the principles described in this chapter." Instead of identifying which of three assessment procedures best agrees with a conceptual model, the student must synthesize his own procedure. A fourth objective could have been constructed at the evaluation level in which the student would have had to render judgments as to whether given preassessment procedures were good or bad. However, this skill is outside the scope of this book.

As a novice package-builder, you should formulate objectives at a higher level than comprehension. For example, suppose you plan to teach in the science area and decide to construct a self-paced instructional package for beginning geology in which the students must familiarize themselves with the characteristics of certain rock types and ultimately be able to classify specimens into the correct rock group. The first step is to write appropriate objectives. The following two objectives will serve as examples.

"Given specific facts about the physical characteristics of five rock groups, the student will be able to recall the characteristics of each group as demonstrated by achieving a score of 80 percent or better on a fifty-question objective examination." (comprehension)

"Given twelve rock specimens, the student will be able to classify at least ten of them into their proper rock categories." (analysis)

As you write your objective, try to reflect what it is that you want your students to be able to do. Don't be satisfied with an objective just because it was easy to write. In addition, your students must be able to discern your instructional intent easily from the objective. If it uses words that will be defined only later in the material, it may be that the objective has no real meaning for the student. If this is the case, we have lost the important contribution that the objective can make in helping the student conceptualize the instructional intent and of guiding him through the learning activities. As has been pointed out in Chapter 1, evidence shows that students who understand the objectives of instruction learn better than those who don't.

STEP 2

The next step in the construction of a self-instructional package would seem to be the preassessment section. However, even though the student will engage in self-preassessment next when he or she uses the package, you as the package writer should develop learning activities and evaluation and then return to structuring the preassessment. There are three basic reasons for this approach. First, the preassessment questions or procedures can usually be more quickly and meaningfully developed if the package writer uses the already constructed learning activities section as a basis for preparing the preassessment. Secondly, the evaluation section will often contain an emphasis that is not readily apparent in the objective, but which can be made clear when the evaluation has been written. Finally, work in the activities section may lead to revision of the objectives and a need to rework the preassessment section anyway.

At this point, you may wish to review Chapters 5 and 6 to refresh your memory regarding possible teaching procedures. All of the instructional techniques ordinarily used in a regular classroom setting can also be incorporated into self-instructional packages. In addition, the use of self-instructional packages encourages the use of mediated instruction. You should first investigate the availability of appropriate mediated materials which have already been produced for inclusion in your package. It will likely be necessary to produce some of them yourself.

Additionally, remember the principles covered in Chapter 1 — perceived purpose, equivalent and analogous practice. These principles should guide and assist you in your learning activities design.

Now consider the two objectives used as examples earlier and attempt to organize a variety of learning activities which will help students achieve these objectives. The first objective requires the student to describe the characteristics of five rock groups. Some of the possible procedures that could be used to accomplish this objective follow:

1. The student could be assigned to read related textbook materials.

2. The necessary information could be included in a specially prepared article written by the teacher.

3. The student could be referred to articles in magazines that cover the material.

4. A commercially produced film or slide-filmstrip may contain the material.

5. The teacher may produce an audiotape accompanied by diagrams and pictures.

6. Students already familar with the material could be assigned to teach the students who are not. The tutor may be provided with a guide to make sure he covers key points.

7. Provision for special help sessions or seminars by the teacher could be made.

8. The student may be directed to complete a simple linear program on the material.

After the teacher has selected the learning method, every effort must be made to make the material interesting and lively. For our model example, the teacher could have chosen to increase the student's understanding of the characteristics of each rock group through the use of a teacher-produced audiotape accompanied by pictures and rock specimens. The student would be instructed in the learning activities section to check out this package of materials from the teacher. The specimens should be clearly labeled and properly referred to in the tape.

In the case of the second objective, it is obvious that the best way to learn how to classify rock samples is through equivalent practice. A rock-identification package similar to the one used for objective one could be developed. However, additional specimens would be necessary.

The two objectives used in this example are relatively easy to design learning activities for. You may experience more difficulty with your own package. Remember that if you choose to build media, a professional job is nice but not an absolute essential. It is more important that your mediated material reflect good teaching principles. With experience, you will be able to add the necessary polish.

You should now begin to design your learning activities for your objectives. Keep the objectives in mind at all times and do not allow your learning activities to stray from the purpose of building the skill required of the students as described in the objective.

Ask yourself the following questions as you design your learning activities.

1. What materials are available?

2. Is the objective important enough to warrant more than one mode of instruction?

3. What are the students who will use this package like? Do they have characteristics that could restrict the range of possible learning activities?

4. What characteristics do the objective or content have that will restrict learning activities?

5. Are there classroom techniques that are particularly effective in accomplishing objectives such as this one?

After you have designed and built in learning activities, you should try them out on a small group of students. Of course, your own situation may prohibit this. If so, you may wish to obtain feedback from peers and your instructor.

STEP 3

The next step is that of building the evaluation section. You may wish to refer to Chapter 14 for a more detailed discussion of evaluation procedures.

The key to any evaluation of a self-instructional package is to make sure that it does indeed check the exact competency described in the objective. Many objectives leave no doubt about the evaluation because they themselves describe the evaluation completely. In our example, it could be argued that the first objective is an en-route objective to the second objective. That is, the teacher's ultimate instructional intent is to get students to be able to classify rock specimens, and being able to describe the characteristics of the categories is a prerequisite skill. Therefore, the teacher may feel that an evaluation consisting of classifying a series of specimens is sufficient for checking both objectives.

On the other hand, the teacher may feel that being able to describe characteristics of the rock categories is a skill that is important in and of itself. If so, then an evaluation opportunity will have to be provided for this objective. In this case, the most obvious procedure would be to administer the objective test mentioned in the objective. In the former case, the objective would, of course, be rewritten so that no examination is mentioned in it.

In some schools that use self-instructional packages, there is a test center available where the student reports for all examinations. If such a center exists in the school, then directions for reporting and taking the examination should be included in the evaluation section.

Assuming that there is no test center, the evaluation section for our example might read something like this:

> After completing the learning activities, you should be ready for the evaluation of both objectives. First, set up a time to take the examination for objective one. After passing the exam, check out the rock specimen set 2-A used for evaluation of objective two and the accompanying answer sheet. Classify each rock specimen into its proper category on the answer sheet.

Sometimes a trial test will be included in the evaluation section instead of the learning activities section. If this is the case, the student could be encouraged to take this self-test as a preliminary check before the actual final examination. Any other unusual circumstances regarding evaluation procedures should be completely spelled out in the evaluation section instructions.

If possible, it is extremely helpful to try out your evaluations on a small group of students or peers before final placement in the package. Test items are often ambiguous, but trying them out in advance and making appropriate alterations will help to improve their quality before actual use.

One of the problems with new test material is setting a proper level. As you develop skill as a package writer and evaluator, your intuitive notions will improve in the area of setting proper levels. Initially, it is best to set a standard at the level dictated by professional judgment with a willingness to adjust if the instrument turns out to be invalid.

STEP 4

You should now be ready to construct the preassessment section. With behavioral objectives, learning activities, and evaluation set up so that they are properly interrelated, you are prepared to construct a preassessment procedure that can help the student quickly determine the areas that need to be emphasized. If the students for whom the package is being prepared know nothing about the objective, the preassessment section may serve only as a study guide. Often, however, the students will already possess part of the background necessary to exhibit the skill described in the objective. In these cases, preassessment questions that are keyed to specific learning activity sections can help students save time by directing them only to knowledge and skills they do not already have. In Chapter 1 of this text, for instance, the specific skills that were considered most important are focused in a series of questions asked in the preassessment section. If students are able to answer all of these questions, they should go immediately to the evaluation without doing any of the learning activities. At this point, you may wish to review Chapter 4 to obtain a better background in preassessment.

In our example, students are expected to be able to demonstrate comprehension of the characteristics of five rock specimen categories by taking an objective test. One way to preassess would be to give them a parallel form of the test, and then give feedback in those areas where weakness was found. In a self-instructional package, however, it is often possible for you, as the teacher, to determine from the preassessment questions the extent to which you must cover each area in the package.

For our second objective, it seems that equivalent assessment would be best. Students can quickly determine if they are able to classify rock specimens into the categories by trying classification. It might be possible to have the student simply classify a series of pictures of rocks included in the package.

You may wish to look at the preassessment sections of several of the chapters in this text to get further ideas for preassessment procedures. Again, after building the entire package, you should make a trial run with selected students to spot flaws that were not initially apparent.

STEP 5

As you get feedback from your trial run and as you examine your package closely, you may feel that some of the additional sections mentioned at the beginning of this chapter may be of importance. For example, you may want to include checklists, trial tests, special scheduling times, etc., as sections in your package. You are the only one at this point who can determine this, but if you feel that such additions would make student success more likely, then by all means include them.

STEP 6

As a final check of your package, use the following questions to guide your inspection.

1. Does the package have the four basic sections: behaviorally stated objectives, preassessment procedures, learning activities, and evaluation?

2. Do the objectives each answer the three questions; What will the student be able to do after completing the package? How well will he or she be able to do it? (criterion level) Under what circumstances will the student be able to do it? (conditions)

3. Is the objective worthwhile?

4. Can the objective be evaluated precisely?

5. Does the preassessment section give students a procedure to find out where he stands in relation to the objective?

6. Is the procedure in the preassessment section workable and not cumbersome?

7. Are there a variety of learning activities in the learning activities section?

8. Is the material cited in the learning activities section easily available and does it provide appropriate practice?

9. Is the material written at a level that students can understand?

10. Is the material interesting?

11. Do the objectives, preassessment, learning activities, and evaluation all complement each other?

12. Does the evaluation section help students identify specific areas of weakness?

13. Would additional sections be helpful?

STEP 7

If you experience trouble with any portion of package building, schedule a session with your instructor to receive help.

EVALUATION

Prepare a package using the following qualitative criteria as a guide.

1. Your package must contain one or more objectives which have an observable behavior, conditions under which the behavior will be exhibited, and a criterion of acceptable performance.

2. The package must have a preassessment procedure that helps students to determine the extent to which they can already achieve the objective and directs them to learning activities which help develop skills they are deficient in.

3. The package should have at least two learning activities with different learning modes that directly assist students in building the skills described in the objectives so that they can select the instructional procedure they prefer.

4. The package should contain a precise description of the evaluation process.

5. Any evaluation instruments, checklists, or criterion guides should either be in the evaluation section itself or accompany the package. If the evaluation is a test, then the test should be appropriately constructed and submitted with the package.

6. Any additional sections included must relate to the other components of the package and be designed to aid the student in completing the package.

7. The objectives, preassessment, learning activities, and evaluation must all complement each other by being properly related to one another.

After making sure that your package complies with the checklist and the criteria, turn it in to your instructor for evaluation.

chapter 8

The Concept Lesson

The concerns of Chapters 8 through 13 are to provide actual practice teaching in a simulated situation. It is particularly useful to have your performance videotaped during these experiences so that appropriate feedback may be facilitated. Where videotaping equipment is unavailable, audiotape recorders are highly recommended. It is important to capture your behavior so that your performance can be analyzed and evaluated. When this data is unavailable, analysis at best is superficial and limited in meaningfulness. Videotaping increases the data available, to include nonverbal information, and its importance should not be underestimated. Analysis may be provided by supervisors during a videotaped replay of your lesson. However, the experience is also designed to provide the opportunity for your own self-analysis, thus adding to the flexibility of the program.

OBJECTIVES

1. From the content in either your major or minor field of study, develop a lesson plan for teaching a concept or principle. The lesson plan must contain the appropriate elements (preassessment, objective, learning experiences, content, materials, evaluation, strategy),

written in the appropriate form as illustrated in the examples given in this chapter.

2. You must be able to teach a fifteen-minute lesson using the lesson plan developed for the objective above. You must also use the interaction style of teaching and adequately demonstrate the skills of set induction, stimulus variation, use of examples, repetition, and closure. You will teach this lesson to a small group of peers or public school students and if possible, have it videotaped by an instructor.

3. You must be able to make a written analysis of your teaching skill from viewing a videotape replay of your lesson. This analysis must be based on the categories of teaching behavior listed on the Critique for Simulated Teaching form on p. 306 *(Note:* The student's lesson may also be analyzed by a Clinical Analyst.)

4. You must also be able to replan and reteach your fifteen-minute lesson, eliminating the problem areas identified in your analysis of the first lesson. If possible, this second lesson should be analyzed by yourself and an instructor from a videotaped replay using the Critique for Simulated Teaching form and a comparison made between the teach and the reteach cycles.

PREASSESSMENT

The following questions reflect the information presented in this chapter. They are designed to aid you in determining your present level of knowledge and skill. Each question is followed by a number that links it to the *Instructional Procedures* included in this chapter. They should be used in guiding you through the various sections presented.

1. What is set induction? *(1)*

2. How does a teacher establish a set for the following types of objectives: psychomotor objective, affective objective, and cognitive objective? *(1)*

3. What are at least three strategies for establishing set? *(1)*

4. When do you use set induction in a lesson? *(1)*

5. What is the relationship of goals to set induction? *(1)*

6. What must be the relationship of set induction to the learning task? *(1)*

7. What should be the relative emotional quality of a set induction? *(1)*

8. What is a stimulus variation? *(2)*

9. What purposes does physical movement have in varying the stimulus? *(2)*

10. What information can be communicated by gestures? *(2)*

11. What rules should be followed in using gestures? *(2)*

12. Why must a gesture fit the verbal message? *(2)*

13. What is meant by the intensity of a gesture? *(2)*

14. What are two ways in which a teacher can use focusing as a means of varying the stimulus? *(2)*

15. What does it mean to alter the interaction style? *(2)*

16. What are two ways to alter the interaction style? *(2)*

17. What effects do pauses have in varying the stimulus? *(2)*

18. How can the teacher shift sensory channels and thus vary the stimulus? *(2)*

19. Why is it important for the teacher to provide appropriate examples? *(3)*

20. Explain how questions are used in the deductive process of understanding concepts. *(3)*

21. Explain how questions are used in the inductive process of understanding concepts. *(3)*

22. Give two positive and two negative examples of a concept. *(3)*

23. Why is it useful to give both positive and negative examples of a concept? *(3)*

24. What must a teacher do to insure that students are able to properly relate examples to the concepts they represent? *(3)*

25. Why are examples from students' interests and experiences usually more effective? *(3)*

26. What is the purpose of repetition? *(4)*

27. What does it mean to differentiate repetition? *(4)*

28. Why should repetition be differentiated? *(4)*

29. What is the purpose of spaced repetition? *(4)*

30. For what purpose would a teacher use cumulative repetition? *(4)*

31. In what part of a lesson is massed repetition ordinarily used? *(4)*

32. What are the different forms which repetition may take? *(4)*

33. Upon whose perception does closure depend? *(5)*

34. In what way is closure related to goals? *(5)*

35. In what way is closure related to set induction? *(5)*

36. What steps can the teacher take to ensure that closure takes place? *(5)*

37. How can a teacher determine whether or not closure has taken place? *(5)*

38. What factors constrain an individual's perception? *(7)*

39. What effect does perception have on communication? *(7)*

40. If we followed Woodruff's model of learning, how would we teach? *(7)*

41. What is the purpose of a trial response? *(7)*

42. Where does feedback fit into a learning cycle? *(7)*

43. How are concepts used in the learning process? 2(7)

44. What are the steps in teaching a concept lesson and how is each step conducted? *(8)*

45. In what two ways can conceptual information be organized and sequenced? *(8)*

46. What is meant by the action of minds on ideas? *(8)*

47. How can a teacher determine when he has communicated with his students? *(9)*

48. What are the elements of an appropriately written lesson plan and how are they related? *(10)*

49. What is used as a basis for evaluating a concept lesson? *(11)*

50. How should a lesson analysis proceed? *(12)*

INSTRUCTIONAL PROCEDURES

INTRODUCTION

The primary role of a teacher is to plan for and execute teaching behaviors designed to bring about purposeful student learning. In planning for instruction, you, as the teacher, must first identify and organize a defensible body of information, from which you can formulate viable instructional objectives which your students must achieve in order to attain a desired level of competency. The second task is to formulate the student learning activities and teacher behavior patterns which can reasonably be expected to lead to student achievement of instructional goals, given the ordinary constraints operating in a classroom. You then must execute your plan with a class, readjusting your behavior and/or class activities as needed in order to meet your goals. Finally, you must evaluate to determine the extent to which students were able to do those things specified in the objective. Chapters 8 through 13 are designed to provide practice in this single most important teacher role. In achieving the objectives of these chapters, you, as a trainee, will learn how to prepare appropriate lesson plans, execute specified teaching skills, and use specified methodologies to help your students achieve objectives. In this chapter, the methodology selected for use is the interaction method. The teaching skills which will be used include set induction, stimulus variation, use of examples, repetition, and closure. Specific definitions of these are given later.

These skills and methods are to be demonstrated in simulated teaching episodes. Simulated teaching consists of short (about fifteen minutes) teaching experiences where you, as the trainee, focus on a limited number of skills and try to increase your ability to use them appropriately. Simulated teaching should be differentiated from the popular method of microteaching often used in the preparation of teachers. In microteaching, single teaching skills are focused upon and analyzed. In the simulated teaching exercises, several skills are to be learned in conjunction with one another, thus increasing the meaning of the experience. In addition, trainees are encouraged to orient their lessons toward achieving specific objectives. Ordinarily, the accomplishment of any objective requires a number of skills used in conjunction with one another. A small group of either public school students or the trainee's peers may be used as pupils in the simulated teaching exercises. The major advantages of simulated teaching for practice is that it lessens the complexities of a normal classroom situation and it provides for increased control of practice. It also provides a means of receiving feedback regarding teaching skills in a nonthreatening environment, thus providing you some basis for improving your performance prior to field-testing. The first teaching skill which will be considered is set induction.

LEARNING ACTIVITY 1: Read the following descriptions of teaching skills and complete the exercises associated with them.

1. Set Induction It is patently obvious that most teachers do very little preparation for classroom activities. Most commonly the ineffectual, stultifying phrase, "Today we are going to talk about . . . ." precedes nearly all classwork. At best, this phrase simply announces the fact that instruction is about to begin. At worst, it may act as a signal for the student to tune out the instructor. In any case, such introductory statements contribute little to the process of stimulating student interest and enthusiasm for the learning they are about to engage in. For the lesson to be successful, you, as the teacher, must motivate the students by providing "setting" experiences.

A set is a predisposition to respond in some prescribed way toward a given learning experience. In order to establish set, you provide motivating experiences which arouse interest and enthusiasm in the lesson. Student enthusiasm should be generated toward the specific learning task. They should be able to visualize the relationship between goals and learning experiences. Depending on the goals, set induction may take different forms.

When the learning task is in the psychomotor domain, a student's physical senses should be stimulated to prepare him or her to act out learning physically. For example, a runner's mind at the start of a race should be focused on the proper execution of the psychomotor movements which will insure a proper start. The instructor may effectively prepare the learner by such statements as, "Remember to lift your knees high and pump your arms hard," and "Don't straighten up until you are at least ten yards down the track."

When the learning task is cognitive, the mental set becomes symbolic and ordinarily the symbol is that of language. Consequently, the learning task and the resultant goals must be expressed in an arrangement of symbols. Suppose for example, that you are teaching a lesson on interplanetary travel. The following set may be used: "Imagine you had the responsibility for devising all life support systems for a flight from earth to the moon and then on to other planets in our solar system. What factors must be taken into consideration and how would you deal with them?"

If the learning task is an affective one, the mental set is emotive. In this case, learning must be primed by emotional sets and the result of learning must be expressed, at least in part, by emotional acts. For instance, if you desire to have the class feel the emotion associated with racial conflict you may have two students of different races simulate a fight and then have the class express how they felt during the episode. Caution is necessary in this case to insure that a riot doesn't break out in the classroom. Students must understand that the fight was simulated.

One way of establishing set is to focus the attention of the student upon some familiar person, object, event, condition, or idea. You then use this as a point of reference with which to link familiar with new material. Also, seeing the familiar about a learning task is more likely to entice student interest. For example many students are familiar with the fact that a projectile fired from a rifle will eventually fall to the earth. You may remind them of this fact and then demonstrate the effects of gravity on projectiles by contriving an experiment where a steel ball is blown by an air gun at the same instant another steel ball is dropped from a magnet. The air-blown ball should be aimed so that it intersects the ball dropped from the magnet at a moment in time. Ask the class to explain why they collide.

Set may also be developed by asking thought-provoking questions which encourage students to become involved in the lesson immediately. Generally, these questions must call for the student to make an analysis, exercise a judgment, or create a divergent response. Low-level questions generally fail to create set. You may say for example, "Imagine that you and twelve of your classmates have just been shipwrecked on a small island in the Pacific Ocean which is well off regular shipping lanes. How would you organize yourselves for survival?"

A short description or story may also serve as a setting strategy as well as short dramatizations or role-playing episodes. You may, for example, ask a group of students to imagine that they are the founding fathers of the United States Constitution. Their task is to formulate a document which can be used as a basis for governing a society similar to that found in eighteenth-century America.

Finally, set can also be based upon the importance or utility of a particular area of study. In this case you can explain how the topic to be studied is important to the students or how they may use the knowledge gained in a useful way. For example, you may say, "Contained in today's lesson are the principles and procedures which form the basis for everything that we will do in making curriculum decisions during our course of study. The same principles can be used in many other aspects of life. What is the first thing that you ordinarily do when confronted with a problem where you find it hard to decide between two alternatives?"

Set is generally used to start a lesson but may be used any time you shift directions in a lesson or when student attention and enthusiasm are waning. Set may also be used at the conclusion of a lesson when students are to be encouraged to engage in some out-of-class activities or when specific preparations are needed for a subsequent lesson. Simply identifying what the learning task will be is not sufficient. Students should be made to see the task in its relationship to some visible goal, and that goal should be presented in such a way that enthusiasm is generated. Suppose you want students to dribble a basketball to the basket and properly execute a lay-up. Preparation for this skill may include dull, repetitive drills dribbling the ball up and down the court with no basket shooting involved. You may explain that the goal is for them to properly shoot a lay-up and that the dribbling drills are designed to help achieve this goal. It may further be added that shooting lay-ups well is necessary for anyone who wants to make the team.

One word of caution should be made with regard to providing sets for students. First, it is essential that the set induction be directly connected to the learning task and that it leads naturally to the learning. Also, one needs to avoid sets which may cause students to remember only the set and not the information that it was designed to lead to. One example of this kind of problem is a case where a teacher was attempting to prepare students for a discussion regarding the effects of discord on interpersonal relationships. She contrived an enactment of an argument between herself and one class member. All seemed to go well until a week later when the teacher was approached by a student who said he was still upset by the conduct of the teacher in the argument and couldn't understand how she could have done such a thing.

Now attempt to formulate a set induction for a lesson you may teach from your major field. Remember that the set should be attention-getting and connected to the lesson in such a way that it naturally leads into the beginning of the lesson. When you have completed this task you are ready to consider the next teaching skill, stimulus variation.

2. *Variation of Stimulus*   Most of us have experienced teaching behavior which has had a tendency to put us to sleep. Most commonly, it is a lengthy lecture where the teacher stands rigidly behind a podium with his only perceptible movement being the shifting of his

weight from one foot to another or the turning of the pages of his notes. Most likely he or she spoke in a monotone and even if the topic was interesting, you found it difficult to follow. Psychological experiments have shown that deviations from standard habitual teacher behavior result in higher pupil-attention levels. In order to maintain interest it is, therefore, necessary to vary teaching behavior continuously.

There are a number of ways that stimulus variation can be achieved. One of the primary ways is through movement. This entails movement by the teacher to various parts of the room. Even though it may be acceptable to move to the back of the room or among students, the bulk of teacher movement should be in the front of the room where students can more readily observe the teacher. Generally, movement causes the student to shift sensory channels from simply listening to watching. Movement can also be used to draw attention to an object in the room, movement toward it will increase the likelihood that students' attention will focus on the object. Also, movement toward the class tends to create a sense of urgency or emphasis about what is being taught. In addition, it causes students to increase their efforts to follow what is being said. It is well-known that movement into close proximity of misbehaving students generally causes them to refrain from their disruptive behavior and follow the lesson.

A second form of movement is gestures such as hand, head, and body movements. These movements help to convey meaning and emphasis in addition to providing variations in the stimulus. Many times oral communications don't convey the whole message. Gestures embellish and fill out the more exact meaning intended. It is important to remember that meaning is not conveyed simply by hand and head movements. It is essential that these movements correspond with the verbal message. If the same movements are used, no matter what the verbal message, students become bored or distracted. They begin to think about the ineptness of your movement and forget to concentrate on the intended communication. It is also imperative that gestures are not overexaggerated. They should fit the message in terms of intensity as well as intent.

Focusing is another way to vary the stimulus. The teacher, through verbal statements and/or gestures, attempts to direct students' attention to specified instructional components. The teacher may, for example, approach the board and point at a diagram while at the same time saying, "Now here's something which is very important." Focusing may also be directed by the voice level of the teacher. This may be accomplished by either lowering or raising the level beyond the normal range.

Altering interaction styles can also help in varying the stimulus and maintaining the interest level of the class. For example, you, as the teacher, may begin by lecturing to the whole class, then speak directly to one student. You may then redirect a student's response to another student for purposes of clarification or comment. You may also ask a student to discover any fallacy in a remark made by another student or to give examples of what another student is saying. Shifting among these interaction styles helps to increase interest in your lesson as well as increase attention overall.

Pauses may also be used to vary the stimulus. This is particularly important when expected responses require some thought. Silence can be used as a natural way of breaking instruction up into easily absorbed units. It also has a tendency to force students to pay attention. Most people are uncomfortable during silence in group situations. Yet it is a very effective way of obtaining the attention of students when they are bored or distracted. Pauses also help provide the variety necessary to appropriate stimulus variations.

Shifting sensory channels is a final way of varying the stimulus. The teacher, in this case, shifts from one mode of communication to another. This causes the student to adjust by changing his means of reception. For example, the teacher may shift from oral messages to diagrams on the blackboard or to tactile attention through handling actual objects. Such required adjustment of sensory channels induces a high level of attention.

The following is an example of how stimulus variation is used in a teaching situation:

TEACHER: Have you ever noticed how hard it is for young children to think in terms of probability? Have you ever wondered why? Today we are going to discuss one man's view of why this is so. After our lesson you should be able to explain the answer to this question as well as identify the intellectual skills which children can demonstrate during each stage of their development. The name of the man whose theory we will be discussing is Piaget. (The teacher writes PIAGET on the board and then steps back and points to it. This type of stimulus variation is called aural-visual switching. This requires the students to use their eyes as well as their ears to receive the message.) Piaget believes that children increase their skill to deal with intellectual tasks by the growth of schema. Jim, what do you suppose schema are? (Here the teacher switches to a student as a source of information to provide stimulus variation.)

STUDENT: I suppose they must be brain cells.

TEACHER: Mark, can you add to what Jim has said and increase our understanding of the nature of schema? (In this case, the teacher uses a different interaction style by redirecting one student's response to another for comment or clarification.)

STUDENT: It seems to me that Piaget must be referring to patterns of connections between brain cells.

TEACHER: Okay. That's very good. (The teacher goes to the board and writes SCHEMA—PATTERNS OF NEUROLOGICAL CONNECTIONS and then moves to the opposite side of the room. This maneuver draws attention to the correct responses, switches from a visual to an auditory mode. In addition, the teacher varies the stimulus by physically altering his or her position in the classroom.) Now let's examine how the development of schema is related to specific behavior patterns. The process is generally one of adapting to environmental situations with the use of schema. There are two ways adaptation may take place according to Piaget. The first is referred to as assimilation. In this case, the individual attempts to handle new environmental situations with his present abilities. The second way for adaptation to take place is called accommodation. Jane, if assimilation is using present schema to handle new situations, what must accommodation be? (The teacher again switches to an interaction model to vary the stimulus, and pauses to allow the student a sufficiently long period of time to answer.)

STUDENT: I'm not sure, but it must have something to do with developing more schema.

TEACHER: (The teacher walks toward Jane and expresses a good deal of enthusiasm when he or she says the following:) That is exactly right! Accommodation is a change in the organism which is necessary

to handle situations that are at first too difficult. (The teacher writes
the definitions of ASSIMILATION and ACCOMMODATION on the board
and points to them as he or she elaborates the definitions, thus
focusing as necessary to vary the stimulus.) Mary, can you learn to
accommodate? (The teacher again employs the interaction mode.)

STUDENT: Not unless you can will your schema to develop.

TEACHER: That is correct. Accommodation must await the
natural growth of the organism. Assimilation, on the other hand, can
be learned. (The teacher walks toward the class and gestures in such a
way as to show the importance of his statements. Walking toward the
class and executing appropriate gestures varies the stimulus and
focuses the attention of the class on the important principles produced in the discussion.)

As an exercise, attempt to write a student-teacher dialogue in
which you portray each of the ways to vary the stimulus. When you
have accomplished this, you are ready to consider the use of examples
as a teaching skill.

3. *Use of Examples*   One of the greatest determiners of teacher
effectiveness is the ability to use appropriate examples. Even though
it is an economy of time and effort to think in abstract terms, learning
about a concept or idea for the first time usually requires some kind of
concrete representation of the abstraction before understanding can
be brought about. If the teacher is unable to provide a concrete
example, the students may not be able to comprehend the idea being
presented. The teacher may also get feedback on student understanding of concepts by asking students to formulate examples.

There are two ways in which examples may be used to bring
about the understanding of concepts. These are deduction and
induction. Deduction is accomplished by the teacher *first* identifying
the concept he wishes students to understand. He or she *then* gives
examples of the concept. This may be accomplished by oral presentation of a literal example, an analogy, or metaphor, or by presentation
in the forms of visuals such as pictures, diagrams, and charts.
Metaphors are figures of speech; words or phrases which are not
literally demonstrable. For example, the phrase "she looks like a sack
full of hog livers" is meant to convey the unbecomingness of dress for
certain body types. An analogy usually highlights similarities or
differences between ideas which are understood and those which are

not, with the goal of bridging the gap between them. For example, an analogy may be made between a camera and the human eye. Caution must be exercised, however, not to use analogies that oversimplify or mislead the student.

The third step in the deductive approach is the process of relating the example back to the concept. The teacher must, in this instance, be careful to compare the example accurately with the abstraction. He or she may also at this point call for students to give examples and relate them to the concept as a means of determining the level of understanding of the class.

A second basic approach to the use of examples is induction. In this case, you as the teacher begin instruction by giving examples of a concept and encouraging students to identify the generalization or concept which the example illustrates. When the students perform the induction erroneously, you either provide additional examples and/or identify the fallacies in their inferences. You should avoid telling students what the concept is, but rather permit them to discover it from examples.

One useful method is to provide negative as well as positive examples. In other words, in addition to providing examples which illustrate a concept, also provide examples that do not. This helps students discriminate more clearly between the concept you are teaching and others that may be related to it.

One problem that often develops in using examples is the tendency to expect students to relate the example to the concept all by themselves. You should not assume that your students will be able to perform this operation. The able instructor will show the way in which the example illustrates the idea and will check to see if it is understood.

For examples to be used effectively, they should reflect the interest and experiences of the learners. If the example is not in their experience, it is unlikely that it will lead to understanding. In addition, if examples are used which are akin to student interest, the probability of understanding will increase.

The following are illustrations of the use of examples and analogies:

Concept:

Personification occurs when an object or abstract idea is described as having human qualities or feelings.

Positive Example: The wind whispers, the shadows danced on the wall.

Negative Example: The wind blew, the shadows fell.

Concept:

Sovereignty is nearly supreme political power or authority.

Positive Example: A Soviet Union dictator.

Negative Example: A United States senator.

Analogies:

A camera is often used as an analogy for an eye.

A heart is often compared to a pump.

A brain is sometimes compared to a computer or a tape recorder.

The structure of an atom is often used as an analogy of the solar system and vice versa.

Complete the following exercise on the use of examples. Where examples are called for, devise them from your teaching major or minor.

1. What is an analogy?

2. Give an example of an analogy.

3. Give a positive and a negative example of a particular concept.

4. Identify a second concept and give two positive examples, two negative examples, and an analogy.

5. Identify several sources a teacher may use for examples.

4. Repetition The major purpose of repetition is to clarify and reinforce major ideas and concepts and to produce a state of over-learning. Research supports the fact that learning beyond initial mastery of a concept aids in the retention and understanding of the concept over longer periods of time. Many students are satisfied when they can perform at some minimum acceptable level. If they stop at this point, however, they will soon forget the material they are attempting to learn. If they continue to practice—to try their responses over and over—they will acquire the new learning so thoroughly that, within limits, it will never be forgotten. Take the case of the alphabet or the multiplication tables. As children we chant these repeatedly and use them in numerous ways in school. Any time the alphabet or multiplication tables are called for we have the appropriate response on the tip of our tongues because they have been overlearned. Overlearning is not, as the nature of the word might suggest, something bad. Rather, overlearning is a more thorough learning than that required to perform well on an immediate test.

Many times learners are unable to identify what the major points of a discussion are or are engaged in mind-wandering when important ideas are taught. Because of these two very natural inabilities, teachers should make a practice of repeating important ideas.

Is is also a fact that limited real communication takes place in the classroom unless you as the teacher take great pains to see that it occurs. Because of the differences in experiences and expectations of students, they develop divergent perceptual mechanisms. Repetition should be differentiated sufficiently to cater to these perceptual differences. In other words, repetition should not always occur in the same form as the initial instruction. This will bring about under-standing for more students as well as add to the understanding of others.

Repetition may be simple, spaced, cumulative, or massed. Simple repetition occurs when concepts are repeated immediately following the initial presentation. This may be given, obviously, in the same or different form as the initial instructions.

Spaced repetition occurs when the teacher repeats a concept at various intervals during a lesson. This is a particularly useful technique because it increases understanding by relating all subsequent instruction to the initial concept being taught. Thus, the major idea can be viewed continually as the guiding principle during instruction.

Cumulative repetition is a procedure whereby all prior concepts in a sequence are reviewed before new points are presented. This technique is particularly useful when it is viewed as necessary to reidentify all concepts in order to conceptually organize new concepts. It is obviously useful to view the total context into which new ideas are being introduced. It should be remembered, however, that overuse of this technique may produce boredom. It should be used essentially when it is decidedly necessary to do so.

Massed repetition is where all major points are repeated together as they are sequenced, or related. This generally is done at the conclusion of a lesson and serves to summarize and assist students to make a final conceptualization of the material.

Repetition, then, provides a means of permitting students to come in contact with already learned materials for the purpose of helping them add to their understanding by relating previously learned material to new concepts being studied.

The forms that repetition may take are varied. The following is a list of possible forms: figures of speech, metaphors, verbal emphasis, analogies, focusing, visual highlighting, and gestures. It is desirable to use a number of these as well as providing the repetition in the same form as the initial instruction.

Complete the following exercise on repetition:

1. Define the following types of repetition:

1. Simple—

2. Spaced—

3. Cumulative—

4. Massed—

2. Give a description of a specific instance of the use of each type of repetition. Use the actual content of your field of study.

5. *Closure*   Closure may be defined as the relative degree of logical organization or integration of learnings and understandings *as perceived by the learner*. Because closure takes place in the mind of the learner, it must be viewed as more than a quick summary of material given at the close of a lesson. Closure entails the students pulling together the major points of the lesson and conceptually relating them to past knowledge and experience in such a way that a sense of achievement is reached. It must be possible for the student to see where he or she has been in terms of development and where he or she is going. Students must view this as a viable and orderly direction for them to proceed in. In other words, students must know the purposes of the instruction and identify them and be able to visualize how each aspect of instruction articulates with these purposes.

Closure is complementary, therefore, to the process of making the goals of instruction explicitly clear and of having logical rationales for these goals. If students do not agree that the instructional goals are viable for them, they will be reluctant to pursue them. If they are unable to visualize these purposes because they are not clearly defined, then they will make only cursory responses to the learning task and obviously obtain no closure.

Closure is also complementary to set induction. Set induction is made many times in a form which establishes a communicative link between a student's past experiences and knowledge and the materials to be presented. The teacher must then follow through and help the student obtain closure on these same terms. You, as the teacher, may, for example, thwart closure for your students by emphasizing subtopics which are of interest only to you, or a certain group of students may entice the discussion away from the proposed purposes thus confusing and disillusioning others. The purposes of the lesson may also be interfered with by outside influences or management problems in the classroom. These problems may interrupt the flow of the lesson and successfully destroy any possibility for obtaining closure.

In addition to providing set induction, explicitly teaching objectives, and avoiding the problems identified above, you, as the teacher, can also engage in a number of other activities for the purpose of assisting students to gain closure. First, you can carefully organize what is taught into a conceptual model, construct, or generalization. Doing this helps the student increase his or her understanding, which obviously assists in bringing closure. Second, you can provide the students with such organizational cues as "There are eight parts to the process" or "This discussion may be organized under three main headings, namely. . . ." Third, you can use appropriate repetition procedures and allow sufficient time at the end of a lesson for a thorough review. Fourth, you can emphasize closure periodically throughout the lesson, rather than attempting closure only at the end. Fifth, you should, as frequently as needed, connect previous learning to current lesson material. You may also attempt to relate previous and current learning to future learning as well. Finally, closure may be achieved by students demonstrating what they have learned and by you, as the teacher, providing feedback on their responses. You also learn in this process the extent to which students are able to achieve the objectives. You should not assume closure for a whole class when only a few students are able to demonstrate their competency. It is, therefore, recommended that you provide all students an opportunity for trial and feedback prior to evaluation.

Closure, then, is the process of helping students perceive logical organization in a lesson to the point where understanding is developed and a sense of achievement is reached. Most important, closure may be aided by the teacher, but it must take place in the mind of the student. You can determine what is in the student's mind only if you require him to make responses which are valid indicators of a particular understanding.

Complete the following exercise on closure:

1. Explain the timing and purpose of closure.

2. Explain how a teacher may obtain closure; i.e., what procedures can be used to advantage in obtaining closure.

3. Give specific teacher strategies for obtaining closure in a lesson from your own teaching field.

LEARNING ACTIVITY 2: *6. What Are Concepts and Principles?* A concept is a word, an idea, an abstraction that represents the essence of what all things in that category share or have in common. In simple form a concept may represent such things as buildings, trees, fruits, and vegetables. More complex concepts include such things as democracy, capitalism, human rights, and evolution. Simple concepts may be understood and characterized by simply naming examples. To explain a complex concept such as democracy would, however, require a rather lengthy and detailed treatise on the components and characteristics of a number of different examples of democracy.

Concepts usually have attributes that differentiate them from other related concepts. For example, take the concept of *lake.* The major attribute which distinguishes a lake from an ocean and sea, on one hand, and from a pool and pond, on the other hand, is size. Oceans and seas are usually larger than lakes, and pools and ponds are smaller. There are, of course, other attributes of *lake* (fresh water and river drainage) but size is perhaps the most fundamental one. The more complex concepts have a greater number of attributes and generally these attributes are more obscure. Many times the teacher will want to reduce the complexity of some concepts by limiting the number of attributes discussed or by combining a large number of attributes into a smaller number of patterns. For example, in teaching about democracy, an instructor may wish to use only American democracy as an example, or talk about only a limited number of the least obscure characteristics of democracies.

Principles are statements of fundamental truth connoting a relationship between two or more concepts. Other terms often used for principles are rules or generalizations. The following are examples of principles:

Example 1. The greater the availability of a particular commodity, the less it will cost to obtain it in an open market. Illustration: When there is an excess of beef cattle marketed, the result is a decrease in the purchase price of red meat, so long as a program of price supports is not used.

Example 2. The volume of gas in an enclosed space is determined by the temperature and the pressure to which it is subjected.

Illustration: If we place a given mass of oxygen in a container and increase its temperature. it will expand and increase in volume. If pressure is applied to the oxygen, its volume will be reduced.

Example 3. The sooner reinforcement follows a particular response, the more likely that the response will increase in frequency.

Illustration: If we provide encouragement for a good performance in math immediately following the performance, good math performances will be more likely to increase than if we provide encouragement later on.

Example 4. A metaphor literally denotes one kind of object or idea which is used in place of another by way of suggesting likeness or analogy between them.

Illustration: A ship *plows* the sea.

Example 5. Territorial aggrandizement is the major cause of war.

Illustration: In the case of both Germany and Japan in World War II the major motivation for making war was to expand their borders and gain control over additional territory.

Example 6. The greater the number of alternatives, the greater the dissonance in the act of choice.

Illustration: If an individual is trying to decide whether to go to college or get married, there is less of a problem choosing one than when a third alternative is included, such as the possibility of going on a mission to Africa.

Ordinarily when making reference to teaching concepts in the classroom, teachers are really referring to concepts as well as principles. It is important that a proper distinction be made between concepts and principles, but the concept lesson you teach may include concepts, principles, or both. A teacher should accept as evidence that students have learned a concept, the ability to render a definition of the concept, and the ability to identify things which are and things which are not examples of the concepts. In giving a definition of a concept, students should be able to state its characteristics or attributes.

LEARNING ACTIVITY 3: 7. *Interaction Model for Concepts and Principles* The following discussion is an explanation of an interaction method of teaching. This method is primarily oriented toward the teaching of complex concepts and principles. This is the model which you as a trainee should use in teaching your simulated concept lesson.

Subsequent to instruction, you should be able to give a description of the model presented and use the method in teaching a concept lesson.

The rationale for using this model (see Figure 8—1) in teaching can be illustrated by the following study: During World War II, the U.S. Navy had a station in a village in the interior of China which was beset by disease. So the sailors there embarked on an instructional campaign to rid the area of many of the flies which were carriers of disease. In the best pedagogical fashion they set out to show the locals why they should reduce the fly population. They brought in a movie projector and a screen, and projected a detailed drawing of the fly to show how germs were carried on the filth trapped on the legs. When the picture appeared, the audience walked out amidst uproarious laughter. Then the befuddled sailors found the reason. The Chinese had never seen flies that were so large. Magnification of a fly or any other object was outside their experience and thus their perception of the image was impaired. In the classroom students are likely to have similar perceptual difficulties. They may be familiar with magnification of such things as flies, but be completely lost when it comes to perceiving unfamiliar objects magnified under a microscope. They will have to be provided with proper reference points in order to perceive phenomena which are outside their normal experience.

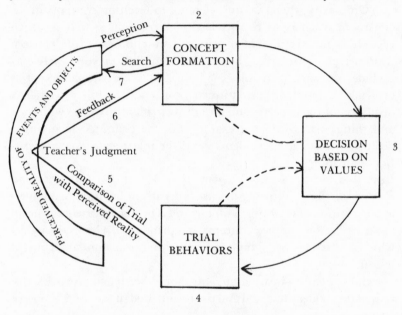

FIGURE 8—1

There are other things besides previous experiences that alter the way in which we perceive our environment. One of these is needs. We frequently perceive our environment in such a way that we exclude those things that are not directly related to the means for meeting our needs. All of our attention becomes focused upon our need deprivation to the exclusion of other factors. Children who come to school hungry provide an example of this. Their learning is greatly hampered because their hunger narrows the range of environmental stimuli to which they are able to attend.

A third item which alters the way in which we perceive reality is that of expectations. This is simply a matter of seeing or hearing those things that we expect to see or hear. It is fairly well-documented, for example, that certain behavioral characteristics are contained in stereotypes about minority groups. People who hold these views are more likely to perceive minority group members displaying these characteristics when indeed they do not. For example, laziness may be associated with a particular minority group. In observing an individual of that minority group, the so-called prejudiced person is more likely to perceive him or her as lazy than someone who doesn't have these perceptual constrictions, even when the facts are to the contrary.

These problems with perception illustrate the point that communication is often difficult because of the different experiences, needs, attitudes, and expectations that we have. In the classroom situation, you, as the teacher, may be expected to deal with students who have had a wide variety of experiences, and who have different needs and expectations. This obviously makes the problem of communicating with children a more complex one. An example is that of a child who has spent his total life in a city environment and has had limited opportunity to observe cows; consequently, concepts related to the concept of a cow may be difficult to teach. The problem for the teacher then becomes one of portraying concepts in such a way that students are able to comprehend them in terms of their present set of experiences. But how does one portray concepts when students come to the learning situation with such a wide variety of experiences and variable readiness? This whole problem of perception and communication implies the need for some kind of feedback system in the communication process in the classroom.

A learning model that illustrates a feedback system is shown in Figure 8—1. Note from the illustration that events and objects in the environment are first perceived and then registered in the central nervous system and related to the present stock of concepts contained there. These perceptions are used by the student to alter his concepts or to change his values regarding the concepts. These new ideas are then used in a decision-making process. The student subsequently decides how these new concepts will be acted out in terms of his or her behavior. This process obviously requires the incorporation of value judgments. The student proceeds to act out his changed conceptions by making a trial response while at the same time comparing his behavior with perceived reality. As he does this, the teacher provides feedback.

If a student shows that he or she has a misconception, you, as the teacher, can assist that student by providing additional experiences or altering the objects or events in the environment to correct it. The student could be asked to make another statement and try out the concept in some other way. One of the significant problems in education is that a portion of this learning cycle is frequently omitted in the process of teaching and learning in the classroom. It is not unusual to find the student engaged in sensory intake and retrieval with little or no time given to decision-making, trial, and feedback. The student more often than not is evaluated on his performance with no opportunity to receive feedback beforehand. This procedure of providing trial and feedback can easily be carried out using a discussion format where the class members are asked to make responses with you providing feedback. This way you as the teacher can provide response-related instruction based on a sample of student behavior as well as get some indication of how well students understand the materials being taught. In some instances feedback can be given to all class members before evaluation takes place. For example, in a math class each student could be required to work a particular problem, with you giving help to those students who are unable to determine the correct answer. In physical education it is also relatively easy to single out individual students who are experiencing difficulty mastering the expected skills and give them individual instruction. In courses like social studies, however, you may have limited opportunity to give feedback on the trial responses of all class members. In this case you will have to depend on sample responses during class discussion. Care should be exercised to avoid sampling the behavior of only the more gifted students.

In introducing a concept to students, there are logical steps to follow that will increase the likelihood that students will understand. First, you as the teacher must provide some kind of motivation. This is the process of establishing set. Next you should engage in a careful and specific outlining of the objective. With this accomplished you are ready to make an initial attempt to teach the concept. Movies and filmstrips are frequently used to clarify complicated ideas. You might also wish to dramatize an experience through role-playing. One might also show the concept in the form of graphs, charts, maps, or diagrams.

Once the instructor has made this initial presentation, the next step is to induce the students to make a trial response. The nature of this trial response depends, of course, on the nature of the objective. The student may be expected to give an explanation of the concept. The teacher then must monitor the student's trial responding and give him or her feedback concerning the correctness of the response. A series of trial-feedback experiences may be necessary before the teacher is satisfied that the students are able to understand a particular point. When you, as teacher, are satisfied with the response of students, your next task is to fix the concept in the minds of the students. This is accomplished by drill or practice. Hopefully, this procedure will assist the student in recalling the concept from memory when necessary. At this point, you are ready to evaluate whether or not the objective of the lesson has been achieved.

LEARNING ACTIVITY 4: The following dialogue represents a concept lesson wherein the teacher demonstrates the teaching skills of set induction, stimulus variation, use of examples, repetition, and closure as well as the interaction model. Read the dialogue and then use the Critique for Simulated Teaching form on p. 306 to rate the performance of this teacher.

8. Concept Lesson Dialogue TEACHER: Many of the questions that you said you'd like answered deal with why something happened, what factors were involved in causing a particular kind of behavior. For example, why are people afraid of the dark? Why are people afraid of doctors who they know can help them? Or why do middle-aged people who use pills put down teen-agers who are on dope? All these *why* questions require that you have a certain bit of knowledge before you can really answer the question. (set induction)

Today we're going to take the first step in trying to figure out how you go about answering a question about human behavior. Before we can figure out or analyze any kind of behavior or any pattern, we have to understand what a drive is and what it does, what part it plays in a whole behavior sequence. Today we'll look at what a drive is and then we'll distinguish between the two types of drives—primary and secondary. After this lesson, each of you should be able to define and give examples of primary and secondary drives and discriminate between examples which I will provide. (objective) We'll define a drive as the following: it is a condition within the organism that initiates a type of action, directs this action, and sustains the action. So a drive does what three things?

STUDENT: It initiates, directs, and sustains action.

TEACHER: Let's take an example: Simon was out in his backyard playing baseball with his friend. He was having a good time when all of a sudden he stopped playing and went inside to get a sandwich, glass of milk, and some cookies. After he consumed these, he went back outside and continued playing. Why do you suppose Simon stopped playing in the first place? Mary? (example)

STUDENT: Because he was hungry and thirsty.

TEACHER: All right, he was hungry and thirsty. (stimulus variation) (Teacher writes on the board) In this case we would say there might have been two drives operating: hunger and thirst. Simon was outside playing, he was hungry. The hunger drive initiated his actions, or his behavior, of stopping his playing and directed him to go inside for lunch. He ate until his hunger drive was fulfilled. So in this case we could say that hunger was the motivator. Hunger was responsible for the change in Simon's behavior. (closure)

Let's take another example, the air-conditioning commercial where the man is out on the hot desert and dramatic music is played. The man staggers to a little hut, opens the door, goes in, and pushes what they call the panic button on the air conditioner. He sits down and with obvious pleasure lets the cool air blow on him. Why do you suppose he went in to turn on the air conditioner in the first place? Jane? (example) (repetition) (stimulus variation)

STUDENT: He was overheated.

TEACHER: Okay, he was hot and wanted to be cooled off. The drive that was working here is what we call maintenance of body temperature. The man was out in the desert working or whatever, the commercial doesn't really show that. In any case, he was overheated and uncomfortable; his body was seeking to maintain a particular kind of balance—maintenance of body temperature. The man stopped whatever he was doing and went in the direction of the house or the source of the cooler air. He stayed in front of the air conditioner until his body had readjusted to a normal level. (closure) Let's look at one other situation. (example) We have Simon again out in the back-yard playing baseball with a friend and his Mom and Dad say, "Okay,

Simon, don't forget we're going to the reception for the new minister this afternoon." So Simon's playing, it's after lunch, and at about 1:30 P.M. he goes inside, bathes, and changes into a suit and tie. He goes to the reception for the minister and he comes home later and changes back into his play clothes and heads for the back yard again. Now why do you suppose Simon changed clothes? Gary? (repetition)

STUDENT: Because he wanted to be accepted socially. If he had gone to the reception all grubby, he would have found that people would not accept him.

TEACHER: Very good. (Teacher approaches student using gestures) (stimulus variation) People might not have approved of someone going to a reception in grubby clothes. Social acceptance is the drive and the motivator involved in Simon's behavior. He was prompted to go in to change his clothes. He wore the clothes until the period of social acceptability was no longer involved in his life. He came home and changed into his grubby clothes. We've talked about two types of drives. We said there's a primary drive and a secondary drive. Take a look at the three drives that have the check marks by them—the hunger, the thirst, and the maintenance of body temperature. These are all examples of primary drives. (closure) Does this give you any kind of clue as to what a primary drive might be? Renee? (stimulus variation)

STUDENT: A primary drive is something you have to have.

TEACHER: All right, something we have to have, something you couldn't live long without. A primary drive is something your body needs for survival. In other words, it's a biological need—it's a very basic need. The body must have these things or it can't function. Social acceptance is what we call a secondary drive. What do you suppose a secondary drive is? Mary? (stimulus variation)

STUDENT: An individual type of thing. I mean not everyone would have it.

TEACHER: Okay, a secondary drive is an individual thing. Where does it come from? Before we can say it is an individual thing we have to know where it came from. Where does it come from? Gary?

STUDENT: You learn it.

TEACHER: All right, you learn it from your environment. Secondary drives are learned needs, they come from the environment. The environment refers primarily to the people we come in contact with and activities we engage in with them. Now, Mary, you mentioned something about secondary drives being individual. (closure) Could you explain a little bit about what you mean? (stimulus variation)

STUDENT: Well, it is something not everyone possesses because not everyone needs it as opposed to the primary drive.

TEACHER: Okay, everyone needs to satisfy their primary drives—the organism needs them in order to survive. Secondary drives are learned needs—you learn them through the interaction of the organism with the environment. These will be much more individual. So when you look at one question, like why are people afraid of the dark, you have first of all to decide what kind of drive is involved, what kinds of needs are being met in the situation, and what are the individual needs that the person has or what are the needs that everyone has? (closure) I think the best way for you to understand these is to give you some more examples of drives and have you tell me if they're primary or secondary. We'll start with hunger. Is hunger a primary drive or a secondary drive? Frank? (example)

STUDENT: Primary.

TEACHER: Okay, how do you know it's a primary drive?

STUDENT: Because you can't survive without food.

TEACHER: All right, the body needs it for survival. Good. How about vocational ambition? Jane? (example)

STUDENT: That would be a secondary drive.

TEACHER: How do you know?

STUDENT: Because not everyone has the same vocational ambition. We vary a lot in terms of what we want our life's work to be.

TEACHER: All right, it would be a secondary drive. What about success at sewing? Janet? (example)

STUDENT: Secondary, because it's something you learn; you're not born with it.

TEACHER: Okay, good, you're not born with the desire for success at sewing. You learn this sometime during life. That's what makes it a secondary drive. It's a drive, because what does it do? It gets people involved in certain kinds of behavior, initiates, directs, and sustains a certain behavior until the person is satisfied in part. (closure) Let's look at another example. Let's take nest–building for a wasp. Jane? (example)

STUDENT: That wouldn't be either one, would it?

TEACHER: What would it be then?

STUDENT: Isn't it an instinct?

TEACHER: Okay, you say it would be an instinct instead of a drive because what? (stimulus variation)

STUDENT: It's inborn; wasps don't have to learn how to do it. I suppose you could say it's a primary drive, but it's not really biologically based.

TEACHER: All right, now we have a bit of comparing here to do. We said a primary drive is something that is inborn, everyone has it, it's biological. Now you're saying that instinct is also something that is inborn. Something that a wasp, for example, doesn't have to learn. (closure) All right, the wasp doesn't have to learn how to build a nest, but what is the difference between an instinct and a drive? Gary? (stimulus variation)

STUDENT: Isn't a drive a condition?

TEACHER: Okay.

STUDENT: And an instinct would be something that they do.

TEACHER: All right, a drive is a condition and an instinct is an activity, an action, or behavior. In this case, the wasp is building a nest in response to something. A drive is a condition. A drive initiates, directs, and sustains the behavior. A drive itself is not behaving. Okay, that's a good distinction between an instinct and a drive. (closure) Let's take another example. How about an eye blink? A cinder falls in your eye and you blink your eye. Is that a primary or secondary drive? Jane? (example) (repetition)

STUDENT: A reflex.

TEACHER: A reflex. Why would it be a reflex? (stimulus variation)

STUDENT: Because you don't really learn how to blink your eye. It's done naturally, you don't even think about it.

TEACHER: Okay, how about primary drives, aren't they things that you don't learn?

STUDENT: Yes, but a reflex is a kind of unconscious action.

TEACHER: All right. Frank?

STUDENT: Couldn't you say it's a drive because you make the eye blink because it wants to keep the eye clear and wet?

TEACHER: Jane?

STUDENT: If you were to say it was a drive then that is not the eye blink itself, that's the force that makes the eye blink. The eye would be what initiates the behavior. The drive is what happens before you blink your eye. You know like if it hurt or something. But the actual eye blink would be a reflex because a drive is not an action, it's a condition.

TEACHER: Okay, that's the biggest distinction or summary of the whole thing. A drive is a condition, it's not something you see; you see evidences of it but you don't see the drive itself. The behavior you see, in this case, is a reflex. Action was involved, some kind of response, some kind of behavior. So in this case, the eye blink would be a reflex. (closure) How about another example—success of working on a car, making a car run. Renee? (example) (repetition)

STUDENT: Wouldn't that be a secondary drive?

TEACHER: Okay, it's a secondary drive. Why?

STUDENT: Because it's something you've learned, not everybody has it.

TEACHER: How about the need for oxygen? (example) Gary? (repetiton)

STUDENT: Primary drive.

TEACHER: Okay, a primary drive.

STUDENT: Biologically, you need it.

TEACHER: Right. It's biological because it's something your body can't survive without. How about fear? (example) (repetition) Jane?

STUDENT: Wouldn't that be secondary?

TEACHER: Okay, a secondary drive. Pain? (example) (repetition) Renae?

STUDENT: Primary.

TEACHER: Okay, pain is a primary drive. How do you know that?

STUDENT: Well, because it's something everybody has, not exactly a need for survival, but . . .

TEACHER: Okay, something people have which motivates them to avoid pain. Pain is a little bit different drive than some of the others we've been talking about. Other drives encourage you to go for something, to seek out food, water, to seek out cool air. Pain encourages you to avoid whatever it is that's causing that pain. It's a condition that directs your action in a certain way. (closure) How about money? Frank? (example)

STUDENT: That's secondary because it's learned.

TEACHER: Okay, secondary drive, good. Love of baseball? Gary?

STUDENT: Secondary, because you learn it and it's not biological.

TEACHER: Good. Let's try one more. Thirst? Mary? (example)

STUDENT: That would be a primary drive.

TEACHER: Good. All right, to review again, a drive is a condition within the organism itself—it initiates action, directs action, and sustains action or behavior until the drive has been reduced. Primary drives are biologically based drives. Something that every organism needs in order to survive. Secondary drives are drives which are learned on an individual basis. Each individual has his own particular kind. (closure)

LEARNING ACTIVITY 5: *Examples of Concept Objectives* Look at the following examples of concept objectives and then attempt to formulate some concept objectives for a lesson you may teach.

1. Students will demonstrate their understanding of the process of osmosis by computing eight out of ten problems correctly and writing the answers.

2. Students will give a complete written description of the process of photosynthesis. The description must include accurate reference to the chemical reactions which take place, the plant structures responsible for receiving light, wave lengths of light absorbed, and the exchange of gases necessary.

3. Students must be able to make a written explanation of the principle of reinforcement in learning. This explanation must make accurate reference to stimulus and response connection and the special conditions which enhance the effects of reinforcement.

4. Students must be able to give a complete and accurate written description of the mathematical principle of set and solve at least 80 percent of the problems illustrating this principle.

5. Students will be able to give a written explanation of the function and execution of the screen in basketball. This explanation must include at least five possible maneuvers which an offensive player may engage in from a properly executed screen.

6. Students will demonstrate their understanding of Charles's and Boyle's Laws by correctly computing 80 percent of the problems involving these laws.

7. Students will demonstrate their understanding of metaphors by composing at least five appropriate examples.

8. Students will be able to make a written explanation of how

CRITIQUE FOR SIMULATED TEACHING:

Concept Lesson

Teacher_____ Date_____
Evaluator _____

	Unable to Observe	Not Achieved	Below Average	Average	Strong	Superior
	0	1	2	3	4	5
1. Set Induction—Was the set induction motivating and properly related to the learning task? How could it have been improved?						
2. Stimulus Variation—Did the teacher change the mode of the stimulus so that there was adequate variation? How could improvements be made?						
3. Use of Examples—Did the teacher use clear and appropriate examples? Did he or she request examples from students? Where would examples have been appropriate when they were not used?						
4. Repetition—Did the teacher provide repetition in appropriate places as a means of enhancing the learning of his students? How could it have been improved?						
5. Closure—Did the teacher make appropriate use of closure? How should this skill have been employed?						
6. Objectives—Were the objectives of the lesson clearly understood by the students? How could they have been improved?						

	Unable to Observe	Not Achieved	Below Average	Average	Strong	Superior
	0	1	2	3	4	5

7. Empathy—Was the teacher empathic in correction of student's misconceptions and did he or she display skill in interpreting the intent of student questions? Give instances where empathy was shown or where there was lack of empathy.

8. Interaction Skill—Did the teacher demonstrate skill in engaging students in interaction?

9. Enthusiasm?

10. Appearance and Mannerisms?

11. Communication Skills?

12. Skill in the Use of Audio-Visual Aids— Did the visual aids add to the lesson or detract from it?

13. Learning Activities—Were learning activities appropriate in terms of the objectives? Describe the ways in which they were or were not.

14. Objectives Achieved—Were the objectives of the lesson achieved?

It is expected that individuals using this form for purposes of evaluation give written explanations and criticisms which correspond to the questions above as well as check an overall rating in each category. It is particularly useful for raters to include suggested improvements for the lessons they view.

chromosome inversions take place and the procedure by which inversion can be detected.

9. Students will be able to formulate a written explanation of sex linkage and show what the characteristics of progeny would be from a series of matings involving a number of different genes. One hundred percent accuracy is expected.

LEARNING ACTIVITY 6:   Complete the following worksheet.

1. What is a concept?

2. What is a principle?

3. Write two examples of a concept and two examples of a principle from your teaching field.

4. Write a concept and give one example and one nonexample of the concept.

5. Why is an interaction method for teaching a concept or principle recommended?

LEARNING ACTIVITY 7:   As you read the following examples of lesson plans, begin thinking of a topic from your own major field which you could use in a simulated lesson. Then organize a concept lesson which facilitates engaging students in interaction. Plan your lesson so that you will be able to demonstrate the skills of set induction, stimulus variation, use of examples, repetition, and closure. Make certain that your lesson follows the format outlined in the examples presented here.

9. Sample Concept Lesson Plans In this section, there are two sample lesson plans presented for your consideration. Notice that each contains the following elements: behavior, preassessment, content, learning experiences, materials, evaluations, and strategy. Notice that the objective is stated in behavioral terms and that it requires students to understand a concept. Notice also that the content section is composed of a statement of the concept as well as subcomponent concepts. This section ordinarily contains whatever conceptual information is necessary for a student to understand in order to achieve the objective.

The section on learning experiences is a list of the activities which students engage in in order to achieve the objective. These experiences should resemble as closely as possible the behavior called for in the objective and should provide practice for the behavior as it will be evaluated. Notice that the learning experiences include a plan for the teacher to give feedback to students prior to evaluation.

The materials section should identify any pieces of equipment and/or materials which will be used in the lesson. It should also be noted in this section when special arrangements need to be made for such activities as field trips.

In the evaluation section, there is ordinarily included either a description of how students will be evaluated or examples of questions which will be used in the evaluation. Even though sample questions may not appear in an actual lesson plan, it is required here so that your ability to write appropriate test items may be checked. You should be certain that the items you include do indeed measure the extent to which students are able to achieve the objective.

The strategy section is another section that may or may not be included in an actual lesson plan. It is included here for the purpose of encouraging you to think about any special problems you might encounter in a classroom which would act as a deterrent to effectively presenting your lesson. Your ability to overcome the normal contraints in helping students to achieve the objectives you have outlined is a crucial skill in teaching. Some of the most common problems include reading dysfunctions, hyperactivity, disruptiveness, inability to concentrate, failure to think criticially, search for peer approval, and so on.

Finally, you should note that each of these lesson plans is

obviously designed for different lengths of time. Sample Lesson Plan 1 can be given in a much shorter period than Plan 2.

SAMPLE LESSON PLAN 1

Class: Senior Psychology
Title: Cognitive Dissonance
Preassessment:

Prior to discussion, determine the level of understanding regarding cognitive dissonance by asking a series of questions covering principles in the content section.

Objective:

Students will be able to write a complete explanation of the concept of cognitive dissonance, giving at least three examples of the concept and explaining how the dissonance may be reduced in each case.

Content:

1. When a person holds cognitions about himself or the environment that are inconsistent with each other, he experiences dissonance.

2. The person tries to diminish dissonance by reducing the number of inconsistent cognitions about himself.

3. The magnitude of psychological dissonance is a direct function of what one has to give up compared to what one obtains.

4. The greater the qualitative dissimilarity of alternatives, the greater the magnitude of dissonance from choice.

5. The greater number of alternatives, the greater the magnitude of dissonance from choice.

6. Greater choice under deprivation results in greater satisfaction and less dissonance.

Learning Experiences:

1. Discuss each of the concepts outlined in the content section and give examples.

2. Ask each student to write an example of dissonance. Collect these and discuss some of them with the class.

3. Have each student develop five examples of dissonance as a homework assignment to be turned in.

4. Give feedback to students on their homework assignments.

Materials: Overhead projector and transparencies of main points and examples.

Evaluation: Sample Questions

1. Give a complete explanation of cognitive dissonance, using at least three examples during your explanation.

2. How would you recommend reducing dissonance in each of the examples you identified?

Strategy:

The members of this particular class generally memorize well but don't attempt to think. For this reason, you could inform them that they should not use examples of dissonance discussed in class but to think of others. You could attempt to get the interest and attention of the class by asking them if they have ever heard anyone rationalize by downgrading what they haven't chosen and upgrading what they have chosen. Then ask them if they have ever wondered why.

SAMPLE LESSON PLAN 2

Class: Senior Biology

Title: Energy Transfer in Biological Systems

Preassessment:

Ask students to define the following terms: energy, potential energy, food chain, biomass, ecosystem, and metabolism.

Objective:

Students will be able to explain satisfactorily the transfer of energy in a food chain, pointing out the influence on energy transfer of the following items.

1. The length of the food chain and available energy.

2. Spontaneity of energy transformation.

3. Size-metabolism relationships and trophic structure of biological communities.

4. Energy loss.

Content: Basic Concepts

1. Energy may be transformed from one type to another but it is never created or destroyed.

2. No process involving an energy transformation will spontaneously occur unless there is a degradation of energy from a concentrated form into a dispersed form.

3. Because some energy is always dispersed into unavailable heat energy, no spontaneous transformation of energy (light, for example) into potential energy (protoplasm, for example) is 100 percent efficient.

4. In each transfer in a food chain, a large proportion of the potential energy is lost as heat.

5. The number of links in a food chain is usually limited to four or five.

6. The shorter the food chain, the greater the available energy that can be converted into biomass. (Biomass—living weight, including stored food.)

7. The smaller the organism, the greater its metabolism per gram of biomass.

8. The smaller the organism, the smaller the biomass which can be supported at a particular trophic level in the ecosystem. Example: Fewer bacteria could be supported than a crop of fish in terms of grams of biomass.

9. The interaction of the food chain (energy loss at each transfer) and the size-metabolism relationship results in communities having a definite trophic structure which is often characteristic of a particular type of ecosystem (lake, forest, coral reef, etc.).

Learning Experiences:

1. Before coming to class, students should have read Chapter 3 in *Fundamentals of Ecology* by Odum.

2. Use the overhead projector to portray the energy flow diagram and discuss it.

3. Discuss the concepts outlined in the content of the lesson and explain how they are related to the concept of energy transfer. Get written responses from every student and provide feedback to them.

4. Direct students to appropriate laboratory experiments regarding energy transfer.

5. Field trip to Lackley Pond to observe food chain relationships.

Materials:

Overhead projector, laboratory equipment, and biological material, bus arrangements.

Evaluation: Sample Questions

1. Explain how energy transfer occurs in a typical food chain. In your answer, explain how the length of the food chain and size-metabolism are related to energy transfer.

2. Identify the various points of energy loss in a food chain including herbs, deer, and mountain lion.

Strategy:

There may be some difficulty for the below-average student in formulating the concept of energy transfer. Because it is so critical to the understanding of the whole field of ecology, plan to give individual assistance to these students during lab time. In order to get the interest of the class initially, plan to give the following set induction: "One of the most critical problems facing man is that of acquiring sufficient fuel and food energy. In order to feed the world population, it is becoming increasingly imperative that new and better food sources be found. In order to solve this problem, a good understanding of how energy transfer occurs in food chains is necessary."

LEARNING ACTIVITY 8: Read the following two sections: How to Analyze a Simulated Lesson and Simulated Lesson Analysis: An Example. These two sections will explain the format which should be used in making an analysis of your simulated teaching. You should read and study them carefully so that you can make a similar analysis of your teaching. Also examine the Concept Lesson Analysis Guide. This guide will be used to aid you in making an analysis of your videotaped lesson. Fill it in as you view a videotaped replay of your lesson and keep it to use when you prepare your written analysis of your lesson.

10: How to Analyze a Simulated Lesson The critique form for simulated teaching should be used as a basis for analyzing your lesson. Each of the teaching skills should be described in terms of the specific way in which you performed during the first lesson and how you could have improved or did improve your performance in the second lesson on that particular skill. For example, if your set induction was not sufficiently motivating, identify the reason it was not and describe exactly what you could have done or what you could have said to improve it, and how you were able to accomplish this in your second lesson.

You should avoid analyzing your lesson by making general

statements regarding your behavior—how you appeared or how you felt. Such statements as "I was really nervous" or "I didn't know what to do with my hands" contribute little to an analysis.

It is important that you understand what behavior is represented by each of the skills. Unless you do, you will be unable to make an appropriate analysis. If, for example, you believe closure to be synonymous with a review, your analysis will disclose your misunderstanding of this term.

When analyzing your objective, it is essential that you make a judgment not in terms of how you stated your objective, but rather on the extent to which your students knew what was expected of them subsequent to instruction. They should clearly understand how they must respond and how you will judge their performance. The purpose of the lesson and how students are expected to respond in terms of the lesson objective should ordinarily be taught at the beginning of the lesson. It is generally good practice to begin a lesson with set induction and follow this immediately with a statement of the expected student outputs.

The learning experiences in which you engage students should contribute to achieving the objectives you have identified for students. You should check your lesson carefully to see if there is a close correspondence between the objectives and the learning activities in which students participated. In your lesson, it is expected that students will enter into a dialogue with you and that you will give feedback on the students' trial responses. This type of learning activity is important because it is usually necessary for the teacher to correct student responses a number of times before they are adequately exhibited. In your analysis, attempt to make a judgment regarding the clarity with which this dialogue proceeds. Are you supportive of student responses? Are you empathic? Do you ask students to clarify ambiguous statements they make? Do you give good examples in addition to asking students to formulate their own examples? These questions will help in making an analysis of your own lesson.

11. Simulated Lesson Analysis: An Example   Set Induction—My second lesson was a significant improvement over my first. Set induction was particularly weak in my first lesson. I simply stated that "Today we are going to learn about stomates." This statement stood for both the set induction and the objective. For my set induction, I could have begun with the statement "A single corn plant may transpire four quarts of water a day. An acre of corn may give off 300,000 gallons of water in a single growing season. How do you think such a large water loss is possible?" I could then have shown the class a magnified picture of a leaf, showing stomates and explain that water is lost through these minute openings at varying rates depending on the size of the opening and the number of openings per unit of area on the leaf surface. I could then have asked if they would expect desert plants to have more or fewer stomates than tropical plants. In my second lesson I did this. I had their immediate attention.

Objective—I would then teach the lesson objective to the students in the following manner: "We are going to study stomates and their functioning. When we have completed this lesson, you should be able to explain the mechanism by which the stomate opens and what factors influence this opening."

Stimulus Variation—In my first lesson, the stimulus variation was good. I think I did an adequate job of using student-to-student and student-to-teacher interaction. I also think that my movements about the room and gestures were natural and expressive. The one improvement that I wanted to make was to include variations in terms of aural and visual stimuli. In order to accomplish this I used the chalkboard to diagram what I was talking about. I believe that student attention as well as understanding was enhanced by this change.

Use of Examples—In my first lesson, students found it difficult to understand how the two guard cells could expand and contract in such a way as to cause an opening and closing of the stomate. For my second presentation, I constructed a mock-up of a stomate using a bicycle inner tube with additional thicknesses of tubing glued to its inner surfaces. As air is forced into the inner tube, it opens in a way similar to stomates. This example clarified the process very well. One thing that I failed to do in both lessons was to ask for examples from the students. I could have asked if anyone knew examples of osmotic pressure and how it operated.

Repetition—In my first lesson I failed to have any repetition at all. I thought I was being understood. Only at the end of the lesson did I realize that students were unable to understand how new information related to previously covered material. In my second lesson I carefully reviewed the concepts of turgor and osmotic pressure before illustrating how the guard cells expanded. This procedure greatly increased the understanding of the students.

Closure—In my first lesson I did not achieve closure at all. I reviewed at the end of the lesson but each part of the lesson was not understood by students in terms of their relationships, and thus a review was pointless. I decided that misconception of the process of osmosis was the basic problem area and the major reason why students were unable to obtain closure. In the second lesson I set up a demonstration of osmotic pressure using a semipermeable membrane to show students that water actually flowed into areas of higher concentration of dissolved substances. I then made a diagram on the board like the one illustrated:

Students were able to obtain closure on stomate opening with a proper conception of osmosis as I explained the diagram.

Interaction and Feedback—One of the major problems in my first lesson was the small amount of student-to-teacher interaction during the time the most complex part of the lesson was presented. I didn't realize this until I was watching the playback. In my second lesson I did a better job of connecting the various concepts. It was still very evident that my communication skill is limited. For one thing, I tend not to complete statements. I just trail off in the end expecting the class to fill in what I don't complete.

Concept Lesson Analysis Guide

1. Cite two instances of giving examples of the concept you were attempting to teach.

2. Cite one example where you asked a student to provide an example of the concept.

3. Cite one nonexample which you used to clarify the concept. If no nonexamples were given, formulate one and identify where it could have been used to advantage in the lesson.

4. What evidence do you have that learners understood and achieved your objective? Cite at least two instances of student behavior which indicate the objective was achieved.

5. Cite at least two instances that give evidence that students were interested in your lesson. How could you have gained more interest in your lesson?

6. Cite two specific instances of how you varied the stimulus in your presentation. What was the student reaction to your maneuver? How could you have improved your stimulus variation?

7. Cite at least two instances where your questions were unclear. How did learners respond to these questions? How could you have rephrased your questions to reflect the appropriate clarity?

8. Identify two specific instances where you tried to obtain

closure. Give evidence, in terms of student responses, that you did achieve closure or identify the reason that you were unable to achieve closure.

LEARNING ACTIVITY 9:   Read the Replanning a Lesson section that follows. One of the skills that should be developed in teaching is that of making appropriate analysis of teaching and formulating alternative approaches to diminish the weaknesses pointed out in your analysis. Since you will be replanning and reteaching a number of lessons, you should carefully consider the points outlined in the following section.

12. Replanning a Lesson   The perfect lesson has probably never been taught. Even with a well-taught lesson, careful analysis invariably reveals weaknesses, which when corrected, improve subsequent presentations. The tendency for the beginning teacher is to say that he or she did all right in asking higher-order questions or in cueing or in demonstrating any of the other teaching skills when, in reality, what was demonstrated was a minimum level of acceptability. In teaching, minimum acceptable levels can and should be improved upon. This requires that a careful analysis be performed regarding the planning and teaching of a lesson and that subsequent planning and teaching reflect revisions designed to overcome the problems. It is desirable that you begin developing sophistication in analyzing teaching and planning so that you don't come to consider mediocre teaching as acceptable or believe you are doing all right when you could do better.

As part of this package, you are required to make an analysis of the presentation of your simulated lesson. Using this analysis as a basis, you must formulate a new lesson plan which will help in overcoming the problems identified in the first lesson. It is essential that in rethinking your lesson, you develop alternative approaches. For example, if in your first lesson you failed to bring about closure for part of the class as a result of questioning only a few students during the discussion, you may alter this procedure by requiring all students to make a trial response during the lesson. This change would be reflected in the Learning Experiences section of your lesson plan.

The trainee should examine each part of his lesson plan and lesson presentation with the intention of altering each of these components appropriately. Some components may not need much change, but each should be carefully considered.

EVALUATION

SIMULATED TEACHING AND ANALYSIS

Teach a concept lesson to a group of pupils using an interaction model and incorporating the skills of set induction, stimulus variation, use of examples, repetition, and closure. (Pupil participants should be asked to provide the teacher with an evaluation of the lesson.) Have an instructor videotape your lesson as you teach it. While viewing the videotape replay, make a self-analysis of your lesson using the procedure explained in this chapter, How to Analyze the Simulated Lesson and Simulated Lesson Analysis: An Example. Also use the Concept Lesson Analysis Guide in making your analysis.

REPLANNING, RETEACHING, AND ANALYSIS

Using the information from the pupil evaluations as well as your own, reorganize your concept lesson and reteach it. Pay particular attention to overcoming the problems identified in your first attempt at the lesson. Identify how you could improve in the use of the following skills: set induction, stimulus variation, use of examples, repetition, and closure. Check to see if your objective was carefully taught to and understood by the class. Identify any annoying mannerisms or poor communication skills. Determine whether or not you could reasonably expect your students to be able to achieve the objectives. It is imperative that the reorganization of your lesson reflect a careful restructuring of your strategy based on the analysis of your first lesson. You should be able to produce a significantly different approach to the lesson. Videotape the retaught lesson. Get evaluations from your pupils. Make a self-analysis of your lesson while viewing the videotaped replay. Use the format outlined in How to Analyze the Simulated Lesson and Simulated Lesson Analysis: An Example.

Note: Supervisory personnel may also provide feedback and evaluation during the simulated teaching experiences.

chapter 9

The Analysis Lesson

OBJECTIVES

1. From your major or minor field of study, you will develop a lesson plan for teaching at the analysis level in the cognitive domain using the guided discussion method. The lesson plan must follow the format outlined in the Sample Analysis Lesson Plan, number 7 of the Instructional Procedures in this chapter.

2. You will teach a fifteen-minute lesson having an instructional objective at the analysis level in the cognitive domain and utilizing the guided discussion method. You must appropriately demonstrate the skills of set induction, cueing, reinforcement, higher-order questions, and closure. This lesson will be taught to public school students or peers and if possible should be videotaped.

3. After viewing the videotape of your lesson, you will make an analysis of your teaching. You must be able to evaluate teaching skill in the use of set induction, cueing, reinforcement, higher-order questions, and closure. You must also be able to determine the extent to which you learned how to perform analysis skills and how skillfully you used the guided discussion method.

4. You must also be able to replan and reteach this fifteen-

minute lesson, eliminating the problem areas identified in your analysis of the first lesson. You must make a written analysis from the videotaped replay of your lesson, using the Critique for Simulated Teaching form (following number 5, Teaching an Analysis Lesson, in this chapter), and include a comparison between the teach and reteach cycles. The format which you must use in making this analysis is illustrated in How to Analyze a Simulated Lesson and Simulated Lesson Analysis: An Example, found in Chapter 8, numbers 10 and 11 of the Instructional Procedures.

PREASSESSMENT

The following questions reflect the information presented in this chapter. Each question is followed by a number that links it to the *Instructional Procedures* included in this chapter. Questions are designed to aid the student in determining his or her present level of knowledge and skill. Use them as a guide to the various sections presented.

1. What is the justification for the use of cueing? *(1)*
2. When is the use of private cueing to be encouraged? *(1)*
3. What does it mean to shape a student's cueing? *(1)*
4. What are the effects of overcueing? *(1)*
5. What is the relationship between reinforcement and the frequency of a particular behavior? *(2)*
6. What is the difference between reinforcement and punishment? *(2)*
7. What does it mean to ignore inappropriate student responses? *(2)*
8. What is the relationship between timing and the strength of reinforcement? *(2)*
9. What is the relationship between deprivation states and the strength of reinforcement? *(2)*
10. What are tangible reinforcers? *(2)*
11. What is pairing of reinforcement? *(2)*
12. What alternatives are there to providing external reinforcement in order to manage the classroom? *(2)*
13. How can a teacher vary the magnitude of his reinforcement in order to vary its effect? *(2)*
14. How is using the ideas of students reinforcing? *(2)*

15. How can a teacher employ success as a reinforcer? *(2)*

16. What is meant by higher-order questions? *(3)*

17. What are the specific things which higher-order questions require the student to do? *(3)*

18. How is Bloom's *Taxonomy* used in the formulation of higher-order questions? *(3)*

19. What are three factors which determine the kind of thinking brought about in the mind of the student by a particular question? *(3)*

20. Give examples of questions which cause students to engage in the following types of mental activities: analysis, synthesis, and evaluation. *(3)*

21. What are the differences between a bull session, an open-ended discussion, and a guided class discussion? For what different purposes are these procedures used? *(4)*

22. What skills are needed in directing a guided discussion? *(4)*

23. What specific consequences should be expected in a guided class discussion? *(4)*

24. What conditions must ordinarily be met if a guided discussion is to function smoothly? *(4)*

25. What are the recommended steps in planning for and teaching a guided discussion? How is each of these steps used? *(4)*

26. If consensus is desired in a guided discussion, how can this be achieved? *(4)*

27. How can a guided discussion be used as a vehicle for initiating research? *(4)*

INSTRUCTIONAL PROCEDURES

LEARNING ACTIVITY 1: Review the descriptions for the skills of set induction and closure found in Chapter 8. Then read the following descriptions of the skills of cueing, reinforcement, and asking higher–order questions, and complete the exercises which accompany these descriptions.

1. Cueing Justification for cueing can readily be made from the fact that wrong as well as right answers strengthen themselves as soon as they occur. Consequently, merely correcting responses will not reduce their tendency to occur. In other words, making inappropriate responses will reduce one's ability to make the appropriate ones subsequently. Cues help to guide the student in making the correct responses. Cues usually are diminished gradually as the student demonstrates the ability to make appropriate responses.

You, as the teacher, must make a decision regarding the timing and nature of cueing. If it appears that a good deal of preparation for an adequate response is necessary, you may have to provide the appropriate cues a day or so in advance. You must also decide whether or not the cueing should be in public or private. Private cueing a day in advance may be the best way to get an overly shy person to participate in class.

Occasionally a particular cue isn't sufficient to prepare students to respond appropriately. A series of successive approximations is recommended as a strategy for gradually helping the student to make the desired response. Several cues may be presented before a student responds. Additional cueing may be engaged in subsequent to the student's response if the teacher desires to clarify the student's thinking. You, as the teacher, thus shape the student responses until they are appropriately given.

One should use appropriate timing when cueing students. Each cue should be followed by a sufficiently long period of silence to permit students to formulate their response. Overcueing in rapid succession exceeds the thinking capabilities of most students and results in the teacher rather than the students giving the desired responses. The length of time you should wait between cues is directly proportional to the difficulty level of the question and the proximity of the cue to the appropriate response. This requires the exercise of judgment. A good deal of experience is usually required to adequately master this skill.

The following are some examples of how cueing may proceed:

TEACHER: If you were going on a trip to Mars, what special systems would have to be developed in order to support life on such a voyage?

CLASS: Silence.

TEACHER: What would you do about food? (This cue helps the student limit the field from which to formulate his response.)

STUDENT: You would have to carry a lot of dehydrated foods and high-energy foods I suppose.

TEACHER: If you couldn't carry enough food with you, how could you obtain it? (This cue is designed to help the student focus attention away from a less plausible response to one that is more reasonable.)

STUDENT: I suppose you could grow it.

TEACHER: What kind of food could be grown in a spaceship that would meet requirements for such a long voyage? (This cue helps to focus the students' attention upon the problem of what kind of food could be grown in limited confines of a spacecraft.)

TEACHER: How do you move off a screen in basketball?

CLASS: Silence.

TEACHER: When and how do you make your move? (This cue limits the field from which the student needs to make his response.)

STUDENT: You want to fake when the screen passes just behind your defensive opponent.

TEACHER: How do you make sure that your opponent doesn't gain a position between you and the player screening for you? (This cue is designed to help the student understand that his response is fragmentary and that he needs to consider additional related information.)

STUDENT: You need to time your fake so the defensive player is set back a step or two and then pass as closely as possible to the player performing the screen.

TEACHER: From the diagrams can you determine whether sodium or nickel would be more reactive?

CLASS: Silence.

TEACHER: How many electrons in the outer shell of each element? (This cue helps the student determine what he needs to consider in making an appropriate response.)

STUDENT: Sodium would be more reactive because it has only one electron in the outer shell.

Complete the following exercise on cueing:

1. Describe different instances where cueing is appropriate.

2. Write a difficult or complex question from your teaching field

and identify the cues you would use in clarifying the intent of the question so that students are able to answer it. (Include questions and instructions that are likely to be necessary.)

2. Reinforcement One of the more fundamental functions of the classroom teacher is to provide appropriate reinforcement to students. Research on the use of reinforcement in the classroom has been extensive and generally conclusive. Reinforcing a response or set of responses increases the likelihood that a particular behavior will occur. In addition, it increases the response frequency. It is important to differentiate reinforcement from punishment because of the widespread misunderstanding regarding these terms. Reinforcement refers to an increase in the number of responses as a consequence of presenting or removing some kind of stimulus. Usually the teacher defines these procedures in terms of what he or she does rather than the effect his or her actions have on the number of student responses. This should not be done.

For example, a teacher who scolds a student who exhibits disruptive behavior usually believes that he or she is punishing the child and that the consequence will be a reduction in disruptiveness. However, it is common for such teacher behavior to increase the disruptive behavior output of some students. In other words, the scolding is reinforcing the student's deviant responses. It is absolutely essential that you, as the teacher, understand which responses are reinforcing and which ones are punishing.

A good model to follow in the classroom is generally to ignore inappropriate student responses and reinforce appropriate ones. The more appropriate behaviors that can be encouraged, the less time students have to be disruptive. There is a tendency for beginning teachers to focus attention on disruptive behaviors rather than ignoring them. It will undoubtedly require considerable thought and practice to develop this skill.

One of the principles that has consistently shown up in studies of reinforcement is that the closer (in time) reinforcement follows the desired behavior, the more influence it has on subsequent behavior. Thus, the longer reinforcement is delayed, the less impact it will have.

Of course, it is not always possible to follow a particular response immediately with the appropriate reinforcement. This has led some teachers to provide students some indication (in the form of a token which can be exchanged) that they will receive the reinforcement later, thus bridging the time gap.

Another principle which the teacher would be wise to utilize in terms of reinforcement is paying attention to the deprivation states of students. A deprivation state refers to a condition where an individual has a strong need or desire for a particular thing at a particular time. The effect of reinforcement is directly related to the degree of deprivation which that particular reinforcer would satisfy. For example, if it can be determined that a student has an intense need to be recognized, the teacher can arrange for the student to be recognized when he or she behaves appropriately.

There is usually a good deal of difference in terms of potency between verbal reinforcers, tangibles, and special privileges. Tangibles are such things as candy, money, trinkets, stars; special privileges are such things as going to the lunchroom early, being the teacher's assistant, and running the projector. Some students can be strongly influenced by any of these but may respond poorly to verbal reinforcement.

One way to get around this difficulty is to pair verbal reinforcement with tangibles or special privileges. Later when the behavior has been brought under control, gradually diminish tangibles and special privileges while continuing to maintain an adequate amount of verbal reinforcement. A good deal of reinforcement may be necessary to encourage appropriate behavior by students initially. It is hoped that this level of required reinforcement can be reduced when the students become more interested in the subject matter itself as a consequence of their involvement with it. Thus, the subject matter itself can provide a reinforcing function and reduce the frequency of teacher reinforcement needed to a manageable level.

It should be pointed out that some educators have developed arguments against the exclusive use of external reinforcers for managing the behaviors of students and encouraging appropriate academic responses. In this brief discussion it can only be noted that these individuals believe differently about human nature and the nature of motivation. They believe that man has purposive motivations built in rather than motivation based on drive reduction or satisfaction in responding as a consequence of reinforcing external stimuli. Rather than organizing the environment to influence behavior in specified directions, they believe that one should be expected, as a result of natural consequences, to develop responsible behavior. This behavior repertoire should help the individual engage in meaningful interpersonal relations which satisfy his social needs. The management procedures used involve helping the individual identify unacceptable behavior and its consequence and formulating acceptable alternatives which can be adhered to and which logically will help achieve relatedness and respect in the real world.

In delivering verbal reinforcement, you, as the teacher, should be careful to temper your response so as to correspond to the responses made by the students. Matter-of-fact reinforcers that usually appear in normal conversation such as "Right," "Uh-huh," and "Good" provide low-key feedback to the student. If a student response is particularly outstanding, the teacher may make such exclamations as "Excellent," "Very good," or may even provide such verbalizations as "Fantastic!" and "Tremendous!" Each of the above verbalizations can be given different connotations simply by varying the tone, expressing differing nonverbal feedback such as smiling, nodding the head, or gesturing with the arms and hands. The important point to remember is that the reinforcement should correspond to the response so that it doesn't appear either bland or gushy.

One very useful kind of reinforcement which you can employ is to use the ideas presented by students to enhance a discussion. You can also explain how important a particular student response is in understanding a particular topic. For example, if the class were discussing the topic of evolution and a student volunteered the fact that without genetic mutation, evolution would be impossible, the teacher could provide reinforcement by saying, "Jim has provided us with one of the most important considerations in evolution. If there were no mechanism for altering the genetic material, there would be no chance for new biological types to be tried out in the environment." In this statement the teacher has identified just how important Jim's contribution was and has gone on to elaborate the concept identified.

You may also draw attention to the importance of student responses by referring the class to earlier statements made by class members and showing how these responses relate to or clarify the present discussion. For example, the teacher might say, "Do you remember a very important statement made by Bill at the beginning of the class which helps to clarify what a social outcast really feels?" The teacher could also say, "Bill made a statement wherein he said that social outcasts have extreme difficulty adjusting to almost any situation and that many never do. How do you think this analysis is related to the problems of encouraging the development of personal identity and integration of races?"

Reinforcement may also be provided students by getting them involved in classroom activities. Participation is self-reinforcing. A good way to encourage participation is to give adequate verbal and nonverbal reinforcement, use student ideas by incorporating them into the discussion, and by dealing with student emotional responses in a positive way. You should also try to reduce the frequency of controlling and criticizing responses.

Success is another strong reinforcer. Too frequently, schools provide that experience to only a select few. This group is usually composed of highly intellectual, convergent thinkers who are able to conform to classroom routine with a minimum amount of dissatisfaction. Their behavior is reinforced by their success in getting good grades. This norm-based model doesn't take into account the need for all students to gain a feeling of success in their schoolwork. Students simply will not pursue those activities in which they don't succeed. The wise teacher will encourage student involvement by formulating strategies which insure success for every student in the classroom. Complete the following exercise on reinforcement:

1. What are the modes of expression of reinforcement?

2. Give an example from your teaching field of how you would reinforce a student response in each of the following ways:

   (1) Extending a student idea.

   (2) Having a student extend his own idea.

(3) Having the student's peers extend his idea.

3. *Higher-Order Questions*   The great majority of questions in the average classroom call for the student simply to recall information. This is done in spite of the fact that educators have maintained that their purpose is to stimulate students to think. A number of reasons may be postulated for the emphasis on remembering facts, but none of them seems justifiable. For example, some educators support the teaching of facts on the grounds that it is too difficult to measure the higher mental processes validly. Others say that a knowledge of many facts is necessary for every properly functioning individual in our complex society. It should be noted that it is not the learning of facts that is to be condemned, but rather their exclusive use. Some facts are necessary, but even many of these should be learned in conjunction with the development of higher mental processes rather than by rote.

Higher-order questions are those questions for which students obtain answers by engaging in the processes of analysis, synthesis, and evaluation. The student has to go beyond factual or descriptive information and learn to compare and contrast concepts and principles, determine meaningful patterns in a body of information, discover principles, make inferences, perceive cause-and-effect relationships, generalize, make predictions, formulate consistent wholes, and evaluate products and possible problem solutions and courses of action. Higher-order questions require the student to discover and use concepts and principles. Rather than the teacher figuring out the answers and requiring the student to remember them, higher-order questions lead the student to figure out the answers himself. One of the key words used in higher-level questioning is "why?" The why question forces the student to go beyond the facts to justify, classify, infer, relate, and organize.

You, as the teacher, must know how to formulate questions that cause students to engage in specific kinds of mental activities. You must also be able to determine whether or not a student response is derived from a specified kind of mental activity. Because the discussion of questioning which follows is based upon Bloom's *Taxonomy of Educational Objectives*, it is necessary that the reader understand the taxonomy sufficiently to formulate objectives at the various taxonomic levels before proceeding. If you need to review the taxonomic levels, see Chapter 3.

There are three factors that determine the kind of thinking brought about in the mind of the student by a particular question. First, one must consider the nature of the question in terms of its classification in the taxonomy. This factor will be the primary consideration of this discussion. Secondly, one must be aware of the knowledge about the subject which each student brings to the classroom. Each student has a different frame of reference based on the sum total of his or her knowledge as well as experiences and values. Consequently, a question which causes one student to engage in higher mental activities may only require another to recall information. For example, if the teacher asks students to differentiate between communistic and capitalistic statements, one student may be required to engage in an analysis activity while another may simply have to recall having read the statement made by a well-known statesman whose political identity could be readily fixed.

The third factor that determines the kind of thinking a student has to do in response to a particular question is the instruction which precedes the asking of the question. If the answer to the question has already been dealt with in class, no opportunity exists to do anything more than simply recall information.

Questions may be formulated by the teacher which require the student to engage in specified mental operations. Bloom's *Taxonomy of Educational Objectives* is one convenient system for helping the teacher identify the kinds of questions which may be asked. It calls the teacher's attention to a number of possible kinds of thinking in which he may help students engage. Without such a classification system, teachers are less likely to provide opportunities for students to develop these skills.

The first level considered in this discussion is analysis. The following are examples of analysis questions. (It should be pointed out that some authorities may consider some of the low-level analysis questions listed here to be in the comprehension level of the taxonomy. Also, some questions may elicit either an analysis response or comprehension response. The examples shown are not limited to formal logical processes. It is assumed that analysis is indeed involved in responding to appropriately formulated questions where formal rules of logic are not necessarily used.)

Analysis is the examination of component parts of a communication or object designed to determine their relationships, inconsistencies, and principles. The following instructions and questions require the student to engage in analysis skills.

1. Compare ancient Greek and Roman cultures in terms of religion, architecture, and government.

2. Which of the two arguments is more conservative?

3. What social rule applies in each of the four situations?

4. Tell why the reasoning in the following quotation is sound or unsound: Governor Ross wants to be elected to the Senate. If you will remember, he was involved with the foreign aid give-away program a few years ago. We all know that corruption has been proven in the State Department. Governor Ross should not be elected to the Senate because he is a crook.

5. What is the relationship between the plants of this particular area and the temperature, rainfall, and soil constituents and pH?

6. In what ways can you differentiate between the works of Beethoven and Bach?

Synthesis questions are designed to cause students to formulate original communication or products from a number of component parts. These communications and products must reflect careful organization and integration of ideas. The following questions require the student to engage in synthesis skills.

1. If you were to embark on a journey to Mars, what would you take with you? Why?

2. Devise a set of principles which explains why students behave the way they do in the classroom.

3. How would you solve the problem of poverty in this country?

4. What are the steps the United States should use in disengaging itself in Southeast Asia?

5. What kind of tax system will encourage economic growth and yet be equitable?

6. How can we organize a plan for insect control that does not violate ecological balance?

The following questions require students to engage in evaluation skills. These questions are designed to cause students to determine the quality of communications or products.

1. Who were the most important literary figures in the United States prior to 1860? Defend your choice.

2. Should capital punishment be abolished?

3. Which of the two articles has the better literary style?

4. Which forward one-and-a-half dive was most expertly executed?

5. Which musical selection best represents the theme of the festival?

6. Which weld best meets all of the criteria of good welds?

Success in teaching depends in large measure on the extent to which you are able to use the appropriate questioning techniques. In order to accomplish this effectively, you must view yourself, not as a dispenser of information, but rather as one who can engage students in purposeful thinking processes. Beginning teachers find difficulty keeping this perspective. It is, therefore, recommended that you, as a teacher trainee, expend the necessary time and energy to bring about competency in this area.

Complete the following exercise on higher-order questions:

1. What is a higher-order question?

2. Identify the levels of higher-order questioning, i.e., what kinds of higher-order questions are there?

3. Write a question at each of the higher-order levels.

LEARNING ACTIVITY 2: *4. Conducting a Guided Discussion* Discussion is commonly engaged in by everyone. The employee must clearly understand the explicit wishes of his employer and often resorts to a discussion of the issues. Examination of political issues, possible solutions to social problems, and many other topics are best handled subsequent to discussion sessions. Because of the wide use of discussion techniques, it seems advisable to differentiate between guided classroom discussions and other forms which discussion may take.

First, guided discussion is not an undisciplined bull session. A bull session is the type of discussion which usually takes place in unstructured situations, but occasionally resorted to by the classroom teacher. Generally, this form of discussion lacks purpose and moves aimlessly among a variety of topics. Any and all inputs are acceptable and conclusions are rarely reached. It is not uncommon in these sessions for irrational ideas to dominate simply because they are sponsored by a more enthusiastic and forceful person. Ideas tend not to be weighed and considered in relation to one another, but rather to simply be asserted and supported. This kind of experience serves a useful function in generating new ideas but has limited utility in developing analytical skills.

The open-ended discussion is a second type of discussion which should be differentiated from the guided discussion. Unlike the bull session, this type of discussion does have a purpose but very little direction. Usually, the purpose is to formulate an original set of ideas for developing a product, accomplishing an action, or understanding a phenomenon. The emphasis is upon the uniqueness of what is produced and thus little direction is given by the instructor. As a matter of fact, the very act of subjecting ideas to analytical procedures and special directions undermine the creative processes.

The guided class discussion has as its purpose the orderly examination of a problem or issue with the intent of exploring all constituent parts and their relationships. Many times group agreement is sought, although this is not always necessary, or even desirable. The important point is that all issues are examined rationally and logically and that possible points of disagreement or divergence be identified and explicated. Essentially, your task as the teacher is to lead the group to bring appropriate evidence to bear on the crucial issues of a problem. You must attempt to clarify student ideas which may be vague and ambiguous. In addition, you must monitor student contributions and relate each new bit of information to the whole problem while at the same time helping the class members to discard those ideas which are irrelevant or inaccurate. You must exercise a high degree of support for students when their ideas are incongruous and help them formulate more appropriate responses. If you fail to be supportive and helpful when inaccurate or inappropriate ideas are offered by students, you will alienate them and reduce or eliminate future participation.

You, as the teacher, must also aid the group to focus on ideas which are related to the problem under consideration, but which no one has thought to consider. For example, if a group is discussing the topic of sex education and no consideration has yet been given to the important issues of community values and the relation of sexual values to specific religious beliefs and customs, you might say, "We have concluded that sex education could be handled in the present school setting, but we have failed to consider how community values and religious preferences may affect its implementation. What effects might we anticipate with regard to the community values if we implemented a sex education program in the schools?"

You should, through appropriate questioning, guide the class to identify inconsistencies in the arguments of one another. Rather than always pointing out these inconsistencies yourself, a good practice is to refer the matter to other students. You might say, after listening to the response of a student, "What do you think, Ned, about Lynn's idea that revenue-sharing is the only way that control at the local level can become more effective?"

There are a number of conditions which ordinarily must be satisfied if a guided discussion is to function smoothly. First, there must be a problem to solve about which the group can maintain some interest. Second, the group must have the requisite skills to deal with the problem and produce viable solutions. Third, the related facts must be at the disposal of the group and become part of the preparation of the group prior to discussion. Fourth, individual values and ideas must find their way into the discussion for possible consideration.

Certain steps should be followed in planning for and teaching a guided discussion. The first is that of identifying the problem or issue to be considered. It is essential that the topic selected is one that students have an interest in. If the topic is not directly related to student interests, the discussion should be developed so as to bear upon student interests. Topics which cannot be so developed are of little value for discussion because little participation will be generated. Controversial issues such as whether or not we should support the sale of grain to Russia lead naturally to discussion. With this type of topic, you, as the teacher, should not be overly concerned with arriving at a consensus, however, Because there are a number of views on controversial topics, there is an increased likelihood that the various positions will be identified and compared. In addition, controversial issues frequently have two or more very plausible viewpoints. Attempting to identify differences and make comparisons among supportable but conflicting positions naturally engages students in discussion and aids in the development of analytical skills in the process.

Once the problem for discussion has been identified, you must begin planning goals and strategy and formulating the lesson plan. It is obvious that you must familiarize yourself thoroughly with the topic. This entails knowing the basic arguments that might be considered on all sides of the problem. You must also direct students to sources of information that will adequately prepare them to engage in meaningful discussion. Lack of preparation by students is a deterrent to a successful discussion. Once you have familiarized yourself with the basic issues involved with a problem, you should next construct an outline of these in the form of questions. They should be organized so that the discussion generated by the questions flows smoothly and sequentially. Your role, as the teacher, then is to pose the questions, clarify questions and comments, direct resolution of different viewpoints, interpose intermittent summaries as needed, and steer the discussion into new areas as the occasion demands. One tendency you should guard against is the practice of occupying too central a role in the discussion—in terms of premature exposure of your personal values on the subject—and performing too much of the analysis yourself. You would be better advised to refer questions to students rather than answering them yourself. Your purpose is to formulate questions and probe the responses of students, redirecting their comments as necessary, not verifying your authority by giving the final word on each issue. A display of authority encourages students to wait for your judgment and analysis rather than offering their own.

The third step has to do with how the analysis of the problem should proceed. The first consideration in making the analysis is to define the terms and limits of the problem. Then you and the class members are to begin to identify each of the issues connected with the problem. Discussion should elucidate each of these issues. It is imperative that the basic assumptions associated with each consideration be identified and their validity checked. For example, if we were to consider the practice of selling grain to Russia, it may be assumed that there would be little or no impact on such things as (1) the balance of trade; (2) the price of farm products; (3) the consumer cost of commodities; and (4) farm subsidies. Careful analysis may reveal the fact that these assumptions are completely erroneous.

Because it is sometimes desirable to reach a consensus in a discussion, it is necessary that criteria for making judgments evolve in the discussion process before conclusions are reached. This involves the skill of synthesis; while the application of these criteria to the process of making a judgment requires evaluative skills. In the example used above, one criterion that can be used in determining whether or not to ship grain to Russia is "What is the greatest good for the greatest number of Americans?" If this is a criterion of high priority, we can easily judge that a consideration of consumer cost may be more important than farm subsidies unless it can be demonstrated that consumer cost is directly related to subsidies. In other words, if selling grain to Russia increases the cost of consumer goods, we might be reluctant to do it. If, on the other hand, withholding such shipments had an adverse effect on subsidies which in turn had an adverse effect on consumer cost, we may have some justification for shipment. It is necessary at this point to add to this situation all other appropriate criteria and facts, attempting all the time to weigh and compare all component parts of the argument and come up with a solution. Frequently, a decision cannot be reached by the group because advantages and disadvantages weigh evenly. In order to avoid this difficulty, it is recommended that when criteria for making judgments are identified, effort be made to arrange them in terms of priority. Then the solution which best satisfies prior criteria can be selected with little difficulty. The solution reached should be held as tentative initially. The purpose of this is to allow students an opportunity to gather additional information or to test out the solution as one would test a hypothesis using the experimental method. The guided class discussion can thus be used as a vehicle for initiating library research and/or empirical investigations. Discussions that lead to consensus tend to be dead-end experiences while those which identify unresolved issues lead to further learning and involvement on the part of the student. Both orientations serve their purposes, and most all classrooms should probably engage in both types of discussions.

LEARNING ACTIVITY 3:   Read Teaching an Analysis Lesson. As you read it, perform a rating of the lesson by recording the appropriate information on the Critique for Simulated Teaching: Analysis Lesson form which follows the lesson.

5. Teaching an Analysis Lesson

TEACHER: Ron is the lion-tamer for the circus. One evening during a performance Leo the lion attacks Ron and injures him. Two weeks later when Ron is out of the hospital he practices with the lions again and is particularly careful with Leo. (set induction) It would appear that Ron is afraid of Leo. Now let's use our principles of operant and classical conditioning and see if we can figure out how this all came about. What you should be able to do after this lesson is to analyze behavioral situations and explain the way conditioning principles are exhibited in the situations. (objective) What's the formula for classical conditioning? Jane?

STUDENT: The conditioned stimulus appears to be a conditioning series and eventually elicits the same response.

TEACHER: Okay, good. (reinforcement) We have an unconditioned stimulus which elicits an unconditioned response. This unconditioned stimulus is paired with the conditioned stimulus and both are able to cause a response. Okay, what is the formula for operant conditioning? Gary?

STUDENT: It is a response with a reinforcing stimulus.

TEACHER: Okay, response followed by the reinforcing stimulus. Now if we're going to put the formulas for operant and classical conditioning together to analyze the sequence of behavior, what would it look like?

STUDENT:
$$\begin{array}{c} CR \\ | \\ R-S-R-S. \end{array}$$

TEACHER: Somebody pick out the operant conditioning for this particular formula. Okay, Frank.

STUDENT: The R-S.

TEACHER: Okay, this will be your operant. Good. (reinforcement) What about classical conditioning? Frank?

STUDENT: The S-R.

TEACHER: The S-R? Anything else?

STUDENT: Yes, plus the unconditioned stimulus.

TEACHER: All right, very good. (reinforcement) Now that we have our formula, we can break down any kind of behavior simply by plugging the parts in. Getting back to Ron, the lion tamer, where is the classical conditioning in this particular situation? Okay, Mary?

STUDENT: The pain was paired with Leo the lion.

TEACHER: Okay, the pain was paired with Leo the lion. Which is the unconditioned stimulus? Gary?

STUDENT: Pain.

TEACHER: Okay, the pain would be the unconditioned stimulus. How do you know that's the unconditioned stimulus? (higher-order question) Gary?

STUDENT: Because it's natural. You don't have to learn anything.

TEACHER: Good. (reinforcement) Pain elicits a response without learning. With a conditioned stimulus, you have to learn to associate it with something to cause a response. If pain is your unconditioned stimulus, what's your conditioned stimulus? Mary?

STUDENT: Leo.

TEACHER: Okay, the lion is your conditioned stimulus. These two are paired together. What is the reinforcer here? What is the reinforcement that connects Ron with being careful with Leo? (cueing) Jane?

STUDENT: The pain.

TEACHER: That's good, the pain is also the reinforcer. What is the operant conditioning in this situation? (silence) Okay, Frank.

STUDENT: The lion tamer's behavior and the attack that caused the pain.

TEACHER: All right. Ron is involved in the performance. The pain of Leo's attack follows this response. You all seem to understand operant conditioning. (reinforcement) So far we haven't talked about why Ron is performing in the first place. What's the motivation behind his being in the ring? (cueing) In other words, what is driving him? (cueing) (Teacher points to the diagram on the board offering additional cues.) Jane?

STUDENT: He has the desire to train the lion.

TEACHER: All right. He has a desire to train the lion and perform with it. (reinforcement) Gary?

STUDENT: He may want money and success.

TEACHER: All right. If he performs, we could assume here that this is his job. If he performs well, he gets paid for it: so we could say he wanted to be successful so he could get paid. This would probably be the drive for success. Is this a primary drive or a secondary drive? (closure) Renae?

STUDENT: Secondary drive.

TEACHER: How do you know that? (higher-order question)

STUDENT: Because it's learned, the body doesn't need it biologically.

TEACHER: What is the formula for habit-chaining that we use to figure this out? Jane?

STUDENT: Response—stimulus to response.

TEACHER: Okay, we would say this is our basic formula that we use. We can always use this to figure out or try to determine the factors involved in any kind of behavior. We observed when Ron was in the cage with six other lions plus Leo that he was especially careful with Leo. This was because Leo had attacked him two weeks earlier. Using what we know about classical conditioning, how it works, the principles involved, and operant conditioning and reinforcement, and also what we know about motivation and drives, we've come up with a fairly good analysis of this situation. So we know what factors influenced the behaviors we saw exhibited. (closure) Okay, you did a good job on figuring these things out. (reinforcement)

Why don't we try a different situation that doesn't deal with animals this time but deals with an inanimate object. It's the second one on your example sheet. This deals with Chuck working on his car. Chuck decided one day to replace the entire engine in his car. He replaced it and the car ran very well. While replacing the engine, Chuck used his own tools. Suppose you're a friend of Chuck's. As you walk down the street, you see Chuck out tuning up his dad's car. You may say, "Hey, I got some tools you might want to use." Chuck says, "No thanks, I got my own," and you say, "But I have a newer model of this particular wrench you're using: it'd be much better." Chuck says, "No, I'd rather use my own, thank you." So now you say to yourself,

"Well, gee, I've got a newer model; it's obviously better than the one he has. Why won't he use it?" Take a look at this sequence of behavior. We'll use our formula again for the sequence of behavior. (cueing) What's the classical conditioning here? (higher-order question) Gary?

STUDENT: Pleasure associated with using tools.

TEACHER: All right, how do you know that's the classical conditioning? (higher-order question)

STUDENT: Because it has a condition stimulus.

TEACHER: All right. What is the conditioned stimulus for this?

STUDENT: The condition that he uses his own tools.

TEACHER: All right, and what was that paired with? Gary?

STUDENT: Pleasure.

TEACHER: Okay, good. (reinforcement) The unconditioned stimulus is paired with the conditioned stimulus. What would be the reinforcement used to strengthen the ties between pleasure and using one's own tools? (higher-order question) Frank?

STUDENT: Success.

TEACHER: All right, if you look at the diagram, would you put success here? (Teacher points to the diagram.)

STUDENT: No. There would be pleasure.

TEACHER: All right, why would pleasure replace the engine instead of success? (higher-order question) Gary?

STUDENT: Success would be a drive, wouldn't it?

TEACHER: Fine, success is a drive. That's true, but what is pleasure in this particular case? (cueing) Gary? (higher-order question)

STUDENT: That would be what the drive is trying to achieve.

TEACHER: Okay, that's what motivates us. It moves us on to finish whatever we are doing. What else do you know about unconditioned stimuli? (higher-order question) Jane?

STUDENT: They're the same as the reinforcer.

TEACHER: Right. (reinforcement) So in this particular case you've already distinguished the two parts of the classical conditioning involved. His own tools were a conditioned stimulus; the unconditioned stimulus is pleasure. (cueing) Therefore, the reinforcement would also be what? (higher-order question) Jane?

STUDENT: Pleasure.

TEACHER: Right. (reinforcement) What is the operant conditioning? (higher-order question) Mary?

STUDENT: It'd be Chuck working on his car's engine and having the pleasure of replacing it.

TEACHER: All right, Chuck is working on his car. Followed by what? (cueing) Mary?

STUDENT: Pleasure.

TEACHER: Pleasure, which is? (cueing)

STUDENT: Operant conditioning.

TEACHER: Okay, and what did we say about operant conditioning? Just operant conditioning in general? (cueing)

STUDENT: That there's an action and then there's a reinforcement.

TEACHER: Good. (reinforcement) Now you've understood what the operant conditioning is in this situation. There's an activity— followed by the reinforcement of pleasure. (closure) Very good. (reinforcement) Now someone mentioned drive before. What is the drive involved in this particular situation? (higher-order question) Gary?

STUDENT: The success of working on the car.

TEACHER: All right, success again. And what do you know about success? This is not just success in general, but specifically, success of working on cars. (cueing) Gary?

STUDENT: It's learned.

TEACHER: All right, you learn in some way. Good. (reinforcement) Is there anything else we need to know about this behavior? Do you think we've pulled it apart and taken all the pieces out and put them back together in some kind of an understandable statement? Could you make some kind of general statement to say why Chuck might have rejected your tools? (closure) (higher-order question) Jane?

STUDENT: Because he had success using his own tools and he probably associated success with the use.

TEACHER: Okay, very good. (reinforcement) That sort of sums up the whole thing. In essence, you've summed up everything referring to the principles of conditioning that we've talked about and used. Why don't we make some final summary statement about Ron and the lion? Could you make a general statement about Ron and Leo? (higher-order question) Gary?

STUDENT: Leo attacked Ron, hurt him, and Ron was sent to the hospital. When Ron came back, he remembered the pain and suffering from Leo's attack; and to keep Leo from attacking again, he was more careful. (closure)

TEACHER: Okay, good, fine. (reinforcement) I think you really have an understanding of this now, so we'll be able to deal with some of the questions that you wanted to have answered, such as why some people are afraid of the dark and some people are afraid of things that are good for them.

LEARNING ACTIVITY 4: Read and study the following examples of analysis objectives. Attempt to write some analysis objectives from your own teaching field. You may wish to obtain feedback from your instructor on the objectives you write.

6. Examples of Analysis Objectives

1. Given a list of political statements, students will be able to identify those which represent each of the following categories of propaganda: glittering generalities, bandwagoning, and name-calling. Eight out of ten correct is the minimum performance level.

2. Given a series of statements, students will be able to correctly describe, in writing, at least one unstated assumption for each statement.

3. From a novel selected by the teacher, students will be able to correctly describe, in writing, the motives of three selected characters.

4. Given a list of facts, students will be able to identify and underline those which are relevant to the validation of a judgment and cross out those which are not, with 80 percent accuracy.

5. Given an improperly functioning automobile and appropriate tools, the students will be able to properly diagnose and record in writing 90 percent of the malfunctions in engine function.

6. From each of a series of videotaped teaching performances,

CRITIQUE FOR SIMULATED TEACHING:

Analysis Lesson

Teacher _____ Date _____
Evaluator _____

	Unable to Observe	Not Achieved	Below Average	Average	Strong	Superior

1. Higher-Order Questions—Did the questions asked require students to use higher-order cognitive skills? What additional higher-order questions could have been asked?

| 0 | 1 | 2 | 3 | 4 | 5 |

2. Reinforcement—Did the teacher adequately reinforce the responses of students? Was it genuine and frequent enough?

3. Cueing—Did the teacher demonstrate skill in cueing students? In what way could this skill have been improved?

4. Objective Taught—Was the objective clearly understood by the students? How could this have been improved?

5. Objective Achieved—Was the lesson objective achieved?

	Unable to Observe	Not Achieved	Below Average	Average	Strong	Superior
	0	1	2	3	4	5

6. Did the teacher engage students in meaningful discussion? Describe.

7. Learning Activities—Were learning activities appropriate in terms of the objective? Describe the way in which they were or were not.

8. Enthusiasm?

9. Communication skill?

10. Appearance and mannerisms? Identify specific mannerisms which may create problems for the individual as a teacher.

11. Skillful use of audio-visual aids?

Individuals using this form for purposes of evaluation should give written explanations and criticisms that correspond to the questions above as well as check an overall rating in each category. It is particularly useful for raters to include suggested improvements for the lessons they view.

students will be able to identify and describe in writing at least one appropriate and one inappropriate instance of executing the following teaching skills: set induction, closure, and reinforcement.

7. From slow–motion movies, students will be able to identify and describe in writing at least one inappropriate component of a golf swing in nine out of the ten examples exhibited.

8. From a series of poor quality baked goods, students will be able through observation, taste, and touch to determine and record what inappropriate procedure is responsible for each improperly prepared product.

9. Given a plot of ground, students must be able to determine and record what factors influence the distribution, size, and number of plants present in the plot.

10. From examination of the scene of a car accident, the students will be able to determine and describe in writing the most likely cause.

Learning Activity 5:   Examine the following Sample Analysis Lesson Plan. Then organize an analysis lesson which can be taught in a fifteen-minute period which facilitates the use of a directed discussion. Plan your lesson so that you will be able to demonstrate the skills of set induction, cueing, reinforcement, higher-order questions, and closure. Make certain that your lesson plan follows the format outlined in the Sample Analysis Lesson Plan following.

7. Sample Analysis Lesson Plan

Class: Senior Social Studies

Title: Recognizing Propaganda Statements

Preassessment:

A pretest of propaganda statements and terms will be administered in order to determine the readiness level of the class.

Objective:

Given a list of propaganda statements, students will be able to identify inconsistencies in logic and the type of propaganda statement being made (i.e., glittering generalities, name-calling, bandwagoning, etc.) by describing, in writing, at least 80 percent of the possible examples.

Content:
    1. What is propaganda?
    2. What is the purpose of propaganda?
    3. How does propaganda influence people?
    4. How do you differentiate it from other types of statements?
    5. How do you differentiate the various types of propaganda techniques?
    6. How do you find inconsistencies in propaganda statements?

Learning Activities:
    1. Engage the class in a guided discussion regarding the questions outlined in the content section.
    2. Provide the students with a series of statements to classify in terms of propaganda techniques. Provide feedback on their responses.
    3. Have students complete the homework assignment on determining logical inconsistencies in various types of propaganda statements. They should identify the inconsistencies as well as classify the statements with regard to propaganda techniques.
    4. Give feedback on homework assignments.

Materials:
Overhead projector, propaganda overlays, and statement analysis overlays.

Evaluation:
Students will be given a series of twenty-five statements which they must classify in terms of logical inconsistencies and propaganda techniques used. Eighty percent is the minimum acceptable level.

Strategy:
I will point out to the class that many people are deceived by propaganda into believing inconsistent and false statements. In order not to be deceived, students need to learn to think carefully about political statements. Preassessment will help determine a starting point for instruction. The various propaganda terms will have to be defined before proceeding with the development of the lesson. Actual development of the required skills will begin in class discussion and proceed to practice in a homework assignment with appropriate feedback provided. All the tech-

niques will be reviewed and compared carefully before students are evaluated.

LEARNING ACTIVITY 6:   Review How to Analyze a Simulated Lesson and Simulated Lesson Analysis: An Example, numbers 10 and 11 of the Instructional Procedures in Chapter 8. These two selections will explain the format which should be used in making an analysis of your simulated teaching. Study them carefully. Examine the following Analysis Lesson Analysis Guide. This form is to be filled out as you view your own videotaped lessons. It will provide a basis for making an analysis of your lessons.

Analysis Lesson Analysis Guide

1. What evidence do you have that students actually engaged in analytical skills? Cite at least two instances. If there was no evidence, what would you have done differently in the lesson in order to engage students in analysis?

2. Cite at least two instances where you helped students differentiate between subcomponent parts of the subject under analysis.

3. What evidence do you have that learners understood and achieved your objective? Cite at least two specific instances of student behavior which indicate that you achieved your objective.

4. Cite at least four higher-order questions which you used in your lesson. Explain, in terms of the student responses to your questions, the extent to which your questions were clear or unclear. How would you rephrase your questions?

5. Identify four specific statements which could be considered reinforcing. How could you have increased the reinforcement value of these statements?

6. Cite at least two instances which give evidence that students were interested in your lesson. How could you have gained more interest in your lesson?

7. Identify two specific instances where you tried to obtain closure. Give evidence, in terms of student responses, that you did achieve closure or identify the reason you were unable to achieve closure.

8. Cite two specific instances of cueing. Explain why the cues were given and the effect they had on learners. How could you have rephrased your cue to improve it?

EVALUATION

SIMULATED TEACHING AND ANALYSIS

Teach a fifteen-minute analysis lesson using the lesson plan which you have prepared. Have the lesson videotaped. Your lesson should be taught to either peers or public school pupils with each learner preparing an analysis of the lesson. While viewing the videotaped replay, make an analysis of your lesson using the procedure explained in How to Analyze the Simulated Lesson and Simulated Lesson Analysis: An Example in Chapter 8 (numbers 10 and 11 of the Instructional Procedures). Fill out the Analysis Lesson Analysis Guide as you view your videotaped replay to use as a basis for making your analysis. In making your analysis, you must be able to identify your problems correctly and formulate viable corrective measures.

REPLANNING, RETEACHING, AND ANALYSIS

Using the analysis information from your lesson, reorganize and reteach your analysis lesson. Pay particular attention to overcoming the problems identified in the first attempt at the lesson. Determine how you could have improved in terms of each of the following skills: set induction, cueing, reinforcement, higher-order questions, and closure. Check to see if your objective was carefully taught to and understood by the class. Identify any annoying mannerisms or poor communications skills. It is imperative that the reorganization of your lesson reflect a careful restructuring of your strategy based on the analysis of your first lesson. You must be able to produce a significantly different approach to the lesson. Videotape the retaught lesson and have the learners evaluate your presentation. A clinical analyst may also evaluate your lesson and provide feedback. Make an analysis of your lesson while viewing the videotaped replay.

chapter 10

The Synthesis Lesson

OBJECTIVES

1. From your major or minor field of study, develop a plan for teaching a simulated lesson utilizing synthesis skills. The lesson plan will follow the format of the lesson plan for teaching a concept lesson given in Chapter 8.

2. You will be expected to use this lesson plan to teach a synthesis lesson in which you will exhibit skill in set induction, probing questions, divergent questions, appropriate use of silence, nonverbal cues, and closure. The lesson will be taught to a group of peers and, if possible, videotaped.

3. You will also be expected to make a written analysis of your teaching using critiques from peers (Critique for Simulated Teaching: Synthesis Lesson, at the end of this chapter). In this written analysis, you will evaluate the teaching skill which you exhibited including: set induction, probing questions, divergent questions, silence, nonverbal cues, and closure.

4. You will then replan and reteach your synthesis lesson, eliminating the problem areas identified in the analysis of your first synthesis lesson. This second synthesis lesson must be analyzed from

a videotaped replay using the critique form. A comparison must be made between the teach and the reteach cycles.

PREASSESSMENT

Make use of these questions to guide you in your study. Each question is followed by a number that links it to the *Instructional Procedures* included in this chapter.

1. Why is synthesis learning important to students today? *(1)*
2. How has it changed the role of the teacher? *(1)*
3. What is synthesis? *(2)*
4. How is synthesis placed in Bloom's *Taxonomy of the Cognitive Domain? (2)*
5. Why is it placed there? *(2)*
6. Where is synthesis in Gagné's model of learning? *(2)*
7. What is synthesis learning? *(2)*
8. How does synthesis learning differ from concept learning? *(3)*
9. What is the position of knowledge in the model given for synthesis? *(3)*
10. What types of learning require synthesis? *(4)*
11. What are the five capacities in which the teacher functions in synthesis learning? *(5)*
12. What are probing questions? *(6)*
13. How are probing questions used? *(6)*
14. What are divergent questions? *(7)*
15. Why are divergent questions useful in synthesis learning? *(7)*
16. Why are divergent questions sometimes disconcerting to traditional teachers? *(7)*
17. What is the teacher's function in using divergent questions? *(7)*
18. What is the function of silence in synthesis teaching? *(8)*
19. What are the three main nonverbal cues that a teacher may use? *(9)*
20. What facial cues may a teacher use to encourage a student to respond? *(9)*
21. What facial cues may a teacher use to curtail an inappropriate response? *(9)*

22. What head movements may a teacher use to aid a student in responding? *(9)*

23. What head movements may a teacher use to indicate disapproval of an inappropriate response? *(9)*

24. How may a teacher indicate he is interested in what the student is saying through body movement? *(9)*

25. How may a teacher use nonverbal cues to help him in knowing the feeling of his students as an indication that he should change the learning experience? *(9)*

26. What are the major criticisms of synthesis learning? *(10)*

27. How valid are the criticisms of synthesis learning? *(10)*

INSTRUCTIONAL PROCEDURES

LEARNING ACTIVITY 1:   Read the following selection, *Planning and Teaching a Synthesis Lesson,* and answer the exercises included in it. Choose a topic from your major or minor field and organize a synthesis lesson in which you demonstrate the skills of set induction, divergent questions, probing questions, silence, nonverbal cues, and closure. Then teach the synthesis lesson which you have planned to a group of peers.

1. Planning and Teaching a Synthesis Lesson   Why synthesis teaching? Although many of today's educators have already reoriented their perception of teaching-learning, the knowledge explosion has forced all educators to face up to a very harsh fact, namely that the traditional role of the teacher as a dispenser of knowledge or facts is being curtailed if not completely eliminated. The availability of libraries with up-to-date reference material, the implosion of the paperback books that lower the cost factor, and other media acting as sources of information have produced a metamorphosis in the relationship between teachers and students. For a teacher to consider himself as a fountainhead of knowledge, even in a very limited and highly specialized area, is fallacious as well as an untenable position, and even the most traditionally oriented teacher who has not mastered the technique of saying to his students "I do not know," is in trouble.

Clearly, there are forceful implications for teachers. First, how are we, as teachers, to function in the classroom in light of this change in the role of the teacher, and second, how are our students to function in life when knowledge is constantly being changed to include new information?

The first of these is a tactical situation but involves your perception of yourself as a teacher, the environment of the school in which you serve, and the perceived role or function of the school itself in the school community.

The second of these considerations is far more complex. If we adopt the philosophy that the major goal or purpose of a student's school experiences is to enable him or her to live (perhaps survive would be a better word), then we must set up educational experiences that will enable students to develop techniques or procedures for handling the reordering of knowledge. This not only includes new knowledge as it is made known, but it implies that they take this knowledge and use it in everyday life situations. Research has shown that it is clearly possible to be the proud possessor of a multitude of facts and yet be totally incapable of using them in order to arrive at a valid conclusion or solution to a problem. The fact that a student has mastered the adding of two numbers by drill does not in itself indicate that he or she will be able to use his or her knowledge of addition in any situation other than when presented with two given numbers in a drill pattern. The new curricular materials in the various disciplines have thus taken the tack that students must discover or formulate knowledge so as to understand rather than memorize and recall.

2. *What is Synthesis?*   Synthesis (you will also find it called problem-solving or discovery) is a highly complex process. Synthesis itself in the hierarchy of Bloom's *Taxonomy* lies at the fifth level in the cognitive domain.[1] If you do not recall the levels of the cognitive domain, reread or review the cognitive domain portion of Chapter 3 (number 2 of the Instructional Procedures). From this, it can be inferred that a student must have passed through four levels of learning before he or she can engage in synthesis. First, students must have the knowledge or facts with which to work. Second, they must be able to demonstrate understanding by being able to manipulate facts or work with them. Third, they must be able to take these facts and apply them in a given situation. Fourth, they must be able to utilize these facts as elements of a whole and analyze them as elements in context or relationship to each other as well as the whole. Then they

arrive at the process of synthesizing. Here students are required to take facts and reconstruct them. They must put them together into a unique form to fulfill unique conditions or requirements.

R. M. Gagné, in his hierarchical model, accepts eight types or categories of learning and arranges them from simple to complex with the assumption that each of the higher-order learnings depends upon the mastering of the one below. Problem-solving is the highest level of his model and is listed as Type 8: "Problem-solving is a kind of learning that requires the internal events usually called thinking. Two or more previously acquired principles are somehow combined to produce a new capability that can be shown to depend on a 'higher-order' principle."[2]

Thus, synthesizing or problem-solving or discovery or inquiry is the process of taking knowledge and restructuring it. In order to engage in synthesis, students must have knowledge, be able to comprehend that knowledge, apply it, use it to analyze the component parts of a given situation, and take that knowledge and reconstruct it so as to enlarge their perceptual field to include a new area.

Define synthesis in your own words.

3. What is Synthesis Teaching? Synthesis teaching employs a variety of techniques to bring about specific outcomes in students. Synthesis teaching seeks to help the student answer the question, how? It explains, it builds upon knowledge, and therefore is not of particular value in merely learning facts.

It is a blending and sorting process. It is a method of dealing with the unknown by manipulation of the known. It can be totally creative or merely restructuring. It differs from trial-and-error learning in which a student merely pulls out one response after another from a repertoire, hoping that one or the other will answer the question or solve the problem. It is more insight than trial and error. It requires internalization of thought processes. It is the reconstrucing or modifying of a student's perceptual field.

The problem-solving technique or discovery method has been stated and restated in varying forms since the time of Dewey, who outlined five steps of thought in analyzing reflective activity. Dewey did not state that the stages must be passed through in any order or that all of the stages were necessary. Nonetheless, these five steps have been elaborated on and thus we have had authors who have reduced the five to as few as three, and others who have increased them to as many as nine.[3] Throughout these elaborations, the labels of the steps have also changed. Irving M. Copi stated them as "the general pattern of scientific research."[4] Edwin Fenton stated them as "steps in a mode of inquiry for the social studies."[5]

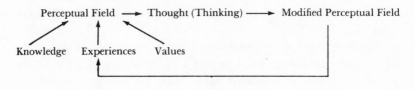

FIGURE 10—1

Once we define synthesis as a restructuring of knowledge into a new construct, the following model may be used.

The perceptual field here represents the status quo of a person. Included in this are his or her experiences, knowledge, and value systems. These three impinge, to varying degrees, upon the reaction of that person to any given situation. They are called upon in making decisions, interpreting data, and relating experiences into an integrated whole. The knowledge, past experiences, and value system a person brings to a particular set are the raw material that a person carries with him. The perceptual field of a person is under constant restructuring as experiences and knowledge and values are added, shifted, rejected, or shaped. The facilitating portion of the model is the central element, *thought,* or *thinking,* or as Dewey stated it, "reflective thinking." Here lies the process of transformation of information. It is in this element that synthesis takes place, and it is here that the teacher involves the students in synthesis. The experiences the teacher provides, the techniques he or she employs, the role the teacher plays all congregate at this point in allowing, encouraging, demanding, and rewarding students engaging in the highest form of intellectual endeavor, thinking. Thus, we have a modified perceptual field as the result of the thought processes.

Using the given model, define synthesis teaching.

4. What Types of Learning Require Synthesis?   Synthesis teaching or the discovery method lends itself to many teaching-learning experiences. It may be used in teaching the social sciences such as sociology, economics, psychology, and so forth, to help students formulate, based on facts, their positions relative to social conditions, trying to answer such questions as "what plan might be used to reduce the need for welfare among urban populations?" "What plan of action should the U.S. government develop to meet the needs of returning servicemen who have become addicted to drugs during their Vietnam service?" "What sequence of experiences could be developed in order to ensure that juvenile offenders do not make the usual transition from first offense to hardened criminal?"

History offers two ways of using synthesis. The first is retrospect, allowing the student to conjecture as to how a given situation might have been solved in order to have achieved a better outcome. For example, retrospect could be employed in answering this question, "What plan might have been used to solve the problem of slavery that would have been acceptable to both North and South without resorting to war?" The second way of using synthesis in history is in projection, such as "Now that we have signed a ceasefire in Vietnam, what plan should the United States adopt as its diplomatic policy in Southeast Asia to insure peace?"

In languages and the arts, synthesis offers the opportunity for the students to engage in creativity. Here a student might actually create a sonnet or a short story or a short play. He or she might compose a song or draw a picture.

In science, synthesis experiences have long been known as the laboratory method although there is a real question as to whether problem-solving occurs when the laboratory work is so highly structured that it would be virtually impossible to come to any conclusion other than the one predetermined by the instructor. In each of these the essential elements of synthesis are present, students processing a perceptual field, and through thought processes modifying that perceptual field.

From your subject area list three examples of learning in which you would use synthesis.

1. _____

2. _____

3. _____

5. *What is the Role of the Teacher in Synthesis?* In synthesis teaching, the role of the teacher changes from one of dispenser of knowledge to one of facilitator. You, as the teacher, are concerned with the central element of the model, thought, and how you can aid your students in the thought process. You have assumed the role of facilitator and that incorporates a number of abilities. According to Byron Massia, some of these are: planner, introducer, sustainer of inquiry, manager, and rewarder.[6]

In other words you, as the teacher, will be concerned with choosing materials and activities that will allow the student to pursue inquiry. Further, as with other curricula, you will carefully structure and sequence these materials and activities so that they foster inquiry. Additionally, you must convey to the students that inquiry must be free and entails examination and possible questioning of content of texts, opinions of teachers and opinions of other students. In order to encourage this inquiry process, you may make use of positive reinforcement by rewarding students for their inquiry efforts as well as products. Perhaps the most important role of the teacher in synthesis is that of creating a classroom conducive to inquiry and keeping run-of-the-mill mundane operations of the classroom running smoothly.

List and define in your own words five capacities the teacher assumes in synthesis teaching.

6. *What Techniques Do I Need in Order to Engage My Students in Synthesis?* In order to facilitate synthesis, you will use four major teaching techniques: probing questions, divergent questions, silence, and nonverbal cues. These are in addition to the techniques previously mastered in teaching a concept lesson and an analysis lesson.

If you do not recall the teaching techniques of set induction, cueing, use of examples, stimulus variation, etc., review or reread Chapter 8.

Probing Questions: The purpose of probing questions is to extend the student's thinking. These questions clarify or elaborate upon the statement that has been made. They help the respondent and listeners find other implications in previous statements. Probes seek to make points more explicit or complete. Probing questions forestall superficial answers by forcing the student to go beyond his first response. Thus, the cue to probing questions lies in the student's response. Without a response, there can be no probe. The probing question used is determined by the student's response. You, as the teacher, can never know beforehand exactly what questions to ask. However, you can develop some techniques that will help you. Indeed, it is a good idea for the teacher to plan a lesson, having in mind certain pivotal questions to use in guiding the lesson.

Three ways to use probing questions are: clarifying, justifiying, and relating responses to another area. If you, as teacher, seek clarification, you can ask such probing questions as "Would you explain exactly what you mean?" "Could you restate that more clearly?" "Would you tell us more about that point?" "Please define your term _____ for us." If you seek to increase the student's critical thinking or justify his response, you might use some of the following: "What facts or conditions are you assuming?" "What is your rationale for your response?" "Are there other component parts that you have not covered?" "If you took the opposite position to this point, how would you respond?" If you wish to have the student relate his or her response to another issue, you might use one of the following: "How is this related to _____?" "Can we analyze your answer?" "If we assume that this is true, what are the implications for _____?"[7]

In the following dialogue, classify each of the probing questions as to its function (*clarifying*, C, *justifying*, J, or *relating*, R).

TEACHER'S OPENING QUESTION: Do you think that the government has an obligation to our returning servicemen?

STUDENT RESPONSE: I think our government has a responsibility to our veterans.

_____1. PROBING QUESTION: Why?

_____2. PROBING QUESTION: Do you think that the government should help them get jobs?

STUDENT RESPONSE: I think that the government should provide jobs for all veterans.

_____3. PROBING QUESTION: Would you define your term "veteran" telling us what group or groups would be included?
STUDENT RESPONSE: I mean the Vietnam veterans.

_____4. PROBING QUESTION: Would you limit it to only the Vietnam veterans?

Answers: You should have classified the first probing question as justification. In the one word, why, you are asking the student to justify or give a rationale for his or her response. The second probing question seeks clarification of what the student thinks the government's responsibility is. The third probing question also calls for clarification in asking the student to define his term. The fourth has as its goal relating the response to other areas, i.e., the government's responsibility to veterans in past wars as well as the Vietnamese.

Now state a topic in your subject area in which you would engage the students in synthesis. _____

_____

_____

Using that topic, construct a dialogue in which you give three student responses, and an example of an appropriate probing question. One of your probing questions should ask for clarification, one for justification, and one seeking the relationship of the response to another area.

Teacher's Opening Question:

Student Response:

Probing Question:

Student Response:

Probing Question:

Student Response:

Probing Question:

7. *Divergent Questions* Divergent questions are another technique that you can use to help a student to synthesize. This kind of question is probably the least often asked in the classroom. In James J. Gallagher's research, it was found that teachers in junior and senior high school English, science, and social studies devoted about 60 percent of their questions to cognitive-memory, about 30 percent to convergent thinking, 6 percent to evaluative thinking, and 4 percent to divergent thinking.[8] If you want your students to develop their creative talents, you must vary your questions. Divergent questions, in particular, help to develop the student's and the teacher's creative dimension. Gallagher also found that slight increases in the percentage of teacher divergent-thinking questions yield a large increase in the divergent production of students.

Divergent questions are questions that have no right or wrong answer, but do have appropriate or inappropriate responses. They are open-ended and require students to use both concrete and abstract thinking in order to arrive at an appropriate response. The student is free to explore the problem in whatever direction he chooses, think creatively, leave the comfortable boundaries of the known and reach out into the unknown. Frequently this is an uncomfortable situation for the teacher. It can easily be seen that a teacher who is authoritarian and "knows" what's "right" would be hard put to engage his or her class in divergent thinking. In using divergent questions, you do not sit in judgment handing down sentences of corect or incorrect. You merely serve to help students in thinking creatively, placing knowledge in a juxtaposition, and seeing if they can come up with a new relationship. You may point out fallacies in the student's logic, offer suggestions by other questions, or reinforce, but you must be careful to refrain from making judgmental statements. Students respond in like kind to their teacher's behavior.

Some examples of divergent questions might be: "What will happen to our schools if the states cannot use property taxes for their support?" "What type of life would you live if you were suddenly transported to India?" "If the world had not allowed Germany to expand into Czechoslovakia, could World War II have been averted?" "If Shakespeare lived today, what do you think he would write about in his plays?"

Define divergent questions in your own words. _____

_____

From your subject area state a topic you would teach using synthesis. _____

_____

List five divergent questions you might use in teaching this topic.

1. _____
2. _____
3. _____
4. _____
5. _____

8. Silence   A third technique that you may use in order to help students in synthesis is that of silence. Silence rarely occurs in the classroom. Some teachers find silence intolerable. Students may use silence to control the teacher's behavior. The teacher asks a question of a student, but the student says nothing. In a few moments, the teacher is uncomfortable and probably breaks the silence himself. He or she may reword the question, give more information, or ask another student. By silence, the student has forced upon the teacher a behavior other than that the teacher had planned to use. Many teachers equate teaching with talking. Thus, many beginning teachers think that if they are not talking, they are not teaching; if they are not teaching, the students are not learning, then the teachers are not earning their salaries. Such thinking is erroneous. There is no way we can stop learning, short of death or total impairment of the mental processes through injury. Teachers merely *direct thinking and facilitate learning.* Silence allows the student time to cogitate, to try out things in his head. It allows for reflection. It allows them time to restructure their thinking to include or exclude new facts as presented. Silence is necessary in using probing and divergent questions. Since students are being asked to extend themselves or to propose to the class an answer to a divergent question, they must have time to reflect on their responses, to "get it together," to think out a support of the answer, to try one response out, discard it, and try another, and another.

List three ways silence may help a student in thought processes.

1. _____

2. _____

3. _____

How can silence be used by students to modify a teacher's behavior?

9. Nonverbal Cues Since synthesis teaching often involves responses through class discussion, three main kinds of nonverbal cues may be used by the teacher to encourage student response. Facial cues are the easiest for the students to detect, and are therefore the most powerful. A smile encourages and tells a student to continue. A frown indicates displeasure, and the response may take two forms. The student may halt his or her response, or he or she may feel that the response must be justified by further clarification.

Other facial expressions that cue the student are: (1) looking thoughtful as the student responds, thus indicating that you are considering the response; (2) continuing to look seriously while the student is responding and thus encouraging him or her to continue; and (3) looking quizzically as though the student's answer was not clear, which generally stimulates the student to reword the answer or clarify it.

In each of these instances, silence is used with a nonverbal cue in encouraging students to continue their responses and encourages other students to respond.

Head movement is another type of nonverbal cue. A smile or nod of the head on the part of the teacher encourages a student. Nodding indicates that the student is on the right track. Likewise, a teacher, by merely shaking his or her head, indicates to a student that the response is unacceptable and the student may change it. To indicate to a student that you are listening to the response, you merely need to tilt your head and ear toward the student and assume a thoughtful look.

The third kind of nonverbal cue is that of body movement. Simply by moving a bit closer to the student responding, you indicate that you are interested in what the student is saying. By assuming a thoughtful pose (fist under chin, etc.), you indicate to the class that you are considering the student's response. In using these nonverbal cues, teachers try to encourage student participation.

Nonverbal cues have another important use. They allow the teacher to "read" his students. If there is little eye contact between students and teacher, if students are looking at their desks, out the windows, or at each other, if they are doodling, fidgeting, slumping in their seats, then these nonverbal cues say to the teacher that it is past time for the learning activity of the class to be changed, that the work is boring or uninteresting, and that more time spent on that particular topic in that way is probably wasted effort. A teacher reading these nonverbal cues knows when to break the silence, change the topic, use an alternative experience, or change activity.

1. What are the three major types of nonverbal cues?

2. What facial cues could a teacher use to encourage a student to respond?

3. What facial cue could a teacher use to curtail a student's response?

4. What head movement could a teacher use to encourage a student to respond?

5. What head movement could a teacher use to curtail a student's response?

6. What body movement could a teacher use to encourage a student to respond?

7. How do nonverbal cues help the teacher in interpreting his student's feeling?

10. What Are Some Criticisms of Synthesis Teaching? It should be apparent that the inquiry method is applicable to many situations and serves equally well in any discipline. In fact, it may be used in teaching specific material and in teaching students a method of study. However, it is not an instantaneous panacea for all teaching woes. The method does have critics. For instance, if a teacher knows the answer to the problem under attack, is it proper to call the ensuing discussion discovery or inquiry? Is the teacher inquiring? Are the students engaging in inquiry or merely discovering what the teacher wants them to discover? Is it inquiry if the teacher asks exactly the right question in order to get the right response? Are students actually inquiring if the teacher so directs it that there is little, if any, chance for the students *not* to discover the answer that was predetermined by the teacher?

Such teaching is sometimes termed "guided discovery," and much of the new curricula falls in this category. Bob Burton Brown calls such guided or structured discovery a mockery of the inquiry method.[9] This raises such questions as, to what extent is it a mockery? Is guided discovery simply a variation of the old lecture and recitation methods of acquiring knowledge? Is guided inquiry a deception of the student since the teacher often plays dumb? Is it a guessing game in which the student guesses what the teacher has in mind? If guided or structured discovery is the only type of discovery that the student and teacher engage in, then we must admit that it is a mockery. However, to the extent that it is a useful teaching method by which the teacher teaches his students the skills of inquiry in order that they may engage in free inquiry, then it is not a mockery and has value.

Three most common problems or criticisms of the inquiry method are as follows. (1) Time/Cost Factor—some claim that the discovery method is too slow and expensive in terms of effort expended by the teacher and students. Students will learn fewer facts and principles simply because they will not have studied them. This objection is often offered by those concerned with covering large amounts of subject matter. Frequently this is a self-imposed situation. Furthermore, such matters as students' interest and encouragement of students to become self-learners may far outweigh time/cost factor.[5] (2) Burden of Learning—it requires that the student correct his or her own mistakes. Many students cannot do this well. Students have learned to listen to the teacher and to return the information given intact on examinations. The inquiry method rejects this and forces students to pursue knowledge on their own. Students must be active participants, not passive learners. (3) Need for Discovery Method—it is possible for more mature students to form most new concepts by directly grasping higher-order relationships. Thus, the discovery method is unnecessary as a student becomes older.

These three problems should be recognized and taken as cautions. No one would advocate using synthesis as the sole method of learning, and likewise no one would advocate eliminating it. It is a valid learning experience, and it is the teacher's professional judgment which must be used to balance methods to fit the situation, employing synthesis when appropriate and other types of teaching when they best fit the learning experience.[10]

1. List three major criticisms of synthesis teaching.

1. _____

2. _____

3. _____

2. Choose one of these criticisms and write a one-paragraph defense of it.

SUMMARY

Synthesis may be defined as a restructuring of a person's perceptual field by thought processes. It is appropriate when a teacher wants his students to learn the process of putting information into a new form and/or exercising his creativity. The role of the teacher shifts in synthesis learning from that of dispenser of knowledge to facilitator. In the role of facilitator the teacher may serve as planner, introducer, sustainer, manager, and rewarder. There are four skills or techniques that you, as the teacher, will use in synthesis: probing questions, divergent questions, silence, and nonverbal cues. Synthesis learning has been criticized as being costly, placing the burden of learning on the student, and not being needed for older students. Some synthesis learning that is highly structured has been criticized as being a mockery of the method. As valid as these criticisms may be, there is a place for synthesis learning. It remains the function of the teacher to balance all methods and use synthesis to accomplish those learning experiences for which it is appropriate.

EVALUATION

1. Teach the synthesis lesson that you have prepared to a group of three or more of your peers.

2. Have each of your peers fill out the form Critique for Simulated Teaching: Synthesis Lesson at the end of the chapter.

3. Make a critique of your lesson using the Critique for Simulated Teaching: Synthesis Lesson at the end of the chapter.

4. Using the critiques from your peers and your own critique, make a written analysis of your teaching noting specific strengths and weaknesses and making specific suggestions of ways that your weaknesses might be strengthened.

5. Using the information from your peers as well as your own critique and analysis, replan your synthesis lesson and reteach it. Pay particular attention to overcoming the problems identified in your first synthesis lesson. Identify how you could improve in your use of the following skills: divergent questions, probing questions, silence, and nonverbal cues. Determine if you could reasonably expect your students to achieve your objective. This reteach lesson should reflect a restructuring of strategy based upon your analysis of your first synthesis lesson, and you should produce a significantly different approach to the lesson.

CRITIQUE FOR SIMULATED TEACHING:

Synthesis Lesson

Teacher_____ Date_____
Evaluator_____

	Unable to Observe	Not Achieved	Below Average	Average	Strong	Superior
	0	1	2	3	4	5
1. Rate the teacher on each of the following skills:						
a. Set Induction						
b. Divergent Questions						
c. Probing Questions						
d. Nonverbal Cues						
e. Silence						
f. Closure						
2. Strategy — Was the strategy appropriate for the lesson taught?						
3. Objective—Clearly taught and understood by students?						

Comments:

NOTES

1. B. S. Bloom, ed., *Taxonomy of Educational Objectives: Cognitive Domain*, (New York: David McKay, 1956).

2. R. M. Gagné, *The Conditions of Learning* (New York: Holt, Rinehart, and Winston, 1965), pp. 58–59.

3. David H. Russell, *Children's Thinking*, (Boston: Ginn and Co., 1956), p. 256.

4. Irving M. Copi, *Introduction to Logic*, 2nd ed. (New York: Macmillan, 1961), p. 433.

5. Edwin Fenton, *The New Social Studies*, (New York: Holt, Rinehart, and Winston, 1967), p. 16.

6. Byron G. Massia, "Teaching and Learning Through Inquiry," *Today's Education*, LVII (5), May 1969, pp. 40–42.

7. Dwight W. Allen, et al., *Teaching Skills for Secondary School Teachers: Questioning Skills*, Teacher's Manual, General Learning Corporation, 1969, pp. 20–21.

8. James J. Gallagher and Mary Jane Aschner, "A Preliminary Report on Classroom Interaction," *Merrill-Palmer Quarterly of Behavior and Development*, 9:183–194, July 1963.

9. Bob Burton Brown, "Acquisition Versus Inquiry," *Elementary School Journal*, 64:11–17, October 1963.

10. Ronald T. Hyman, *Ways of Teaching*, (Philadelphia: J. B. Lippincott Co., 1970), pp. 121–122.

chapter 11

The Psychomotor Lesson

OBJECTIVES

1. From your major or minor field of study, you are expected to develop a lesson plan for teaching a psychomotor lesson. This lesson plan must contain the following elements: an instructional objective in the psychomotor domain, a preassessment, modeling (demonstration) of the skill, practice, and evaluation of the skill. The lesson plan will follow the format of the lesson plan for teaching a concept lesson in Chapter 8.

2. You will use the lesson plan developed above to teach a psychomotor lesson in which you will exhibit skill in the following: preassessment, modeling (demonstration), use of practice, and evaluation. In addition, you will demonstrate competence in using the following teaching skills: set induction, stimulus variation, repetition, reinforcement, and closure. The lesson will be taught to a group of peers and, if possible, videotaped.

3. You will also be expected to make a written analysis of your teaching using the critiques from peers (Critique for Simulated Teaching: Psychomotor Lesson at the end of the chapter). In this written analysis, you will evaluate your competency in using preassessment, modeling, use of practice, and evaluation.

4. You will also be expected to reteach your psychomotor lesson eliminating the problem areas identified in your analysis of your first psychomotor lesson. You will analyze this second psychomotor lesson from a videotaped replay, if possible, using the Critique for Simulated Teaching: Psychomotor Lesson at the end of the chapter. A comparison must be made between the teach and reteach cycles.

PREASSESSMENT

Make use of the following questions to guide your study. Each question is followed by a number that links it to the *Instructional Procedures* included in this chapter.

1. What are psychomotor skills? *(1)*

2. Why are psychomotor objectives considered easier to write? *(1)*

3. In what subject areas are psychomotor skills appropriately taught? *(2)*

4. What subject areas are traditionally thought of as being primarily psychomotor? *(2)*

5. What is the relationship of the psychomotor domain to the cognitive domain? *(1)*

6. How might psychomotor skills be incorporated in teaching your subject area? *(3)*

7. What are some psychomotor skills that you would wish to teach in your subject area? *(3)*

8. How are psychomotor skills classified? *(2)*

9. What are the major classifications of psychomotor skills according to Kibler? *(2)*

10. What are some examples of each of these classifications? *(2)*

11. What teaching skills are needed to teach a psychomotor lesson? *(3)*

12. What is meant by the term preassessment? *(3)*

13. How does preassessment aid the teacher in individualizing instruction? *(3)*

14. What is meant by the term, modeling? *(3)*

15. What are some ways by which modeling may be accomplished? *(3)*

16. How does verbal facility (explaining) aid in modeling? *(3)*

17. Define in your own words the term practice. *(3)*

18. What is the purpose of practice? *(30)*

19. What is the difference between whole and part practice? *(3)*

20. When would you use whole practice? *(3)*

21. When would you use part practice? *(3)*

22. How is feedback during practice used effectively? *(3)*

23. What are some factors for using practice correctly? *(3)*

24. How is evaluation of psychomotor skills accomplished? *(4)*

25. What are the difficulties in setting criterion levels for psychomotor skills? *(4)*

26. What is meant by extrinsic criterion levels being imposed on psychomotor skills? *(4)*

INSTRUCTIONAL PROCEDURES

LEARNING ACTIVITY 1:   Read the following selection, Planning and Teaching a Psychomotor Lesson, and answer the exercises included in it.

1. What Are Psychomotor Skills?   Lee J. Cronbach has stated that all psychomotor tasks involve intellectual abilities such as are found in pencil-paper tests.[1] The teaching of psychomotor skills is indeed an important part of the responsibility of many secondary school teachers. The learning process is unique in that it requires more than intellectual activity: it includes muscular coordination as well.

Psychomotor skills consist of sequences of motor activities that are performed in a coordinated way. They have received little attention in curricular planning and writing because the objectives in these areas are, according to Robert J. Kibler, easy to write since they involve an observable skill.[2] Indeed, they are much more easily written than those in the affective domain where indication of achievement is based on inferences that imply attainment of the objective. Psychomotor skills or objectives include an observable skill or behavior which can be evaluated.

The teachers who are most concerned with psychomotor skills are generally in physical education, home economics, vocational education, and the artistic subjects. But an analysis of other subjects that are generally thought to be "academic" will prove that they also have specific psychomotor skills either esoteric to that subject or that are used in evaluating portions of that subject. For instance, geometry is generally thought of as an highly academic subject requiring only the higher thought processes of analysis and synthesis, but in the manipulation of these thought processes, psychomotor skills of accurate measuring by use of rulers, compasses, protractors, etc., and in the construction of geometric shapes, are utilized daily. When history seeks to become more than a "book" subject, psychomotor skills come into play. The construction of maps (particularly topographical maps), dioramas, and models requires the teaching or development of psychomotor skills.

In physical education, psychomotor skills become the focus for much of the class activity, but increasingly this is tied to cognitive skills of knowledge of rules, application of rules, and formulating a game strategy. In addition, analysis skills are used in analyzing films or tapes of games in order to correct errors in play both of purely psychomotor skills and in errors of judgment that require higher cognitive skills. Home economics uses a combination of all three domains. Vocational education courses and the artistic courses both require many psychomotor skills to be developed. It has recently come to the attention of the authors how closely the domains are interrelated and how one domain may be used in evaluation of another.

One example occurred in a music class for elementary children. The children had been studying song form and were to be able to recognize the rhythm of the music being played and to recognize when either of two themes in a given piece of music (ABA form) occurred. The evaluation of this was accomplished by their stepping in place in time to the music, thus demonstrating that they recognized the beat and then raising their right hand when the first melody was played, and their left hand when the second, or counter, melody was played. Clearly, the objective called for them to demonstrate behavior in the cognitive domain at the analysis level, but they were using a finely coordinated psychomotor skill in indicating their analysis of the piece of music (hand-foot-ear movement). Thus, we must not ignore the fact that psychomotor skills, to varying degrees, involve other kinds of behavior found in the cognitive and affective domains. Bach said of playing the organ that it was a simple task. All one did was press the right key at the right moment and the organ did the rest. To view psychomotor skills in this apogee of simplistic description is to blind ourselves to the position that psychomotor skills occupy in education. We must define psychomotor skills broadly, expunge the idea that they are only valid objectives for athletics, and encompass them where proper in our curricula planning.

State your subject area:

Analyze your subject area and then list five psychomotor skills, appropriate for your area, that you would want to teach.

1. _____
2. _____
3. _____
4. _____
5. _____

2. How Are Psychomotor Skills Classified? Unlike the cognitive and affective domains, the psychomotor domain has not been clearly defined or a taxonomy generally accepted. The editors of the *Taxonomy of Educational Objectives* found few objectives in the educational literature in the psychomotor domain and thus felt that it was not as essential to formulate a taxonomy for it at the present time. Nonetheless, the psychomotor domain does exist and is used in curricular planning. It has received considerable attention in the field of testing. Much of this work was done as a result of involvement of the armed services in training personnel. Edwin A. Fleishman, in his research, has attempted to list the factors in psychomotor performance. He made no attempt to classify or organize the factors into a taxonomy, but attempted to identify those factors which would properly lie within the psychomotor domain.[3]

Robert J. Kibler, Larry L. Barker, and David T. Miles[2] have developed a classification of the psychomotor domain. As with Fleishman, their classification is not presented as a taxonomy because the skills listed do not necessarily form a hierarchy. Much of their work is derived from studies in child growth and development. From this they have subdivided the psychomotor domain into four main classifications: gross bodily movement, finely coordinated bodily movements, nonverbal communication, and speech behaviors. A cursory study of child growth and development lends credence to their classification. A child does develop gross bodily movements such as kicking before developing finely coordinated movements such as picking up objects, and in like fashion, nonverbal communication is developed (gestures such as pointing to an object which the child wants) before speech.

Kibler et al. further subclassify the classification of gross bodily movements into three logical divisions: movements which would involve the use of upper limbs (arms, shoulders); movements which would use lower limbs (feet, legs); and, movements involving two or more bodily movements (arm and leg movement, or movement using the entire body).

In their second main classification, they consider finely coordinated movements. As the title of the classification implies, this group of behaviors is comprised of coordinated movements utilizing two or more parts of the body. Such coordinated movements may involve hand-finger, hand-eye, hand-ear, hand-eye and lower body. Their third main classification of nonverbal communication includes such factors as facial expressions, gestures, and bodily movements. These are used to attempt to convey a message without the use of words although they are frequently used in conjuction with words to more clearly convey a message.

Speech behavior is the fourth major area of their classification. This area is concerned with the ability to produce sounds capable of conveying a message. Thus, the babbling of an infant would not be classified as speech. This classification contains behaviors concerned with sound-word formation and the projection of that sound.[4]

1. The classification of the psychomotor domain by Kibler et al. depends greatly upon studies in: _____

2. The four major classifications of the psychomotor domain according to Kibler are:

   1. _____

   2. _____

   3. _____

   4. _____

3. Give an example for each of the four major classifications listed above.

   1. _____

   2. _____

   3. _____

   4. _____

3. What Skills Do I Need in Order to Teach a Psychomotor Lesson? After formulating and writing an instructional objective in the psychomotor domain in your subject area, there are four skills that you will need in order to teach it. These four skills are preassessment, modeling, practice, and evaluation. Of these four, two are discussed in other chapters in this book. Preassessment is discussed in Chapter 4 and evaluation is discussed in Chapter 14. You may want to go over these chapters if you need further clarification of the relationship between these components.

Preassessment in psychomotor skills includes not only the total skills, but also the component skills that constitute the total skill. Your preassessment, therefore, is twofold. First, to determine if the student possesses the total skill; and second, which of the component skills he or she also possesses. For instance, a student being preassessed for the skill of swimming may possess the total skill equivalent to the minimum criteria for the objective, but still have many component skills included in swimming which could be improved.

Preassessment makes several demands upon you, as the instructor. First, you must have firmly in mind the model against which the student is to be compared. Second, you must be objective in your preassessment of the student and be careful to preassess only the total skills called for in the objective and not to confuse it with related but uncalled-for skills. Third, you must be analytical in your preassessment and be able to assess the component skills as well as the total skill.

Preassessment may be brought about in a variety of ways. Frequently, it takes the form of questions in which the students are asked if they possess a specific skill. Upon receiving negative feedback, you can them proceed to modeling. But preassessment may also take the form of allowing the student to attempt to perform the skill. An example of the latter would be preassessing the proper grip of a golf club by handing out golf clubs to the students and asking them to demonstrate how they would grip the club. Visual preassessment by the instructor would follow, and then modeling.

Regardless of the method used in preassessment, it must be constructive and one that minimizes embarrassment to the student. In some areas such as physical education, you must use preassessment techniques that take into account handicaps of students, and you may have to devise preassessment techniques that would only assess those skills which lie in the range of the physical limitations of the handicapped student.

Preassessment offers several avenues to the instructor for further teaching. First, it allows you to group your students for more individualized instruction. This grouping helps to avoid the negative aspects of a student who constantly compares his performance with those who already possess the skill. Second, it assists a student in obtaining a general idea of the abilities of other students. Third, it helps the teacher adjust objective and teaching activities and evaluation in keeping with the abilities of the student. Fourth, it will keep the teacher from boring the student who possesses the skill by forcing him or her to participate in the activities designed for those who do not possess the skill.

1. In your own words, define preassessment.

2. List two demands preassessment makes on a teacher.
    1. _____
    2. _____

Once preassessment has been accomplished, you, as the teacher, will utilize two major instructional procedures. The first of these is *modeling*. Modeling or demonstration procedures refer to those techniques that the teacher employs to give the student a perceptual model of the skill called for in the objective. It is imperative that the students have this model before they can be expected to demonstrate the skill. The modeling, therefore, assumes major proportions. It must be exact in as many details as possible. It must be exemplary of the best skill. A poor modeling begets nothing but poor skill. It is the authors' opinion that little is gained in the primary stage of attaining the perceptual model if the student is introduced to models that are not exemplary. After the student has acquired the perceptual model on the basis of positive teaching or "do it this way," then models that are faulty may be used in sharpening the students' analytical skill. But for the primary introduction of the perceptual model, it is essential that it be good. Indeed, students who already have a perceptual model of the skill or who possess faulty component skills are faced with a twofold problem. First, they must form the correct perceptual model and at the same time they must unlearn the incorrect one. Examination of your own experience will give you instances of skills which you learned incorrectly and the difficulty encountered in correcting them.

If you possess the skill to be attained, model it for your students.

Usually, this modeling will be accompanied by a verbal explanation. Such explanations may include identifying the various component skills in their sequential order, which muscles are being brought into play, stress points, position of arms, legs, body, etc. Verbal facility in explaining the skill should not be underestimated. It allows for multisensory reception on the part of the student and aids in the correction of this skill, using verbal as well as visual feedback. If you do not possess the skill to the degree of proficiency that is necessary for modeling, then use motion pictures, illustrations, charts, diagrams, or another person such as another instructor in the school. It must be stressed here that although it is expected that the instructor will be able to model most of the skills he or she teaches, it is by no means imperative to do so. To teach only those skills which the instructor is capable of modeling severely handicaps the instructor and eliminates teaching skills students may need. The necessary portion of modeling is not who does the modeling, but how well it is done and that the students form the perceptual model of the skill. How the modeling is done lies in the discretion of the teacher in choosing the best model and presenting it to the students. We must also remember here that the instructor who no longer possesses the ability to model complex skills may function quite capably as an instructor of those skills. The athletic coach may consistently be able to teach skills to the team long after age or injury may have curtailed the ability to perform them. The ballet dancer may teach with great effectiveness long after his or her physical strength allows a demonstration of a complex step. Both of these will rely heavily upon verbal facility in explaining, using other ways of modeling, and using their analytical ability to help students in correcting component skills.

Modeling can be said to be a clarification of the instructional objective in that it communicates to the student visually, as well as verbally, the skills that he or she is expected to attain. The major component of modeling is not the way in which it is accomplished, but the fact that the student attains a perceptual model of the skill expertly performed.

1. Define modeling in your own words.

Since learning a psychomotor skill is based on developing muscle coordination, i.e., coordinating the acts of the muscles required for a particular skill to the point that they produce that specified skill, *practice* is required. Two basic types of practice are employed by the teacher. These are part practice and whole practice. In part practice, the student masters the component skills independently before practicing them in sequence. For example, in teaching typing, position of the hands and finger placement and stroke are component skills. The student practices each of these component skills until he or she is sufficiently proficient to proceed in performing the entire sequence. Using part practice does not preclude modeling of the total sequence of skills. This modeling is essential regardless of which type of practice is used. In part practice, it is essential for motivation since it allows the student to see how the component skills will be sequenced together to form the total skill. Part practice offers the advantage of individualizing the instruction so that you can have each student practice those component skills in whichever he or she is deficient.

In whole practice, practice is directed toward the integrated performance of the skills in proper sequence. Practice of parts (in this setting) occurs during practice of the entire sequence of skills. The choice of part or whole practice is contingent upon the type of skill involved. If the skill is one in which the component skills are easily attained, and the skill requires well-coordinated sequencing, then whole practice would be indicated since the procedure emphasizes sequencing. Skills whose component parts require unusual or difficult behaviors lend themselves to part practice.

After considering the skill and deciding upon whether to use part practice or whole practice, you must provide opportunities for the students to practice under proper supervision. During this practice, make suggestions and/or corrections. Here you will use your analytical skills to see if the student is performing the skill properly and if component skills need additional attention. You will sometimes find this type of practice termed "guided practice." In providing practice, you, as the instructor, also provide feedback to the student. This feedback is essential for motivation of the student to continue over a long period of time. It allows the student to note his or her progress and correct deficiencies.

In order for practice to be viable, you must use it properly. If the skill is a complex one, such as proper articulation in speaking a foreign language, then practice in speaking the foreign language should be provided during each class hour for the entire semester or year. At the same time, practice sessions must be controlled in length. Practice can become boring, and consequently, the student accomplishes little in relationship to the time expended. Thus, a number of short concentrated practice sessions may yield far better results than few long practice sessions. Practice activities must be varied if long practice sessions are used. If you plan for the students to practice a skill for an entire class period, then you will need several activities, each one of which allows the student to practice the skill but in a different way.

The students need clear, concise directions as to what they are to practice. This is particularly important if you have grouped your students and have them working concurrently on different skills. If directions are not explicit, then time and effort will be wasted. Practice activities must coincide with the sequential skills to be learned. Thus, the student will practice the skills in sequence rather than haphazardly. Special consideration must be made for plateaus in development. Students will develop a skill sometimes rapidly to a certain point and then seem to stop. Speed in typing is a prime example of this. After a certain speed is built up, the student may make little progress in gaining skill for a time. During such plateaus, the instructor must give positive feedback as to techniques that will enable the student to begin progressing and must also carefully point out to the student that learning curves contain plateaus.

1. What is the purpose of practice?

2. What is part practice?

3. What is whole practice?

4. What is feedback?

5. State six factors in using practice correctly.

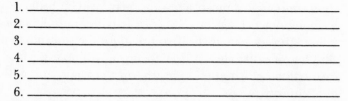

1. _____
2. _____
3. _____
4. _____
5. _____
6. _____

4. Evaluation   This is the final step in teaching psychomotor skills just as it is in teaching cognitive skills. There are two sources of the evaluation of psychomotor skills available. One of these is the feedback from the teacher as he or she observes the student in practice, confirming appropriate attainment of skills and correcting incorrect performance. The formal mode of the evaluation here consists of your keeping records of the student's performance over a period of time and making them available to the student. This allows the student to see his or her progress, and to engage in further practice on those skills that do not meet criteria levels. The other source of evaluation of psychomotor skills is from students. In this case, the students learn to monitor themselves. They develop analytical skills to the point that they can analyze their own performance, compare it to the criteria level and to the perceptual model, and not to their own progress. In each of these, the students are striving to attain the skill at the criterion previously stated in the objective.

Establishing criterion levels for evaluation of psychomotor skills is both extremely simple and difficult. It is a very simple thing to set criterion levels for performing the skills and thus be able to see, through the student's performance, if he or she can or cannot demonstrate proficiency in that skill. The difficulty arises in setting the criterion levels for complex psychomotor skills. For example, why would you arbitrarily set the minimum level of performance for first-year typing at thirty net words per minute? Why not twenty or forty or any other number? If the instruction is individualized, then each student will have his or her own level. Here, the teacher can help the student to set a realistic criterion level.

Another difficulty in evaluating psychomotor skills is students' fear of demonstrating failure before peers. You, as the teacher, can aid the student by providing support and not singling out students as negative examples.

Not to be overlooked as a problem is that some evaluation is imposed extrinsicially. Thus, a vocational course composed mainly of psychomotor skills may have evaluation criteria imposed upon it by the job market, funding agencies, or government. Vocational courses such as those on the building trades state their objectives behaviorally, and the courses are constructed so as to enable the student to enter that job at a minumum level. In some instances, this may entail not only preassessment, but using preassessment as a form of screening which would reduce the failure in the course.

1. What are the two sources of evaluation of psychomotor skills?

1. _____

2. _____

2. List three difficulties in setting criterion levels for psychomotor skills.

1. _____

2. _____

3. _____

3. How are extrinsic criterion levels imposed on psychomotor skills?

4. Give an example for 3.

In conclusion, in order for you to plan and teach a psychomotor lesson, you must first state an instructional objective in the psycho-motor domain, then provide a preassessment procedure to determine if the student possesses the skill and to what extent he must then provide modeling or demonstration of the skill called for, provide practice of the skill, and evaluate the student's achievement of the skill.

LESSON PLAN FORMAT
FOR TEACHING A PSYCHOMOTOR LESSON

1. Instructional Objective (What skill do I want the student to learn?)

2. Preassessment procedure

3. Modeling or demonstration strategies (How will I clarify the objective by modeling or demonstrating?)

4. Practice activities and feedback

5. Evaluation

LEARNING ACTIVITY 2:

1. State your subject area.

2. State a psychomotor skill in that area you want to teach.

3. Write an instructional objective for that skill.

4. List two ways you could achieve preassessment.
    1. _____
    2. _____
5. List three ways you could achieve modeling.
    1. _____
    2. _____
    3. _____

6. What type of practice would you use?
Why?

7. Give three ways you could vary the practice of the skill within a class hour.

    1. _____

    2. _____

    3. _____

8. What evaluation procedures will you use? Why?

EVALUATION

1. Teach the psychomotor lesson that you have prepared to a group of three or more of your peers.

2. Have each of your peers fill out the form Critique for Simulated Teaching: Psychomotor Lesson which follows.

3. Make a critique of your lesson using the Critique for Simulated Teaching: Psychomotor Lesson which follows.

4. Using the critiques from your peers and your own critique, make a written analysis of your teaching, noting specific strengths and weaknesses and making specific suggestions of ways that your weaknesses might be strengthened.

5. Using the information from your peers as well as your own critique and analysis, replan your synthesis lesson and reteach it. Pay particular attention to overcoming the problems identified in your first psychomotor lesson. Identify how you could improve in your use of the following skills: preassessment, modeling, use of practice, and evaluation. Determine if you could reasonably expect your students to achieve your objective. This reteach lesson should reflect a restructuring of strategy based upon your analysis of your first psychomotor lesson and you should produce a significantly different approach to the lesson.

CRITIQUE FOR SIMULATED TEACHING:

Psychomotor Lesson

Teacher_____ Date_____

Evaluator_____

	Unable to Observe	Not Achieved	Below Average	Average	Strong	Superior
	0	1	2	3	4	5
1. Instructional objective clearly defined.						
2. Preassessment procedure adequately measures instructional objective.						
3. Modeling or demonstration appropriate for objective.						
4. Verbal description of skill adequate.						
5. Part practice used appropriately.						
6. Whole practice used appropriately.						
7. Feedback provided for student.						
8. Evaluation-measured student achievement of instructional objective.						
9. Set Induction						
10. Stimulus Variation						
11. Repetition						
12: Reinforcement						
13. Closure						
14. How could this lesson be improved? List at least two specific ways which suggest improvement or alternatives which could be used.						

NOTES

1. Lee J. Cronbach, *Essentials of Psychological Testing*, (New York: Harper and Row, 1960), p. 301.

2. Robert J. Kibler, Larry L. Barker, and David T. Miles, *Behavioral Objectives and Instruction*, (Boston: Allyn and Bacon, 1970), p. 101.

3. Edwin A. Fleishman, "Psychomotor Selection Tests: Research and Application in the United States Air Force," *Personnel Psychology*, 9, 1956, pp. 449-468.

4. Robert J. Kibler et al., *Behavioral Objectives and Instruction*, pp. 66-75.

chapter 12

The Affective Lesson

OBJECTIVES

1. From your major or minor field of study, you will be expected to develop a lesson plan for teaching a simulated lesson in the affective domain. The lesson plan will follow the format of the lesson plan for teaching a concept lesson given in Chapter 8.

2. You will use the lesson plan developed above to teach an affective lesson in which you exhibit skill in set induction, factual recall questions, probing questions, higher-order questions, appropriate use of silence, nonverbal cues, reinforcement, and closure. The lesson will be taught to a group of peers and, if possible, videotaped.

3. You will make a written analysis of your teaching using critiques from your peers (Critique for Simulated Teaching: Affective Lesson at the end of the chapter). In this written analysis, you will evaluate your teaching skill in these areas: set induction, factual recall questions, higher-order questions, probing questions, silence, nonverbal cues, and closure.

4. You will also be expected to replan and reteach your synthesis lesson eliminating the problem areas identified in your analysis of your first affective lesson. This second affective lesson

must be analyzed from a videotaped replay using the Critique for Simulated Teaching: Affective Lesson which appears at the end of the chapter. A comparison must be made between the teach and reteach cycles.

PREASSESSMENT

Use the questions below to guide your study. Each question is followed by a number that links it to the *Instructional Procedures* included in this chapter.

1. What is the affective domain? *(1)*

2. How does Krathwohl define it? *(1)*

3. How does Krathwohl classify it? *(2)*

4. Why is the affective domain ignored in favor of the cognitive? *(3)*

5. What is the place of teaching in the affective domain in the schools? *(1)*

6. Why is teaching in the affective domain controversial? *(1)*

7. How does Kohlberg classify moral reasoning? *(2)*

8. How is the affective domain related to the cognitive? *(3)*

9. How do I write an affective objective? *(4)*

10. What are the two major types of affective objectives? *(4)*

11. What teaching skills do I need to use in teaching an affective lesson? *(5)*

12. What type of set inductions might be used in teaching an affective lesson? *(5)*

13. How would I use factual recall questions? *(5)*

14. How would I use higher-order questions? *(5)*

15. How would I use probing questions? *(5)*

16. How would I use silence, nonverbal cues and reinforcement? *(5)*

17. What type of closure might be used in teaching an affective lesson? *(5)*

18. What three instructional tactics could I use in teaching an affective objective? *(6)*

19. How can I measure my teaching in the affective domain? *(7)*

INSTRUCTIONAL PROCEDURES

LEARNING ACTIVITY 1:   Read the following article and answer the exercises included.

1. What Is the Affective Domain? When you, as the teacher, incorporate any material into your teaching, you must be aware that there are two distinct and important aspects of that material to the learner. These are first the content, concept, or skill itself, and second the meaningfulness, value, or importance of the content to the learner. In recent years, teachers have spent much of their teaching focusing on the first aspect of the relationship, the content. That is, they have been intent upon the transmission of a given body of facts only. To say that teaching content is wrong would be fallacious. Indeed, most teachers try to incorporate both types of teaching in their learning activities. Objectives in the affective domain, then, focus on the second aspect of content to learner, that is, the meaningfulness of that particular concept to the learner. As such, the affective domain represents the identification, clarification, and exploration of beliefs, values, appreciations, emotions, and attitudes. It may also validly represent the teacher's attempt to inculcate within the learner specific values or attitudes.

David R. Krathwohl et al. have defined the affective domain as being that domain which emphasizes a feeling, or emotion, or degree of acceptance or rejection. They further state that objectives in the affective domain vary from simple attention to selected phenomena, to complex yet internally consistent qualities of character. In their survey of objectives, they found numbers of objectives expressed as interests, attitudes, appreciations, values, and emotional sets or biases.[1]

Thus, we may view the affective domain as the emotional set with which each person interacts with content. It is comprised of values, attitudes, interests, appreciations, feelings (both positive and negative), for, or toward, a given body of content or segment of content, or person teaching it. It determines the uses to which the student will put cognitive material. Whereas the cognitive domain deals with student performance of certain manipulations with content, the affective domain deals with the value he or she will place on those capabilities of cognitive manipulation.

The affective domain deserves careful attention, exploration, and evaluation. This is the domain of the politician, minister, the attorney, and the advertising man who seek not to appeal to the cognitive, but to the feelings of persons and so persuade them to pursue a particular course of action. Unfortunately, far much less has been done in the affective domain than in the cognitive. And there are valid reasons for this. First, there is a common belief that what a person holds as his or her value system is a personal and inviolate area and that the teacher should keep hands off and not attempt to teach values, or force his or her own value system upon students. It is imperative that teachers recognize the danger of imposing their values and make special checks to safeguard against that imposition occurring in the classroom. This position is peculiar to the American way of life. We wish to remain individuals and we do not part easily with the idea that every person is entitled to his or her own opinion, values, and attitudes. If it is granted that the person does remain the possessor of a value system, and that the school may be trying to force another value system upon a person, the question still remains: Why give a person massive amounts of information and then not give him a wit of direction or directions by which to assess that information? For example, to give students information as to the ecological systems of the earth and the relationships between those systems without instilling in the student a value for the ecological system of the earth and how it may be used but also replenished is to commit the offense of destroying our earth itself by misuse of natural resources. Thus the schools do have a valid affective objective in teaching students to care about, value, their environment, and further, to evidence that valuing by not polluting it and seeing that others do not do so. The school does have a place in attempting to teach values to the student in order to direct the use of information gained.

It must be pointed out that the teaching of certain values in the public schools is more controversial than the teaching of content and skills. One major reason for this is that objectives in the affective domain are much harder to write and even more difficult to evaluate. Another reason is that society determines to a great extent the values that are acceptable as educational concerns. Thus, some values such as democracy, truthfulness, self-reliance, are acceptable values in American high schools. But teaching specific religious or political ideologies would not be.[2]

Teachers must be constantly aware that they are in a position to force their value systems upon their students and therefore must employ the safeguard of specifying their affective objectives and making certain that they are consonant with those that most teachers in that field would hold. Perhaps they may have to work consciously on becoming more accepting of ideas from their students and thus be capable of creating a climate in their classroom in which students will be able to express their values. The best criterion for objectives in the affective domain is that they deal with the valuing of the subject matter or commonly accepted moral values of the community in which they are taught. To overstep and try to teach one's own moral tenets or values, particularly on controversial issues, is to invite student, parent, and community backlash.

Define the affective domain in your own words.

Why has the school ignored teaching in the affective domain?

Why is teaching in the affective domain controversial?

2. How Is the Affective Domain Classified? Krathwohl et al. classified the affective domain into five major classifications: receiving, responding, valuing, organizing, and characterizing. These classifications are hierarchical in nature and presuppose that a person in developing an affective domain passes through these stages in consecutive order. The continuum is developed on the premise that a person internalizes his or her values and develops them from a point of merely being aware that a specific affect exists to that of the affect becoming a control of his or her life. For a further discussion of Krathwohl's classification, see Chapter 3, Taxonomy of Instructional Objectives.

Lawrence Kohlberg has formulated a theory of how children and adults reason about moral problems.[3] His theory draws heavily upon the work of Piaget and is one of developmental stages. According to Kohlberg, there are six major stages of moral reasoning. People move from one stage to another as they mature. Thus, the development is sequential and hierarchical. His classification calls for three levels:

preconventional, conventional, and postconventional or autonomous. Within each of these levels, there are two discernible states. At
the preconventional level, generally ages four to ten, the person bases
his or her moral judgments or affective behavior upon the terms of
pleasant or unpleasant consequences. Thus, behavior is governed by
punishment, reward. The first stage in this level is that of obedience
and punishment orientation. In this stage, the motives for moral
action are controlled by the person wishing to avoid punishment.
Moral decisions are determined to be either good or bad on the basis of
the consequences. Here the person has an unquestioning respect for
power. At this level, a person responds to rules and labels of good and
bad, right and wrong derived from his parents and siblings. But his
judgment of what is right and wrong is a one-sided view of authority.
He or she values power for power's sake and accepts the values of good
or bad without question as to the underlying moral order or respect.
He or she is concerned only with the consequences of his or her
actions, by those consequences as deemed either good or bad. Developmental state Two at level One is egoistic in its orientation. Here the
person conceives of actions being right or wrong in relationship to
how they satisfy his or her needs and possibly the needs of others.
Moral actions or affective behaviors here are governed by desire for
benefit or reward.

Level Two, according to Kohlberg, is the conventional level. As
might be expected from the label, at this level the person's affective
behaviors are aimed at maintaining and supporting the conventional
order. The person tries to perform good or right behaviors. Also at
this level the person supports the family, group, or nation. He or she
exhibits a behavior of conformity and loyalty to the group. Therefore,
behavior is governed and controlled by expectations and rules of the
group. This level is divided into two stages. At developmental stage
Three, the person's affective behavior is aimed at gaining approval
from the group. Moral actions are governed by the group's approval
and disapproval. They are concerned with what others think. Developmental stage Four has a social-order-maintaining orientation.
Law and order come into play. Here the person's affective behavior is
concerned with doing his duty and showing respect for authority.
Maintaining the given social order is one of his goals. Here the
person's moral judgments are defined by fixed rules which are deemed

necessary to maintain order. Actions of a person at this stage arise from anticipation of dishonor caused by disobeying laws or rules of the group or society. A person at this stage also considers what is deemed best for society when deciding what is right. He or she considers the consequences to society in general.

The third level in Kohlberg's classification is that of postconventional or autonomous. At this level the person moves toward making his moral judgments on the basis of moral principles. These principles are seen as having validity not derived from the authority of the groups of persons and/or from the individual's identification with those groups. This level is also divided into two stages. Development stage Five concerns itself with social contract, constitutionalism, and higher law orientation. Right actions or affective behaviors here are defined in terms of the general values that have been agreed to by the whole society. A person at this level governs his actions by concern for maintaining self-respect. His or her frame of reference is the community or society, not family or immediate group. His or her moral values also include individual rights and standards which have been approved by the whole society. He or she recognizes that in matters of moral judgment, the individual determines what is right action except in matters where right has been agreed upon through proper procedures. This results not in a legalistic point of view, but one tempered with the possibility of changing the law to better meet the needs of the society. Developmental stage Six is the highest stage of moral development, according to Kohlberg. This stage is at the conscience or principle orientation level. Here the person governs his or her affective behavior by applying universal principles of ethics. These principles are not unique to any given group or society, but are elements of a larger sphere. An example of these would be the Golden Rule. These principles are abstract and would pertain to any society. A person at stage Six defines right actions in accordance with self-chosen ethical principles. Among these principles would be justice, equality of human rights, and respect for the dignity of the individual.

Kohlberg, in his research, has found that these stages in moral development are developmental and a person cannot skip a stage. The developmental process proceeds at different rates for different persons. Some move rapidly in their development and move from one stage to another quickly. Others move slowly and never reach the higher levels. Kolhberg has also found that moral reasoning is directly related to behavior, that the movement from stage to stage is a long-term process, and that only about 20 percent of the adult population reaches stages Five and Six.

Each of the two classifications of affective behavior has value to you as a teacher. The Krathwohl taxonomy is possibly the best known and therefore, when you state objectives in its terms, it may be easier to communicate your objectives to others. The Kohlberg classification, however, has much to recommend it since it does have empirical research as a basis for its formulation.

The three levels of Kohlberg's theory of moral reasoning and the six major stages are:

Level 1

Stage 1

Stage 2

Level 2

Stage 3

Stage 4

Level 3

Stage 5

Stage 6

3. What Is the Relationship Between the Cognitive and Affective Domains? Much research has been done on the relationship between the cognitive and affective domains. The fact that the two were treated separately by Bloom and Krathwohl does not negate the fact that the two are inextricably bound. The facts of the matter remain that the two domains are parts of the organism and any division is therefore impossible. The division has been made merely in order to facilitate analysis. Martin Scheerer states it thus, "Behavior may be conceptualized as being embedded in a cognitive-emotional motivational matrix in which no true separation is possible."[4] Milton Rokeach points out that when one analyzes the cognitive behavior of a person, he or she is also working with the affective behavior of that person. Each cognitive behavior is seen as having an affective counterpart.[5]

The usual varieties of objectives concern themselves with specifying behavior in only one domain. In general, in schoolwork we have stressed the cognitive, but nearly all cognitive objectives possess an affective counterpart. Most teachers hope that their students will, through gaining knowledge about a particular subject, also gain an appreciation or value for that subject. In general, we have moved from the cognitive to the affective. That is, we approach the affective through cognitive means. An observer in a classroom can see this in action. We try to instill an appreciation of a given work of art by having the students study and analyze it. That the relationship between cognitive and affective is always positive is erroneous. The fact that a person does possess information about a particular item does not in itself assure that that person will have a positive feeling for that item. Indeed, the opposite may occur. One example of this would be the required study of literature ostensibly pursued in order to instill a love or appreciation of great literature may have just the reverse effect and instead produce a feeling of alienation from literature. This value may even be generalized to include all forms of literature.

One of the major types of affective objectives which are used in order to attain cognitive objectives is that of developing interest or motivation. Since motivation is critical, the affective domain assumes vast proportions. The new curricula, such as the University of Illinois mathematics program, make use of the cognitive in simultaneously achieving cognitive and affective goals. It does this through the use of the discovery method using materials that are interesting to the students. J. Richard Suchman's inquiry training[6] illustrates the attainment of both cognitive and affective objectives simultaneously. In his work, he achieves the affective goal of interest in the material by discovery learning and builds attitudes toward intellectual activity by developing the child's ability in inquiry. His method utilizes the teacher as a data-giver and the students ask questions about the material seeking to arrive at an explanation of the puzzling phenomenon.

In the cognitive domain, we are concerned that the student possess the capabilities of performing some task when required. In the affective domain, we are concerned with the fact that he or she will perform a particular behavior under certain conditions. Obviously, the cognitive is much easier to measure and thus, the tendency for the cognitive to drive out the affective is clearly seen.

Briefly state how the cognitive and affective domains are related.

4. How Do I Choose an Affective Objective?   Teachers have always incorporated affective behaviors within their teaching. Every teacher desires to teach his or her students to appreciate or value the subject matter. Generally these are incorporated into objectives in very loose terms such as: The student will develop an appreciation of his American heritage. Immediately after stating this the teacher resumes teaching important people, events, dates, etc. that occurred within a given chronological period and expects the student to learn them and demonstrate that learning in a number of ways, the most frequent of which is the essay test. To say that the student, by learning the cognitive facts of history, has developed a positive appreciation of the American heritage is tenuous at best and at worst it may be totally fallacious. Students may have developed an opinion, but it may be a negative one. In other words, instead of developing an appreciation of the American heritage, he or she may well have developed an abhorrence of the study of American history. Thus, it follows that if we assume that all behavior is learned, then affective behaviors are also learned. If they are learned, then we must structure learning situations that assist the student. The implication is clear that if we state affective objectives, then we must be clearly aware that we must provide educational opportunities for the student to achieve those objectives and provide some way or ways of measuring the achievement of those objectives.

Affective objectives not only grow out of the discipline (much as the cognitive or psychomotor objectives), but there are also some affective objectives that are appropriate to every subject area. For example, the science teacher teaching the proper laboratory technique also teaches safety. Thus a valuing of safety is developed. This same objective would be appropriate in a home economics course, wood shop, physical education, and or driver training. The differences would be in the behaviors that the teacher would accept as evidence that the student had indeed developed a behavior of safety. Thus in the laboratory it might include absence of horseplay, following directions meticulously in mixing chemicals, using protective clothing and ventilation devices. In home economics, it might include proper use of cooking utensils such as pressure cookers, handling knives, operation of machinery such as mixers, blenders, etc., care in handling food so as to avoid contamination. In wood shop, it might include using approved techniques in operating machinery, use of protective clothing, and use of ventilation devices. In physical education it might include wearing proper protective equipment, and utilization of athletic equipment in approved or accepted ways. In driver training, the range of behaviors which might be accepted as evidence of the student developing a behavior of valuing safety might include such mundane things as locking the door of the car each time he enters, to perceptive driving in which the driver tries to anticipate the actions of other drivers and implement strategies that would compensate for those actions. From this it should be clear that an affective objective may be of two types. It may be one of developing a positive feeling for a particular discipline or it may fall into the range of affective behaviors that are accepted as necessary for our society, but which are taught in several or all subject areas.

In selecting objectives in the affective domain for your subject area, the first procedure is identical to that of choosing cognitive objectives. You must ask yourself the question, what affective behaviors do I want my students to exhibit after instruction? Once you have listed the affective behaviors you wish to incorporate, then you must specify the responses that you will logically accept as evidence that the student is exhibiting this behavior. Thus, you have two parts to an affective objective. First, you state the affect (valuing, intent, etc.) and then the responses (behaviors) you will accept as evidence of having attained the affect.

The two major types of affective objectives are:

The three steps in selecting and writing affective objectives are:
1. _____
2. _____
3. _____
Write an affective objective for your subject area.

5. What Teaching Skills Could I Use in Teaching an Affective Lesson? Suppose you want to teach a lesson at the organization level of the affective domain. Your objective in this lesson would be to elicit students reactions to a given idea and to assist them, through open discussion, to examine, and to compare and contrast the various viewpoints or reactions different persons may have. Your objective may then be twofold: enabling the student to become aware of, and capable of, verbalizing his or her own responses or point of view and having him or her compare and contrast this point of view with those of other students.

In stating your instructional objectives in behavioral terms, it is most important that you name the idea, concept, or other stimulus to which you wish the students to react, and indicate some forms this reaction *may* take. Some examples of acceptable behavioral objectives at the organization level of the affective domain might be:

1. The student will verbally state whether he or she chooses tennis, swimming, or another form of physical activity for his or her own preferred reaction. He or she will support this choice by making statements like the following: I prefer individual or group recreation. I typically choose recreation which challenges me to develop a skill; or which allows me social activity.

2. The student will, in a one-page essay, state whether he or she prefers the paintings of Van Gogh or Monet; defending that choice in

terms of form, line, color, texture, and other dimensions which the student may suggest.

3. The student will, a a two-page essay, compare and contrast his or her own feelings about nature with those expressed by the romantic poets studied in class. He or she will support these statements regarding the feelings of the poets with examples from their writings.

In writing behavioral objectives in the affective domain, you will probably accept a variety of responses as satisfactory. For example, you would not insist that all students prefer group recreation or water sports. Your objective is not that the student prefer a particular idea or object over another but that he or she be able to verbalize and support that preference. You certainly would not insist that the student adopt your preference.[7]

Set Induction: An effective way of focusing student attention on the stimulus (idea, object, performance), to which you want them to react, is by asking a question to indicate the topic of discussion. Some examples might be: What kind of music do you prefer? What should the political and economic policy of the United States be with regard to developing countries? How do you feel about the Women's Liberation Movement? Such questions focus on the topic of discussion. You may wish to precede them by a provocative statement that would relate the question to material or content the class has studied.

Other devices in conjunction with a focusing question may be used in set induction. For example, a history teacher might read a newspaper editorial and then ask for student reactions to it. A teacher in a music class could play recordings representing two types of music and then ask the students which they prefer and why. Pictures, movies, anecdotes, and role-playing also may serve as stimuli for students to react to. After the target area for discussion has been defined, questions become the major strategy used in enabling students to verbalize and clarify their responses.

Factual recall questions may be used in establishing the relationship to a concept, idea, event, or performance to be discussed. They are particularly helpful in establishing a common terminology to be used by students in describing their reactions. Prior to a discussion of the students' reactions to a recent political event, for example, the teacher should be sure that students are aware of the facts surrounding the event and are using a common terminology in discussing them. Questions such as, "What groups are lobbying for and against this bill?" and "What do the terms, 'conservative' and 'liberal' mean?" are important for preparing students to react to an event they all know about in terminology they all understand. The music teacher asking students to react to two musical compositions may need to have students define terms like popular, classical, rock, jazz, or country, because these terms may be used by a student.

Higher-order questions may be used in encouraging students to explore and explain their own reactions or to understand those of someone else. These questions would require the student to go beyond recall or comprehension of facts and look for relationships, trends, applications, and outcomes. Examples of such questions are: "What is present in the one piece of music that is not present in the other?" "What effect do you think prisons have on inmates who eventually return to society?" "Why do you think minority groups are so interested in political representation today?"

Probing questions: After a group of students has been asked to respond to a question which elicits values, the teacher may use probing questions in helping students clarify their own responses, or to compare and contrast their reactions with other viewpoints. They can also be used to open new areas of discussion and to probe for possible diversity when a class initially appears to have unitary response.

If the topic under discussion is: "Should the sale of marijuana be legalized?" and discussion is foundering because everyone has answered with a simple yes or no, questions like the following might be utilized to help the student explore his response in greater depth:

Do most of your friends feel this way?

Do older people generally feel the way you do about this?

What kinds of people tend to feel differently than you do about this issue?

What rationale do you use to support your opinions or beliefs about this issue?

Does your response apply to all instances? (Should marijuana be sold to no one? To everyone?)

Silence and nonverbal cues are important aids in facilitating a discussion. The teacher who answers his or her own questions, or who asks a series of questions before allowing students time to think and respond, should not wonder why students are not getting into the discussion. Silence, and a relaxed physical posture say to the student, "I am giving you time to think so you can answer."

A teacher who wants students to carry on the discussion among themselves may use nonverbal cues, such as pointing to a student who wants to react to another student's statement, rather than verbally giving permission to speak. To indicate that you are participating as a discussant, not as a central figure whose permission must be sought before entering discussion, you might move from your desk and sit in the group.

Reinforcement in a lesson in which students are to verbalize and organize their own reactions should not be construed as rewarding.

No student response should be punished which represents a personal value, belief, or opinion. In a discussion of a particularly volatile issue, an instructor may choose to move away from expression of opinions and appeal to facts, or to role-playing, or to asking students to restate the opponent's point of view to the opponent's satisfaction before continuing discussion. These devices can be utilized to keep a discussion from degenerating into a shouting match. They keep you, as the teacher, in the role of discussion leader, rather than forced into the role of a disciplinarian when discussion threatens to get out of hand.

Closure in an open discussion in an affective lesson frequently consists of summation statements such as, "What appear to be the two main viewpoints present in today's discussion . . . (followed by a summarization of the two)?" "Would someone give the three aspects of the Women's Liberation Movement we have talked about . . . (followed by enumeration and summary description)?" If your instructional objective requires students to express their own points of view, closure will not be an attempt to force the class to adopt a common viewpoint. It will take pains to recognize all points of view or reactions expressed.

In summary, questioning is a major strategy utilized in teaching in the affective domain. Other strategies are role-playing a situation in which one's own reactions or those of another person are expressed, asking a student to restate to the satisfaction of his or her opponent in verbal debate the opponent's point of view before continuing the debate, and asking students to distinguish between fact and opinion.

Using the objective you wrote in the previous exercise for your subject area:

1. Describe a set induction which you might use.

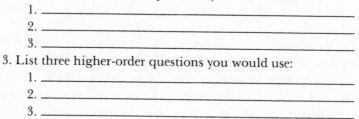

2. List three factual-recall questions you would use.

1. _____

2. _____

3. _____

3. List three higher-order questions you would use:

1. _____

2. _____

3. _____

6. What Instructional Tactics May I Use in Teaching an Affective Objective?   In order for an affective objective to be taught, it must have a behavior which can be observed. In other words, you must have identified a category of behaviors which you will logically accept as evidence that the student or students have achieved the objective. Once that objective and its concomitant behaviors have been identified and specified, then you are faced with the problem of how to instruct so that the students reach the objective.

Three instructional tactics the teacher may use in teaching affective objectives are: modeling, modifying environment to make it more conducive to achievement of the objective, and reinforcement.[8] Research tells us that considerable modification of behavior of learners can be achieved by modeling. We model our behavior after others both consciously and subconsciously. To be successful in modeling, the teacher must provide a personal model for the pupils in hopes that they will accept and emulate that behavior. It follows then that the teacher who wishes to teach an affective objective of instilling a value for a discipline in his or her students must possess and model that value. A teacher who is not interested in the subject he or she is teaching will not model interest in that subject to the students. A teacher who does not possess an interest, value, and appreciation for this subject will not model those affects to students. Frequently this modeling requires nonverbal behavior. The facial expressions, the tone of voice, the approach to a learning task that the teacher takes, all convey to the student the ways in which the teacher feels about the subject. A lackadaisical attitude toward a subject, a statement either explicit or implied that the material is there and simply must be covered but is not of great value ring loud and clear to the student. They respond in turn with a what-does-it-matter attitude. Thus to be successful in teaching an affective objective, you must model it positively and in order to do this you must plan approaches that include modeling. One note should be added. A teacher may model behavior designed to help his or her students achieve an affective objective that is not the exact behavior desired. In other words, you may convey to your students a value for the subject you are teaching in many ways and still provide a model for the students.

The second instructional tactic that a teacher may use in teaching an affective objective is that of modifying environment. This consists in examining the conditions surrounding student behavior, the elimination of adverse conditions, and the inclusion of conditions that would be conducive to students making the correct response. To do this, the teacher analyzes the conditions of the classroom in context with the learner's behavior and changes them so that they contain favorable stimuli to help the student in achieving the objective. Frequently this includes modifying the physical surroundings as well as the psychological surroundings. For instance, if a teacher wishes the students to value reading for pleasure, then books of all kinds and at all reading levels and that are of interest to the students must be available. The teacher simply provides conditions which would make the achievement of the objective more readily possible by manipulating the environment to contain situations which the student will associate positively with achieving the objective.

The third instructional tactic which may be used in teaching affective objectives is that of reinforcement. Reinforcement has been treated in other chapters as it related to the cognitive objectives. Its application here in the affective is similar in nature. Briefly it consists of the teacher rewarding the student for achieving an objective. In general, positive reinforcement is the type used by teachers. The factors concerning the use of reinforcement in the affective domain remain virtually the same as those in the cognitive as regards the time lag between response and reinforcement, partial reinforcement, etc. A difference might be that a teacher in teaching an affective objective would reward for partial achievement.

The three instructional tactics I could use to teach in the affective domain are:

1. _____
2. _____
3. _____

7. How Can I Measure the Achievement of Affective Objectives? As stated before, the measurement of affective objectives is far more difficult than in the cognitive domain. However several ways are open to the teacher.

Verbal types of behavior may be measured by observation and noting responses of students in class. Care must be exercised in this in order that you do not assume that students not making verbal responses in class are not changing their values. Nonverbal behaviors are also difficult to assess. However, some behaviors may lend themselves to measurement on interest-inventories checklists, Likert scales, and semantic differential scales. The following is an example of an objective being measured by a semantic differential scale.

OBJECTIVE

After studying selected writings of Shakespeare, the students will develop a value for this work as evidenced by their indicating on a semantic differential scale that they would read other writings of the author.

Semantic differential scale item:
I would read other writings of Shakespeare.

    Yes—now   Yes—sometime   Maybe   Never again

Such scales can be used to indicate whether or not you are teaching a genuine value. You, as the teacher, must be cognizant of some pitfalls. One, the students may "put you on" and simply "love" Shakespeare for fifty minutes a day for six weeks. Second, in order to be useful, they must be anonymous so that students do not have the fear or threat of displeasure of the teacher. To insure validity, you must insure that the student's response carries no threat. One way of using scales effectively is by establishing class averages on pre- and post-instructional scales. In this case, the teacher would have the students fill in a scale form prior to instruction in a given area and establish a class average as to the valuing of that subject. Then after instruction, in that area, the teacher would administer another scale (equivalent or parallel form) and again obtain a class average. If the second score obtained is more positive, then you may rightfully claim that through your instruction, the students developed a positive valuing for your subject.

Two ways I could measure my teaching in the affective domain are:

1. _____

2. _____

EVALUATION

1. Teach the affective lesson that you have prepared to a group of three or more of your peers.

2. Have each of your peers rate your lesson by filling out the form Critique for Simulated Teaching: Affective Lesson, which follows.

3. Make a critique of your lesson using the Critique for Simulated Teaching: Affective Lesson, which follows.

4. Using the critiques from your peers and your own critique, make a written analysis of your teaching, noting specific strengths and weaknesses and making specific suggestions of ways that your weakensses might be strengthened.

5. Using the information from your peers as well as your own critique and analysis, replan your affective lesson and reteach it. Pay particular attention to overcoming the problems identified in your first affective lesson. Identify how you could improve in your use of the following skills: set induction, factual-recall questions, probing questions, silence and nonverbal cues, reinforcement, and closure. Determine if you could reasonably expect your students to achieve your objective. This reteach lesson should reflect a restructuring of strategy based upon your analysis of your first affective lesson, and you should produce a significantly different approach to the lesson.

CRITIQUE FOR SIMULATED TEACHING:

Affective Lesson

Teacher_____ Date_____

Evaluator_____

	Superior	Very Good	Average	Below Average	Very Poor	Not Applicable
	5	4	3	2	1	0

1. Rate the teacher on each of the following skills:

   a. Set induction

   b. Factual-recall questions

   c. Higher-order questions

   d. Probing questions

   e. Silence and nonverbal cues

   f. Reinforcement

   g. Closure

2. Strategy—Was the strategy appropriate for the lesson taught?

3. Objective—Was the objective understood by the students?

Comments:

NOTES

1. David R. Krathwohl, et al., *Taxonomy of Educational Objectives,* (New York: David McKay, 1964), p. 7.

2. Sharon F. Davis, "Planning for Teaching in the Affective Domain," *Professional Sequence Guide,* Normal, Illinois, Illinois State University Foundation, 1972.

3. Lawrence Kohlberg, "The Child as a Moral Philosopher," *Psychology Today,* Vol. 2, No. 4, September 1968, pp. 25–30.

4. Martin Scheerer, "Cognitive Theory," *Handbook of Social Psychology,* Vol. I (Cambridge, Massachusetts: Addison-Wesley, 1954), p. 123.

5. Milton Rokeach, *The Open and Closed Mind,* (New York: Basic Books, 1960).

6. J. Richard Suchman, *The Elementary School Training Program in Scientific Inquiry,* Title VII, Project Number 216, National Defense Education Act of 1958 (Urbana, Illinois: University of Illinois, 1962).

7. Sharon F. Davis, "Planning for Teaching," p. 146.

8. *Instructional Tactics for Affective Goals,* Prentice-Hall Teacher Competency Development System (Englewood Cliffs, N.J.: Prentice-Hall, 1973), p. 9.

chapter 13

The
Evaluation
Lesson

OBJECTIVES

1. From your major or minor field of study, you must be able to develop a lesson plan that will aid you in evaluation skills. Your lesson plan must be formed around an objective at the evaluation level and must list the strategies considered necessary to attain that objective. The lesson plan must also contain the appropriate elements as illustrated in the Sample Evaluation Lesson Plan in *Learning Activity 2* of this chapter.

2. You will also teach a fifteen-minute lesson in which you exhibit the following skills: set induction, use of examples, higher-order questions, probing questions, divergent questions, and closure. Students may be peers or public school pupils and must be engaged in the development of evaluation skills.

3. You must also be able to make an appropriate analysis of your fifteen-minute simulated lesson while viewing it on a videotaped replay. The analysis must follow the format outlined in How to Analyze the Simulated Lesson and Simulated Lesson Analysis: An Example in Chapter 8.

PREASSESSMENT

Use the questions below to guide your study. Each question is followed by a number that links it to the *Instructional Procedures* included in this chapter.

1. Why is it unusual for evaluation skills to be developed in secondary schools? *(1)*

2. What mental activities are included in evaluation skill? *(1)*

3. What does evaluation skill consist of? *(1)*

4. How are evaluative criteria developed? *(1)*

5. How can you tell when judgments have been made from supportable criteria? *(2)*

6. How can judgments be made when alternatives meet criteria equally well? *(3)*

7. Why do many teachers believe that their subject areas do not lend themselves to the formulation of evaluation skills? *(3)*

8. What is the most important principle to adhere to when selecting learning activities? *(3)*

9. What is equivalent practice? *(3)*

10. What procedures should be used in teaching evaluation skills? *(3)*

11. In testing for evaluation skills, what should be the nature of the test? *(3)*

INSTRUCTIONAL PROCEDURES

LEARNING ACTIVITY 1:   Read the following descriptions of Evaluation Skill, Evaluation Goals, and Learning Activities in Education and complete the exercises associated with them.

1. Evaluation Skill   Evaluation skill is one of the most necessary and yet neglected competencies which the schools purport to develop. Little or no effort is made to help students master this high-level cognitive process because so much time is taken up in the memorization of facts. There are, however, some instances where students are called upon to state their preferences, but this cannot be passed off as evaluation because more often than not, well-articulated rationales supporting preferences are neither required nor encouraged. Evaluation is the highest level of cognition according to Bloom's *Taxonomy of Educational Objectives.*[1] Because the taxonomy is arranged in a hierarchical fashion, each mental skill below evaluation has to be engaged in as part of the evaluative process. Therefore, it is imperative that learning activities which are aimed at increasing skill in evaluation include as prerequisites the development of analysis, synthesis, and comprehension skill.

Evaluation consists of appraisals or judgments about things, people, events, products, or ideas. The judgments which are rendered must be based upon well-defined criteria. The criteria adopted may be from some authoritative, established source, or they may be generated by you, as the teacher. If you generate the criteria, it is particularly important to be able to support them logically. If defensible criteria are not insisted upon, judgments tend to be made from values alone which have no reasonable basis. Judgments so rendered are an exclusive part of the affective domain and require little or no cognition. It should not be concluded from this that evaluation is completely value-free, however. The evaluative process consists of an appropriate blend of the affective and the cognitive with the affective components being supported by rational considerations.

Essentially, what is expected in evaluation is for the student to make judgments regarding the quality of some object or performance, either in terms of its absolute merit or as it relates to similar objects or performance. The student may thus be expected to determine if something is good or bad, right or wrong, ugly or beautiful, acceptable or unacceptable; or may have to compare things and decide which is the best, the most beautiful, or the most acceptable. As already mentioned, these judgments have to be made on the basis of defensible criteria.

One procedure for determining whether or not judgments have been made from supportable criteria is to require the students to explain why they made a particular judgmental response. This necessitates the exposure of the criteria used and requires a rational reason for inclusion.

Judgments are sometimes complicated by the necessity of choosing between alternatives which meet the criteria equally well. If more than one criterion is used in making the judgment, it may be necessary to determine which is the most important. The object or performance which satisfies the most important criterion to the greatest extent can then be judged as best. The above process entails not only making judgments about the use of particular criteria but

also making judgments about the criteria themselves. Both procedures require rational input.

2. Evaluation Goals   The formulation of objectives at the evaluation
level is an essential part of the teacher's responsibility. These goals
have to be formulated in such a way that they clearly convey the
instructional intent and specify what evaluative skills the student
must exhibit subsequent to instruction. There is a tendency for some
teachers to exclaim that their subject area does not lend itself to the
development of evaluation skills. However, all teachers deal with
content or skills from which viable evaluation objectives may be
derived. It is because most teachers have not viewed their subject areas
as anything more than a body of facts to be remembered or psychomotor skills to be mastered that the development of higher-order
cognitive skills has not been fostered.

A more thoughtful appraisal is necessary to determine how the
content of each school subject may be used as a means of developing
higher-order mental operations. To do otherwise is an abrogation of
responsibility by the teacher. The following are examples of evaluation objectives from various areas.

1. Given the definitions and characteristics of proper hole-
borings in steel, the student will observe five samples of borings
and write his or her assessment of the acceptability or unaccep-
tability of the borings based on these definitions and
characteristics.

2. From a videotaped presentation of twelve golf swings per
player, the student will use a golf point-rating scale to determine and name which of six golf players has the best golf swing.

3. Using facts and examples from established pro-and-con
arguments regarding the legalization of abortion, the student
will be able to state why abortion is a good and/or bad practice.

4. Given the factors underlying successful placement of a
shopping center, the student will be able to select the geographic location in the city which most closely fits those factors and
explain in writing how this selection is consistent with these
factors.

5. Given a series of written essays, the student will judge the
essays on the following qualities: (1) the reader is able to
understand the basic message of the writer; (2) the essay is well-

organized and sequenced; and (3) the writer uses language which is not cliche-bound or trite. The student must give a valid rating of strong, average, or poor for each quality on each essay.

Now write three objectives from the evaluation level for your subject area. Underline the behavior, put a double line under the conditions, and place a wavy line under those parts of the objective which represent the standard of performance expected.

3. Learning Activities in Evaluation The most essential principle which must be adhered to when selecting learning activities is to be certain that they provide appropriate practice for achieving the lesson objectives. In the case of evaluation objectives, students should spend at least a portion of their time practicing the actual skill called for in the objective. Student time need not be limited to equivalent practice, but it should consume as much of the available time as necessary to insure mastery of the terminal behavior.

In an evaluation lesson, it is likely that students will need to first receive some descriptive information about how to use evaluation skills. You, as the teacher, may then show examples of evaluation procedures and call attention to the principles involved. This would be followed by your coaching the class as a whole through an evaluation experience. This procedure necessitates the involvement of students in trying out their skills with the teacher offering feedback on their trial responses. The teacher thus guides the class through the steps involved in evaluating. In doing this, you must formulate questions which direct students to produce defensible criteria and apply them in making judgments. Your responsibility as teacher is not to tell the students what the criteria should be, but rather to question students about the logic of their selection and to help them identify inconsistencies which need further consideration. The teacher's role, then, is to call attention to items which the students may overlook and to redirect student responses so that they benefit from the input of their peers in clarifying their thinking. You should withhold judgment at this point and permit students to develop their own reasoning powers during the interaction process. The same kind of role should be used by you in applying criteria to the evaluation process. In the evaluation process, it is necessary that you direct the discussion so that inconsistencies are eliminated and valid judgments are applied.

Many of these inconsistencies can be ferreted out in the discussion by calling attention to overlooked areas of consideration, asking probing questions, and redirecting student responses. The important point for you to remember is that students need to try out evaluation skills and receive feedback on them rather than simply listen to your descriptions about how to evaluate or by observing students demonstrating the evaluation process.

Descriptions and examples represent important preliminary instruction, but the major teaching process should be actual practice and feedback sessions with the students. In the fifteen-minute simulated teaching experience, this in-class trial and feedback session is generally the extent of the lesson. In an actual teaching situation, where more time is available, the teacher should provide students the opportunity to try their evaluation skills independent of the influence of the teacher and peers. Students should then be provided feedback on this experience prior to the time judgments are made on their competency in evaluation processes.

The rating of the students' evaluative skill should be made with materials other than those practiced within the classroom. Otherwise, students have only to recall information generated in the class discussion rather than exhibiting their own evaluation skills. It should be remembered that the facts and concepts dealt with in teaching evaluation skills are incidental to the more important consideration of developing evaluation processes. The teacher's objectives, learning activities, and evaluation should all be oriented toward the mental process of evaluation rather than the acquisition of knowledge.

Now list the learning activities which would help students achieve the three objectives given earlier.

Objective 1

Objective 2

Objective 3

LEARNING ACTIVITY 2: Examine the Sample Evaluation Lesson Plan which follows and then construct a lesson plan for teaching evaluation skills using the same format.

SAMPLE EVALUATION LESSON PLAN

Class: Senior Art
Topic: Evaluating Art Products
Instructional Objective:
> Students will formulate at least six criteria for judging the quality of art objects along with a written justification for each criterion. The student must then apply his or her criteria in making a valid judgment about which of twelve art products is best.

Preassessment:
> Students will be shown three oil paintings and asked to judge which one is best and tell why. The level of sophistication of evaluative skills should be evident.

Content:
The following are some examples of possible criteria for judging the quality of oil paintings:

1. The skill of drawing is evident in the relative size of components of the subjects in the painting.
2. Perspective is appropriately used to give the painting proper depth.

3. Light is used in a way which approximates the natural light which would be available.

4. Color is properly used to highlight appropriate components of the painting.

5. The painting displays an original portrayal of the subject.

6. The painting displays a unique sensitivity in understanding the affective components of the subject.

Learning Activities:

1. The teacher will give a description of the evaluation process.

2. The teacher will explain how the evaluation processes are used in a sample situation. The example which will be used is evaluating artifacts of the Egyptians during the period of 2000 B.C. to 1000 B.C.

3. The teacher will lead a directed discussion where students are to formulate and defend a set of criteria for judging the quality of oil paintings and then apply these criteria in judging the relative worth of six oil paintings.

4. Students will be given an assignment to develop criteria and make judgments regarding the quality of Aztec jewelry. This assignment will be turned in and each student will receive teacher feedback on his work.

Evaluation:

1. Students will be asked to prepare (1) at least six criteria for judging the quality of examples of modern pottery, and (2) a rationale for their list of criteria.

2. Students will apply their criteria in making judgments about which of twelve examples of modern pottery best meets their criteria and explain why.

LEARNING ACTIVITY 3:   Review the principles of analysis discussed in How to Analyze the Simulated Lesson and Simulated Lesson Analysis: An Example in Chapter 8. In analysis of your evaluation lesson, remember that you will be examining the skills of set induction, use of examples, closure, higher-order questions, divergent questions, and probing questions. You may wish to review each of these skills. Set induction, use of examples, and closure are covered in Chapter 8; higher-order questions in Chapter 9; and divergent questions and probing questions in Chapter 10. Also examine the Evaluation Lesson Analysis Guide which follows. You will write your responses in this guide as you evaluate your lesson.

In making the analysis of your lesson, you should also focus your attention upon how well you were able to get the students to exhibit evaluation skills. Determine if your questions were formed so that students had to demonstrate higher-order mental operations in order to respond. Ask yourself the question, "If I were to require the learners to display evaluation skills in a different but related area, would they be able to do so?"

One of the most important skills which you should develop in teaching your simulated lessons is that of making an accurate and detailed analysis of pupil-teacher and teacher-pupil interactions. As a teacher, you cannot rely upon supervisors and administrators to provide you with a basis for improving your teaching performance. Their presence in the classroom is too sporadic to be sufficiently effective. If you are to become a better teacher, you must assume the responsibility for accomplishing this task. It is therefore recommended that you make certain that you understand the concepts discussed in the chapters on simulated teaching and that you are able to recognize the behaviors which they represent in a lesson. In addition, it is necessary that you are able to determine the relative effectiveness of these behaviors and how to formulate alternative behaviors for increased effectiveness.

As you make your analysis, identify the specific areas of your presentation that are unsatisfactory in any way and then attempt to formulate alternative ways to achieve better results. You should proceed both microscopically and macroscopically with your analysis by examining both the larger problems and inconsistencies as well as the minute difficulties.

4. Evaluation Lesson Analysis Guide

1. What evidence do you have that the students actually engaged in evaluation skills? (i.e., made judgments based on established criteria.) Cite at least two instances. If there was no evidence, what would you have done differently in the lesson in order to engage students in evaluation?

2. If possible, cite two instances in which you helped the students differentiate between what was based on fact and what

was based on opinion or values. If there were none, why was it not necessary to help in this differentiation?

3. When you compare your objective stated on the lesson plan to that which the pupils listed on the critique forms, state how they are similar or different. What evidence do you have that the pupils understood or did not understand the objective of the lesson? Cite at least two instances.

4. Cite at least two questions you asked which were of a recall type and two which were probing questions.

5. Cite at least two higher-level questions you asked.

6. Based on questions four and five, how could you have improved the phrasing of your questions in order to encourage *pupil* participation or to have communicated more effectively? State at least two ways.

7. What evidence do you have that the pupils were interested or uninterested in the lesson? Cite at least two instances. How could you have made it more interesting right from the beginning (set induction)? Cite at least two other specific ways you could have made it interesting.

8. How might high school students have reacted differently to

the lesson than your peer group did? Cite at least two ways.

9. In terms of the basic skills (set induction; use of examples; probing, recall, higher-order, or divergent questions; and closure), state at least three ways you would improve this lesson (or consider other alternatives) if you were to reteach it.

LEARNING ACTIVITY 4: OPTIONAL

1. Read Chapter 8, "Evaluation," pp. 141–154, from *Classroom Questions: What Kinds?* by Norris M. Sanders.
2. Read pp. 185–200 in the *Taxonomy of Educational Objectives: Cognitive Domain* by Benjamin Bloom.

EVALUATION

1. *Simulated Teaching:* Teach a fifteen-minute evaluation lesson based on the lesson plan you have prepared, in which you demonstrate skill in set induction, use of examples, higher-order questions, probing questions, divergent questions, and closure. You must also engage your pupils in evaluation processes. Obtain feedback from learners by having them fillout the form Critique for Simulated Teaching: Evaluation Lesson. A clinical analyst may also evaluate your lesson.

2. *Lesson Analysis:* Using the Evaluation Lesson Analysis Guide in this chapter and following the format for analysis explained in How to Analyze the Simulated Lesson and Simulated Lesson Analysis: An Example, in Chapter 8, make a written analysis of the videotaped replay of your lesson.

CRITIQUE FOR SIMULATED TEACHING:

Evaluation Lesson

Teacher_____ Date_____

Advisor_____

	Unable to Observe	Not Achieved	Below Average	Average	Strong	Superior
	0	1	2	3	4	5

1. Which of the following skills were used effectively? Comment about each skill in terms of possible improvements or alternatives:

   a. Set Induction

   b. Use of Examples

   c. Higher–Order Questions

   d. Probing Questions

   e. Divergent Questions

2. What was the objective of this lesson? (State it behaviorally as you recall it.)

3. Were the strategies, content, and learning activities consistent with the objective as you understood it? Why or why not?

4. Did the teacher allow the students to discuss the issue? Cite instances which illustrate that the teacher wanted pupils to participate or did not want them to participate.

	Unable to Observe	Not Achieved	Below Average	Average	Strong	Superior
	0	1	2	3	4	5

5. Were you asked to give your opinion on something without relating it to some standard or criteria? Give an instance which explains your answer.

6. To what degree were you interested in this lesson? How could it have been more interesting to you?

7. How could the teacher have improved this lesson? State at least two specific ways which suggest improvement or other alternatives that the teacher could have used.

NOTE

1. Benjamin S. Bloom, *Taxonomy of Educational Objectives* (New York: David McKay, 1956).

chapter 14

Evaluation

OBJECTIVES

1. Given information on evaluation in general, normative and criterion referenced evaluation, levels of mastery, and evaluation in the cognitive and affective domains, you will demonstrate an ability to utilize these principles in practical application by achieving a score of at least 80 percent on a written objective test dealing with this ability.

2. Given objectives at any three levels of the cognitive domain, you will be able to write one evaluation item for each of the three levels selected.

3. Given two objectives in the affective domain, you will decide on techniques for evaluating the objectives.

4. Given objectives at various levels of the cognitive domain and evaluation items for the objectives, you will decide whether the evaluation items are valid.

5. Given objectives in the affective domain and evaluation items for the objectives, you will decide whether or not the evaluation items are valid, and if not valid, will suggest a change in the evaluation item so that validity is effected.

6. Given a number of evaluation items with assigned difficulty points, you will determine the minimum pass level with 100 percent accuracy.

PREASSESSMENT

Use the questions below to guide your study. Each question is followed by a number that links it to the *Instructional Procedures* included in this chapter.

1. How can evaluation procedures help teachers in dealing with students? *(Introduction)*

2. How can evaluation procedures help teachers in working with the curriculum? *(Introduction)*

3. What is the difference between normative and criterion referenced instruction? *(1)*

4. What kinds of information can be provided from norm-referenced evaluations, rather than criterion-referenced? *(1)*

5. What are the advantages and disadvantages of norm-referenced evaluations? *(2)*

6. What is the short-form for finding standard deviations? *(2)*

7. What elements should norm-referenced test items possess? *(2)*

8. What is the basic focus of the curriculum when a criterion-referenced evaluation instrument is used? *(3)*

9. What is the minimum pass level and how is it determined? *(5)*

10. What is the intent of a knowledge-level question, and how can this intent be implemented? *(6, 7)*

11. How do questions at the comprehension level differ from those at the knowledge level? *(8)*

12. How do application and analysis questions differ from knowledge and comprehension questions? *(9, 10)*

13. Can a synthesis-level question require specifics from the student? *(11)*

14. Why, at the evaluation level, should a student have the material or object to be evaluated readily available to him or her when this is not generally true at the lower levels of the cognitive domain. *(12)*

15. What types of instruments should be used to provide information about particular students? *(13, 14, 15)*

16. Of what value are sociometric techniques? *(14)*

17. What is the value of semantic differential techniques? *(15)*

18. What are the values of both odd-numbered and even-numbered semantic differential scales? *(15)*

INSTRUCTIONAL PROCEDURES

INTRODUCTION

For any program of instruction to be effective, there must be an adequate system of evaluation. Regardless of the form the evaluation might take (to be discussed later), it must provide certain basics for the students involved, for the teachers and administrators, and for others viewing the programs or even the process of evaluation.

From your viewpoint, evaluation must indicate whether students do or do not know the information required, whether they can or cannot perform certain precise skills, and whether or not they can apply these skills, analyze situations, synthesize knowledge, and/or evaluate results. Secondly, your evaluation must also provide the student with adequate feedback. Within certain time limits (before the student has lost all interest in his results), the evaluation results must provide students with the knowledge that they succeeded or failed the evaluation, or their relative standing with others. It is hoped that the evaluation results might also show a student where his or her problems lie. Should students not succeed in the program initially, they then have some solid basis for retracing their steps, finding the area(s) that need(s) more work, and then rebuilding an information system so that they can succeed at a later date. Should they succeed, they still want to know how well they did in relation to peers or in relation to the criteria developed for success. They may also want to know the answers to specific items that piqued their curiosity or drew them into a new line of thinking.

Most educators are feeling different needs for evaluation. One of the least substantive of these needs and yet a very real one in most educational systems is to provide grades at certain points during the school year. Secondly, many teachers need to know exactly what the student knows in relation to a specific subject area before instruction begins. With adequate preassessment, students can be (1) guided to areas of instruction most suitable for them; (2) moved past materials they already know to higher-level applications of these materials; (3)

moved past materials if necessary, to take advantage of more efficient teaching techniques or to make maximum use of limited resources; (4) provided with prerequisite materials not previously available; (5) encouraged toward certain learning modes for most efficient instruction; (6) excluded from instruction in these areas because of their high level of expertise; or (7) given new objectives that more precisely reflect the desired student reaction.

Yet a third need for evaluation includes the assessment of a particular instructional program. Since teaching procedures are constantly changing and since new curricular materials are flooding the markets, teachers need to know what types of techniques and/or materials result in a change in student learning from that gained via the previous techniques or materials. Only with sophisticated evaluation instruments and procedures can satisfactory results be obtained. When new instructional programs are introduced, their value must be assessed in relation to the previous programs. Or, if the instructional program is moving into a new area, adequate evaluation can provide clues as to the effectiveness of this program.

While all of the previous reasons for evaluation are quite useful at a particular time, and preassessment is essential to any solid criterion-referenced program, the most general need for evaluation is to determine what a student knows when instruction has been completed. If a student successfully completes his or her final evaluation, few questions are asked by either the student or the instructor. If, however, a student fails the final evaluation, many possible questions could be asked: Did the student work hard enough? Were the objectives unambiguous? Did the student direct his or her learning to the specific objectives? Were the questions clear enough? Did the evaluation refelct the objectives? Did the preassessment direct students to their weaknesses? Were the learning activities free of ambiguity or were they at a level the student could perceive? Was there some flaw in the evaluation instrument?

These same needs teachers have for evaluation are also felt by administrators as well as others viewing the program from the outside. This latter group would include parents, curriculum experts, educators, and lay people interested in a particular program, as well as evaluation experts. Admittedly, while the needs for evaluation by the above groups are the same as that of the teacher, their view of the evaluation process, the evaluation results, and even of the particular evaluation items might be notably different from that of the teacher.

LEARNING ACTIVITY 1: *1. Normative and Criterion-Referenced Evaluation* Most of the evaluation procedures in our schools today are norm-referenced. In other words, the evaluation results might answer the following questions: How did the student do in relation to other students in his or her class? How did he do in relation to others working on the same material in the school? in relation to all others in the school? in relation to others in the state or geographical area (something the New York Board of Regents exam or the National Assessment project might determine)? in relation to others nationwide (e.g., Scholastic Aptitude Test, National Teacher Examination, Graduate Record Examination)? In all of the above cases, the student was evaluated in relation to others.

Criterion-referenced evaluation has an entirely different base. Rather than determining how well a student has done in relation to peers, criterion-referenced evaluation tries to determine how well the student has done in relation to a certain established level of competency. For instance, assume a person owned a small motor that suddenly did not work. After some testing, a mechanic decided that the only reason for the motor not working was a faulty spark plug. Assume further that an apprentice mechanic is on hand and called on to remove the faulty spark plug and replace it with one that will work. In this case the level of competency expected would be 100 percent. The customer will only be satisfied when the spark plugs are properly exchanged so that the motor will then run. The apprentice proves a level of competency in this area by showing the customer that the motor will run with the new spark plug.

Compared to this high level of competency, we may instead require a much lower level. For example, in a third-grade classroom, by the end of the school year, the teacher may expect each student to read correctly 80 percent of the sight words provided for the third grade, and 50 percent of the sight words designated at a 4.3 grade level. In this case, as in many others, the level of competency may be determined arbitrarily yet utilizing the best judgment of the teacher or a committee of teachers.

2. Norm-Referenced Evaluation Since all of the chapters of this book require a criterion-referenced evaluation, norm-referenced evaluation will receive less emphasis. Virtually every school system in the nation uses norm-referenced evaluation procedures at one time or another; and in most school systems, norm-referenced evaluation is the standard for providing the grades that eventually are used to determine success or failure for a particular student or students.

While a move to nongrading persists and is perhaps strengthening, most schools traditionally give grades. A partial move toward nongrading has occurred in some systems that provide grades of S (Satisfactory) and U (Unsatisfactory). This compromise sometimes brings about other problems. Unless a written explanation accompanies the S or U, or a parent interview is used to explain in depth the meaning of these two grades, the parent (and perhaps the child as well) is unaware of what the student can or cannot do. One would wonder whether a particular student's S is as good as an A or as bad as a D. Or could an S mean working up to potential (perhaps F grades) while a U might mean working below potential (work that was average but that should have been far above average)?

Norm-referenced evaluation, as stated previously, is an attempt to show one student's relationship to other members of his or her class. If everyone were to receive the same grade or nearly the same grade, the intent of showing plausible relationships would be defeated. Therefore, many teachers in building a norm-referenced evaluation instrument attempt to provide enough difficult items so that a spread in grades occurs. Thus, the goal in too many norm-referenced situations is not only to determine a student's mastery of a particular body of knowledge but also to spread the grades adequately so that later report-card grades can be justified to students, parents, and administrators.

In some instances, the attempt to provide difficult items leads to the use of questions that come from the minutiae within a text, items that call for much memorization. Virtually every college student can remember at least one course in which he or she was required to memorize or pay close attention to the footnotes in order to do well in the exam. In the few instances where the above has occurred, the main emphasis of the course has been minimized by trivia.

A large percentage of the standardized tests now available are norm-referenced. They have been designed to show relationships among students having different levels of ability. Consequently, the first items on these tests often are relatively easy with successive items increasing in difficulty. Should a standardized test be considered for a particular system, the faculty would want to look closely at the norm groups used for the tests under consideration. Other things being equal, one would logically select a test with a norm group that approximates the selecting school's population.

In a typical norm-referenced situation where letter grades are given, following a test or at the end of the grading period, the teacher would (1) place all the grades (or averages of grades) on a continuum, (2) find the normal breaking points—shaded areas on the continuum where no grades occur—and (3) make these points the division points between grade groupings. An example follows with each X indicating a student score at that point.

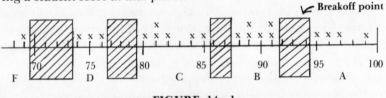

FIGURE 14—1

For the above class of twenty students, a teacher could easily rationalize grades of A, B, C, D, and F as noted above.

Those teachers who are more mathematically inclined or interested in a more precise method of giving grades will perhaps determine the standard deviation. Assuming a normal distribution of scores, a fast method of finding the standard deviation, proposed by W. L. Jenkins, follows:

$$\text{Standard deviation} = \frac{\text{High } 1/6 \text{ of scores} - \text{Low } 1/6 \text{ of scores}}{\text{Half the number of students}}$$

The detailed procedure can be found in an Educational Testing Service booklet.[1] Once the mean and the standard deviation are found and an arbitrary decision is made determining whether the middle grade encompasses one or two standard deviations, the rest of the grades are quickly determined mathematically.

When norm-referenced teacher-made tests are developed, they should possess, at least to the degree possible, the following:

(1) validity—the test measures what it is supposed to measure; (2) reliability—when the test is given a second or third time to the same individual(s), the same approximate scores will result; and (3) usability—easy to administer, economical in terms of cost and use of teacher time, easy to score, and meaningful. Almost any good measurement book will provide added information on any of the above points, but a very readable discussion is provided in John A. Green's *Teacher-made Tests*.[2]

Since norm-referenced evaluation items are designed to spread grades, the person building the instrument must be sure that the items do indeed discriminate among those students who are good in the tested area and those who are not. Before building norms on a test, therefore, each item must be analyzed to be sure it truly discriminates. This can be done most easily after a test has been taken. A detailed procedure that can be utilized quickly and easily in any classroom is described in detail in the Educational Testing Service pamphlet.[3] Should an item not discriminate, many authorities advise not counting the item for that particular testing situation. For later tests the item would either be revised or omitted.

3. Criterion-Referenced Evaluation In establishing how well a student has done in relation to a certain standard of competency, the evaluation instrument could in fact be quite similar to that used for norm-referenced instruction. Both criterion-referenced and norm-referenced tests, for example, could be multiple-choice tests. These instruments often do not vary in degree of difficulty. For example, both norm-referenced instruments and criterion-referenced instruments may be equally difficult. Both types of instruments are expected to be valid, reliable, and usable. Also, it is possible that they both could test the same subject matter or the same process—whether cognitive, affective, or psychomotor.

The basic difference in the instrument lies in the intent of the person building it. First, since the most important question considers how well the student does in relation to an established level of competency, each item in the instrument must relate specifically to this competency. Items that do not relate to the objective have no use in this type of evaluation instrument. Second, since in criterion-referenced evaluation there is no attempt to provide a spread in grades, items from a norm-referenced instrument designed for spreading grades may be eliminated. Hence, the student no longer worries about memorizing the little tidbits of information provided in each course. He or she instead focuses on material that will lead to the successful completion of the objective. In preparation for a criterion-referenced evaluation, the student becomes so cognizant of the objective that should extraneous reading be required, he or she is quick to criticize the inclusion of this material.

A third difference between norm-referenced and criterion-referenced evaluation lies in the degree of mastery required, In norm-referenced evaluation, a student's grade is related to that of peers. If he or she scores higher than peers, he or she generally receives a higher grade. If he or she scores lower than peers, the grade generally reflects this as well. The student is not *required* to achieve a passing average for each evaluation. He or she is required to achieve only a passing average for all evaluations. Failure to do so would result in having to take the course over. In criterion-referenced instruction, the student is expected to pass each of the evaluation instruments at or above the level specified. Should he or she get a higher score than the specified level, the grade received represents his or her level of achievement. However, since grades are not often tied into criterion-level instruction, the reward for achievement considerably above the criterion level is limited to an intrinsic recompense (which may be the greatest reward of all). Should a student get a score lower than the specified level, he or she would probably be forced to retake a different form of the evaluation instrument until able to pass it at the appropriate level.

4. Mastery of Objectives   One could well wonder at what point one shows mastery of a particular situation. The answer is not nearly as clear-cut as criterion-referenced evaluators would like it to be. First of all, one must remember that the evaluation of any objective contains only a sample of the questions or situations that represent the whole. To have selected the precise sample that will indicate whether mastery has or has not been obtained is always subject to question. Couple this with the fact that while teacher-made tests are relatively reliable, they still lack in most cases the reliability achieved by most standardized tests.

Another factor of great importance to be considered is the type of objective itself. Many examples in the literature have illustrated that in the surgical profession anything less than complete mastery cannot be accepted. Similarly, if anyone is to be able to work with an objective on sentence construction at any high level, he or she would first have to know (memorize) and be able to identify all eights parts of speech in relatively simple situations. Anything less than this complete mastery will not be acceptable. There are obviously many objectives for which total mastery is not as crucial. While it might be considered beneficial for students to be able to recite the names of all the presidents of the United States, the typical social studies teacher would probably accept much less than this. In fact, he or she might suggest that only a few need to be memorized. Similarly, when psychomotor skills are demanded, any mastery level of a demanding skill must be less than 100 percent if human differences are taken into account.

In most cases, mastery level is arbitrarily set by the teacher or teachers, using their best possible judgment. However good this method might be, teachers usually consider some of the following guidelines compiled by D. Cecil Clark:[4]

1. Some objectives require complete mastery or nearly complete mastery because of the nature of the objective (the surgical example).

2. Objectives that will be used later in the schooling process should have a higher level of mastery than those that will not be used again.

3. Mastery should be set at a higher level than that which could be achieved merely by guessing.

4. When only a few items have been prepared to measure an objective, the mastery level should be higher than when a large number of items have been developed.

As can be seen from this brief discussion, the careful instructor does more than just pull out any percentage level and use it for mastery. This discussion should not imply, however, that once mastery levels are set, they cannot be changed. Even using the above guidelines can lead to many problems with students succeeding at the resulting mastery levels. Any problems in evaluation items must be reflected in the mastery level. If, after evaluation items are carefully reviewed and considered acceptable, and, if most students are still not achieving the prescribed mastery level (and they appear to be doing the work), the instructor should consider lowering the level. Conversely, if all the students (regardless of whether they study or not) are passing at a particular mastery level, the instructor might consider raising the mastery level.

5. *The Minimum Pass Level* While the minimum pass level is actually an extension of the mastery level topic, the method herein described of establishing a criterion level useful with multiple-choice items would probably be accepted by all instructors. The early practitioners of the minimum pass level (MPL) suggested that it is suited specifically for a "single community of scholars who share a common concept, however vaguely defined, of what constitutes acceptable professional performance."[5] The writers suggest that the application of the principle might not be limited to such a select community. Like the criterion level, the MPL is based largely on subjective judgment—and this judgment can always vary. What the MPL does is try to arrive, as clearly as possible, at the relative difficulty of each item and of the test as a whole.

Following is a procedure used in arriving at an MPL:[6]

A. After reading the item carefully, place an *X* in the difficulty code space of the *One Best* alternative response. This will count as 2 points in later calculations. (In the examples below, the best response is 4.)

Example: (With this example, assume students have been given general information regarding graduation trends.)

1. In 1970–1971, the percentage of 18-year-olds in the United States who graduated from high school was approximately:

   1. 50%
   2. 65%
   3. 73%
   4. 77%
   5. 79%

Difficulty points

   1. *0* 2. *0* 3. *1* 4. X(2) 5. *2*

2/5 difficulty points = 40 percent criterion level

Example:

2. In 1970–1971, the percentage of 18-year-olds in the United States who graduated from high school was approximately:

   1. 10%

2. 25%

3. 50%

4. 75%

5. 100%

Difficulty points

1. *0*   2. *0*   3. *0*   4. X(2)   5. *0*

2/2 difficulty points = 100 percent criterion level

B. Each of the remaining responses should be classified according to its *degree of difficulty* to the *barely passing student* (i.e.,
the student who in your estimation has just enough understanding of the relevant facts and concepts to make it through the
program). Using the following criteria, assign the remaining
responses difficulty points ranging from 0 to 2:

  0 points. This is assigned to responses the barely passing
  student is expected to recognize as incorrect and therefore
  avoid. (See responses 1 and 2 in the first sample which were
  judged accordingly.)

  1 point. This is assigned to responses about which you are
  undecided. Some barely passing student may have difficulty with this and other similar students may not. (See
  response 3 in example 1 above.)

  2 points. This is assigned to incorrect responses which the
  barely passing student is unable to discriminate as such.
  (See response 5 in example 1 above.)

  Note: If these categories do not precisely fit a response,
  the use of decimals (e.g., 1.5) is acceptable. This would
  be particularly true if the response seems to lie between 1
  and 2.

C. Once the difficulty points are determined, the total number of
difficulty points for all items are added together. To determine
the criterion level for the test, the number of test items multip-
lied by 2 is divided by the total difficulty points. To find the
criterion level for one item, divide the number of possible points
by the total number of difficulty points. For the first example, the
criterion level would be 40 percent; for the second, 100 percent.
Of course, a typical evaluation instrument would have many
more items, but assuming ten questions with difficulty points of
2, 3, 3, 2, 5, 2, 2, 3, 2, 3 (Total = 27 difficulty points), the resulting
criterion level (or/MPL) would be 20 ÷ 27 = 74 percent.

While the preceding method seems quite precise, it should be remembered that the difficulty points are initially the arbitrary judgment of the instructor or instructors involved. After a number of persons have tried a specific evaluation item, better criteria can be used for determining difficulty points and thus the minimum pass level or criterion level. Practice Exercise 1 will give you assistance is using the minimum pass level.

PRACTICE EXERCISE 1: DETERMINING THE MINIMUM PASS LEVEL.

Directions: Using the procedure outlined in determining the minimum pass level, determine the level for each of the three problems below. Correct answers are found at the end of the chapter.

Exam 1	Item No.		Difficulty Points			
	1.	a. 0	b. X	c. 0	d. 0	e. 0
	2.	a. 0	b. 1	c. 2	d. 0	e. X
	3.	a. X	b. 2	c. 0	d. 1	e. 0
	4.	a. 0	b. 0	c. 0	d. X	e. 2
	5.	a. 1	b. 0	c. X	d. 0	e. 1
	6.	a. 0	b. 1	c. X	d. 2	e. 1
	7.	a. 0	b. 0	c. 0	d. X	e. 0
	8.	a. 2	b. X	c. 1	d. 0	e. 0
	9.	a. 1	b. 0	c. 1	d. 0	e. X
	10.	a. X	b. 0	c. 0	d. 1	e. 1

MPL = _____

Exam 2	Item No.		Difficulty Points			
	1.	a. 0	b. 0	c. 0	d. 0	e. X
	2.	a. 1	b. 0	c. X	d. 0	e. 0
	3.	a. 0	b. 0	c. X	d. 2	e. 0
	4.	a. 0	b. 0	c. 0	d. X	e. 0
	5.	a. 0	b. X	c. 0	d. 0	e. 0
	6.	a. 0	b. 1	c. 0	d. 1	e. X
	7.	a. X	b. 0	c. 1	d. 0	e. 0
	8.	a. X	b. 0	c. 0	d. 0	e. 0

9.	a. 0	b. 2	c. 1	d. X	e. 0
10.	a. 0	b. X	c. 0	d. 0	e. 0

MPL = _____

Exam 3	Item No.			*Difficulty*	*Points*	
	1.	a. X	b. 0	c. 0	d. 0	e. 0
	2.	a. 0	b. X	c. 1	d. 0	e. 0
	3.	a. 0	b. 0	c. X	d. 0	e. 0
	4.	a. X	b. 0	c. 0	d. 0	e. 1
	5.	a. 0	b. X	c. 0	d. 0	e. 0
	6.	a. 0	b. 0	c. 0	d. X	e. 0
	7.	a. 0	b. 0	c. 0	d. 1	e. X
	8.	a. 0	b. 0	c. 0	d. 0	e. X
	9.	a. 0	b. 0	c. X	d. 0	e. 0
	10.	a. 0	b. 1	c. 0	d. X	e. 0

MPL= _____

6. Evaluation in the Cognitive Domain   Evaluation items at various levels of the cognitive domain differ little from each other. The main concern involving any item, regardless of its cognitive level, is whether or not the item evaluates the objective specified. If students cannot see the relationship between an evaluation item and the objective after a discussion with the instructor, then the instructor should weigh carefully the merits of including that item on future examinations.

Objective tests can be constructed at any level of the cognitive domain. Often, however, for a variety of reasons (e.g., lack of time in preparing the exam, desire to gauge students' abilities to record their thoughts, etc.), instructors prepare subjective examinations to test above the knowledge level. While the intent is not to criticize this type of examination, several words of warning may be appropriate. When this type of examination is used, the criteria for grading should be stated precisely either on the examination paper or on the objective. Students should know in advance the basis upon which a subjective evaluation is to be given. Too often teachers without previous written criteria, after looking at a few of the exceptional papers in a class, have revised their hastily perceived criteria for grading in the midst of a grading session. The dangers of this are obvious. A further discussion of subjective examinations will be limited to the brief discussion of the affective domain.

7. *Knowledge Level*   The various levels of the cognitive domain were discussed in Chapter 3. Rather than repeating information presented there, it is assumed that you have an adequate familiarity with that chapter. Since the intent of a knowledge item is to learn what a student can recall or remember, the item must be exact enough so that the student will recognize the information when seeing it again. Many different types of questions can be used for the knowledge level including the following:

1. Visual recall

   Write the meaning of the following musical symbols in the space provided:

   p = _____
   f = _____
   > = _____

2. Repeat definition

   Write the definition of a mammal.

   _____

   _____

3. Completion

   Washington Irving's home was called:

   _____

4. Multiple choice

   Who was the author of *The Child Buyer?* (Circle the correct answer)
   a. Harper Lee
   b. John Hersey
   c. Ernest Hemingway
   d. MacKinlay Kantor
   e. Graham Greene

5. True or False

   Place a *T* in front of the item if it is true, or an *F* if it is false.

_____ a. F. D. Roosevelt was elected president four times.

_____ b. The New Deal was established by President Hoover.

6. Matching

Identify the authors of each musical composition by placing the letter which appears before the correct author in the blank beside the title.

_____ 1. "The Pines   a. Beethoven
         of Rome"   b. Copland
_____ 2. "New World   c. Respighi
         Symphony"   d. Offenbach
_____ 3. "Emperor   e. Dvorak
         Concerto"   f. Mussorgsky
_____ 4. "Afternoon   g. Debussy
         of a Fawn"
_____ 5. "Pictures at
         an Exhibition"

Other types of objective questions as well as variations of these types are acceptable as long as the information is in some easily recognizable form.

8. Comprehension Level   As Benjamin Bloom has stated in his book on summative·and formative evaluation, "material for translation, interpretation or extrapolation must not be the same as was used in instruction, but it should have similar characteristics in terms of language or symbology, complexity, and content."[7] While there will not be an attempt to show how each type of objective question can be used, representative samples will be given for translation, interpretation, and extrapolation as follows:

Translation:

1) Robert Frost, in his poem "The Road Not Taken," used poetic imagery to arrive at a deeper or more profound meaning than the words seem to imply. In a paragraph of your own words, state what you think Frost's profound meaning might be.

2) Translate the following German phrases into English.

a. Setz dich— _____

b. Guten Tag— _____

c. Nahmen Sie Platz—_____

3) Which of the following is the best literal translation of the German idiom, Setz dich?

a. Set the table.

b. Sit by my side.

c. Sit down.

d. Sit in this place.

e. Set it down.

Translation, Interpretation, and Extrapolation

1. After looking at the following graph and reading statements 1, 2, and 3, use A, B, or C to indicate your

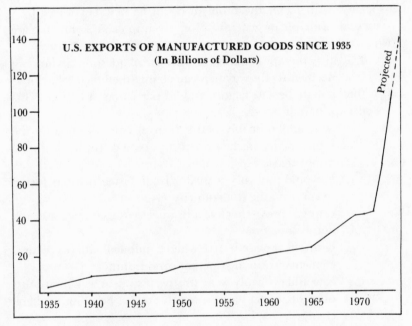

U.S. EXPORTS OF MANUFACTURED GOODS SINCE 1935
(In Billions of Dollars)

answer.

a. The statement is *not* supported by the information provided on the graph.

b. The statement is supported by the information provided on the graph.

c. The statement is *neither* supported nor contradicted by the information provided on the graph.

1. The U.S. exports of manufactured goods have risen each year since 1948. (translation)

2. If the increases in exported goods over the past five years were to continue at the same average rate, the exports in 1980 would be $200 billion. (extrapolation)

3. The total of U.S. exports is much higher during years of high inflation than during years of moderate or low inflation. (interpretation)

9. Application Level At this level of the cognitive domain, the student is faced with a problem that is similar to one provided in instruction yet which has some elements of uniqueness or newness associated with it. Or the problem could be new but solved by a particular principle or generalization given in class. Following are two possible questions:

1. Reality therapy demonstrates the use of questions in helping students identify the way they can change their own behavior so that it will be satisfactory in the particular situation. This disciplinary method:

    a. would probably be ineffective if used only after the fourth occasion the student has been disruptive with the same offense.

    b. would probably be ineffective if the teacher were forced to confront the student privately.

    c. might prove effective if limited to use with two students at the same time.

    d. might prove effective when combined with procedural elements involving operant conditioning.

    e. would probably be ineffective if student was questioned until he or she stated a way his or her behavior could be changed.

    (It must be assumed that the specific information in the above question has not been previously mentioned.)

2. Your employer has recently agreed to purchase an irregular-shaped lot. Most land in this area has been selling at $10,000 for 40,000 square feet. Since you are now taking a math course, and since he does not know how to figure square footage for this shape of lot, you are to help him. Of the choices given below, which one would be the fairest price for the lot?

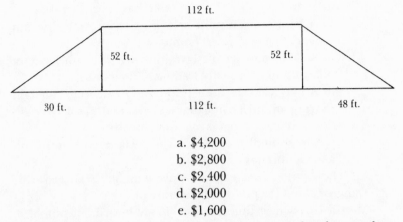

a. $4,200
b. $2,800
c. $2,400
d. $2,000
e. $1,600

10. Analysis Level At the application level, the student faces evaluation problems which are similar to those in his or her experience, yet with a degree of newness. At the analysis level, however, the problem situation must be new or different from that faced in instruction. This new problem situation must be available to the student for referral as he or she tries to solve the problems or find answers to the questions, as the two examples below demonstrate.

After reading this portion of the poem "Thanatopsis" by William Cullen Bryant, complete the test items that follow it.

Thanatopsis

So live, that when thy summons comes to join
The innumerable caravan that moves
To that mysterious realm, where each shall take
His chamber in the silent halls of death,
Thou go not, like the quarry-slave at night,
Scourged to his dungeon, but, sustained and soothed
By an unfaltering trust, approach thy grave
Like one who wraps the drapery of his couch
About him, and lies down to pleasant dreams.

1. In lines 2 and 3 of this section, the more profound meaning of "innumerable caravan that moves / To that mysterious realm," is best described by:

a. A large number of people who have met their death.

b. A long caravan train belonging to an Arab chieftain moving to a new desert home.

c. A large number of slaves moving to another day of difficult toil, eventually leading to their deaths.

d. A long caravan train belonging to an Arab chieftain moving toward a battle that will eventually lead to certain death, yet death that is met individually.

e. A large number of people who are faced with dreary toil and an uncertain future.

2. "Thou go not, like the quarry-slave at night, / Scourged to his dungeon," has the profound meaning of:

a. Do not meet this situation bloody, bowed, and humbled.

b. Do not meet this situation under the fear and threat of slavery, with beatings and confinement facing you each evening.

c. Do not go, in this situation, as a slave would be led or forced to go, under duress.

d. Do not accept this situation as a tired, beaten quarry-slave would, with fear and abject hopelessness.

e. Accept this situation even to the point of joyously seeking or welcoming it.

11. Synthesis Level   At this level, like the previous one, the problem or situation should in some way be new or different from that faced during instruction. Since the idea is to use divergent thinking while applying all the previous knowledge one has, the student would logically be allowed to use any materials previously studied—in essence, an open-book exam. Since the student is to be creative, neither time factors nor other controlling limitations should be overly rigid. Instead, he or she is to use the various materials studied and, within reasonable time limitations, synthesize these materials and finally come up with a new or unique idea, communication, outlook, plan, or procedure. Within the prescribed guidelines, the student's final product is to be a unique creation.

Norris M. Sanders, in *Classroom Questions: What Kinds,*[8] provides eight different approaches to synthesis questions. He also notes the weaknesses associated with synthesis questions: often lacking in significance, sometimes too difficult for the student, and difficult to evaluate fairly.[9] Another good source for the synthesis subject is Benjamin Bloom's book.[7] Following is a sample question.

A. The need for reform in political campaign contributions in national elections dominated the newspapers during the Watergate debacle. The logical extension of this reform movement is application at the local level. Write a paper for or against reform in campaign contributions in city, county, or school elections. The following guidelines apply:

1. The paper must concern itself with the moral as well as the social issues involved.

2. Specific examples from elections within the past fifty years must be cited. These may include elections results, court cases involving elected officials, or court decisions relating to local levels. In all cases, however, the examples must apply to a local election situation.

3. This paper should consist of a logical argument with supporting reasons for your stand rather than a recitation of your own feelings.

4. Concise expression is important to this paper. Do not belabor any specific point. Rather, cite your argument, reasons for it, and move on.

5. The nature of your argument, pro and con, will have no effect on the grade. Instead, grades will be based on the power of your argument, the specificity of the examples, and the criteria for arguments developed in class.

It should be noted that synthesis evaluation is not limited to writing exercises. A house plan in industrial arts, an original musical score, a dramatic presentation, a finished art piece, or a speech could all fill synthesis requirements.

12. Evaluation Level When evaluating at this level of the cognitive domain, the material or situation must always be new or different from that originally presented to the student. He or she then evaluates this new material or situation against criteria that have been previously established. When possible, the student should have the material or situation available during the evaluation for easy referral.

When some material or situation is judged better than another according to specific criteria, or when various materials are placed in some type of rank order, the evaluation level is being met. Examples of this level follow:

1. Of the more famous lines from *Macbeth* is the following:

"a tale Told by an idiot, full of sound and fury, Signifying nothing."

Which of the following is the best interpretation of this quotation?

—Life is totally meaningless; nothing is left for the future.

—The noise and blatancy (sound and fury) of life are meaningless as compared to the contemplative moments.

—Life takes on idiotic moments when much noise is made, but little occurs.

—Life, as described by most of us, is idiotic; but its more important aspects can be seen by the perceptive.

—The meaningful moments in life are not illustrated by noise or other sounds.

2. In a town having seven major religious organizations, the local board of education recently allowed one local religious organization free use of school premises each Sunday, for the next ten years. The school will provide janitorial services without charge. Evaluate a property owner's chance for success in a lawsuit enjoining the school from providing these premises for the use of one religious organization, using a principle from *McCollum* v. *Board of Education* as a base.

PRACTICE EXERCISE 2: WRITING EVALUATION ITEMS FOR COGNITIVE OBJECTIVES

Directions: Write an evaluation item at the proper level for each of the following objectives.

1. The student will, shown six international road signs, write the meanings of any five.

2. Given the grades of thirty-two students on a test, the student will identify the standard deviation that is within .3 of the correct answer.

3. Given three similes from a sixteen-line poem, the student will

identify those that promote the general theme as compared to those that are neutral or descriptive.

4. Given a graph of economic cycles for the past fifty years, the student will select the best prediction of the economic trend for the next four years.

Note: The previous four objectives were at the following levels: 1–knowledge; 2–application; 3–analysis; 4–comprehension.
5. Write your own objectives, and write proper evaluation items at each of the proper cognitive levels.
Objective:

Evaluation Item:

PRACTICE EXERCISE 3:
SELECTING VALID EVALUATION ITEMS
FOR OBJECTIVES—COGNITIVE DOMAIN.

Directions: Following are objectives in the cognitive domain and evaluation items designed for those objectives. In the blanks below each evaluation item, state whether the evaluation is valid for that objective. If not valid, state your reason for its not being valid, and on a separate sheet of paper write an alternative evaluation item that is valid. Responses to this exercise are at the end of the chapter.

1. The student will be able to form the past tense of five verbs with 80 percent accuracy.
Evaluation: Following are five verbs with a blank upon which you should write the past tense of each verb.

        1. lie   _____

        2. lay   _____

        3. sit   _____

        4. set   _____

2. Define from memory all of the following words as they are used in regard to minorities: *bigotry, persecution, prejudice, intolerance.*

Evaluation: Following are four words related to minorities. Match the definition of each word as it is used in relation to minorities with the word.

_____ 1. bigotry   a. injury or damage to one's legal rights

_____ 2. persecution b. behavior ensuing from one's total devotion to his own race

_____ 3. prejudice   c. state of unwillingness to grant equal freedom of expression

_____ 4. intolerance d. an irrational attitude of hostility directed against a different race

           e. act of harassing one who differs in race.

3. Translate the following German phrases into English.
Evaluation: Select the best literal translation of the German idiom "Setz dich":

1. Set the table.
2. Sit by my side.
3. Sit down.
4. Sit in this place.
5. Set it down.

Select the best literal translation of the German phrase, "Guten Tag":

1. Good day.
2. That was a good tag.
3. Have a good day.
4. Have a good tag.
5. This is a good day.

4. Given the assets and liabilities of a corporation, the student will construct a simple balance sheet with no errors.

Evaluation: Listed on the handout was all the information necessary to prepare a simple balance sheet. In the blanks below fill in the necessary amounts:

Total Assets   _____

Total Liabilities   _____

Net Worth   _____

13. Evaluation in the Affective Domain The section of Chapter 3 that deals with the affective domain goes into some detail regarding the problem of evaluation. Regardless of problems, there exists a real need to evaluate the many affective objectives to which schools seem to subscribe.

No matter what type of evaluative device is used, if the students feel that the results will be reflected in grades or in either rewards or penalties, the validity of the resulting scores must be questioned. Students tend to give teachers what they think the teachers want.

14. Affective Instruments—Student Information To preserve validity, students can be asked to provide adequate feedback through *anonymous* responses. This is particularly useful when teachers need to evaluate the affective curriculum rather than an individual student. There are times, however, when identifying students is important for the proper development of the students' affective needs. In these latter cases, teachers must assure the students that their grades will not suffer from test results.

Among the affective evaluation techniques involving the student are the following:

    1. Incomplete-sentence survey: (the student finishes the sentence)

        a. When I read . . . .

        b. On Saturday evenings I . . . .

        c. When I get my report card . . . .

        d. Secretly I wish . . . .

The danger with the above approach is that students are often reluctant to express their true feelings in such a survey. A variation by J. W. Getzels and J. J. Walsh[10] gives students the opportunity to project their feelings through someone else:

    2. Variation of incomplete-sentence survey.

        a. When I read . . . .

        b. On Saturday evenings I . . . .

c. When I get my report card . . . .
d. Secretly I wish . . . .

a. When Sue reads . . . .
b. On Saturday evenings Mary . . . .
c. When Sara gets her report card . . . .
d. Secretly Brenda wishes . . . .

Whenever projective techniques, such as the two above, are utilized, one must also be aware that the following also exist:

a. Even when projecting feelings through someone else, a student will be reluctant to discuss items of extreme concern for those items are considered too personal.

b. A person's feelings vary from day to day and even, on occasion, from hour to hour. A student filling out an incomplete-sentence survey just after a traumatic emotional experience would be expected to respond quite differently than if the hours preceding the questionnaire were relatively uneventful.

c. A student's relationship to the teacher (particularly if highly negative or highly positive) is likely to result in a variation of possible responses. When feasible, teachers might want to give specific attention to those students whose responses are likely to be influenced by such a relationship.

While responses students make regarding themselves can be useful, the reactions of their peers can also be of value. A student's inability to react favorably with his or her peers could have obvious consequences involving his or her work within that class. To judge peer reaction, various methods are available such as the "guess who" technique or a sociometric device.

3. "Guess who" method. This method, developed by Remmers and Gage, is used when a group of students within one class show their reactions to their peers. The directions adequately describe the procedure:[11]

Here are some little word-pictures of some children you may know. Read each statement carefully and see if you can guess who it is about. It might be about yourself. There may be more than one picture for the same person. Several boys and girls may fit one picture. Read each statement. Think over your classmates, and write after each statement the names of any boys or girls who may fit it. If the picture does not seem to fit anyone in your class, put down no name, but go on to the next statement. Work carefully, and use your judgment.

    1. Here is the class athlete. He (or she) can play baseball, basketball, and tennis, can swim as well as any, and is a good sport.

    2. This one is always picking on others and annoying them.

Additional statements describing specific students can be developed by the teacher, although description is particularly important should a teacher elect this option.

    4. Sociometry. To develop the interrelationship of students within a class—to see who is most popular, least popular, isolate, etc.,—the students might be directed to select a certain number of students to work with in their class for a particular assignment. An example of such an assignment might be to tell students to "Write the names of three persons you might like to work with on (name a specified class project). Be sure to include the person you prefer to be with, not necessarily someone you are working with now. Number your paper 1, 2, 3, placing your first choice beside number 1, etc."

    After the choices are made, the teacher then graphically charts the number of times each student is selected, the mutual selections, and so forth. As with any such peer selection, one must be aware that in any given day a student's peer approval may rise or fall. If this type of measure is utilized by two or three different teachers or two or three different times during a year, an averaging effect would tend to affect any momentary deviations from the expected. A sample sociogram is presented below: As can be seen from the sample sociogram, Dale and Ivan (who have the most arrows pointing to them) are the two most frequently selected boys in the class, while Elise and Ellen receive similar distinction. Neither Tom nor Mae were selected by any of their peers. While one can easily determine who was selected most frequently, it is an entirely different matter trying

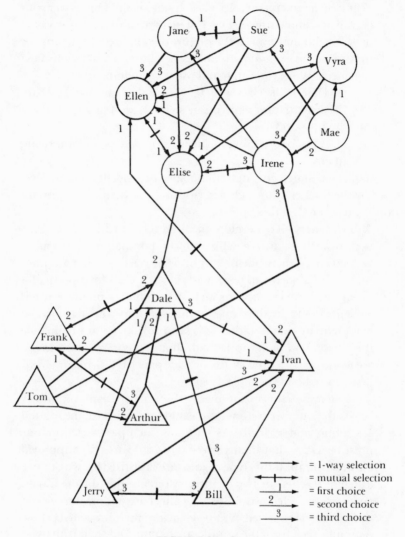

FIGURE 14—2

to decide *why* someone was or was not selected. In fact, the reasons students were not selected could vary from assignment to assignment.

15. *Affective Evaluations—Curricula and Teaching* The previous four evaluations involved the student—either his

reactions to himself or others' reactions to him. While this is of extreme importance to any teacher, equal importance is often afforded reactions to subject matter or subject areas. The following are examples of evaluation instruments that elicit student reactions to the affective curriculum:

5. Yes-No Attitude Response (type used in the *San Diego County Inventory of Reading*).

_____ Yes _____ No   Are you interested in reading fiction?
_____ Yes _____ No   Do you read the newspaper each day?
_____ Yes _____ No   Are the types of books you enjoy available in your school library?

6. Intensity of agreement or disagreement response. The respondent is asked whether he strongly agrees (SA), agrees (A), disagrees (D), strongly disagrees (SD), or is undecided (?).

__SA__A__?__D__SD   The general mathematics course taught the basics of being a good consumer.
__SA__A__?__D__SD   The freshman English course helped students learn to read faster and with more understanding.

7. Semantic differential techniques. The student checks a blank to indicate his relative position between two polar adjectives. When eliciting opinions of a particular course, the semantic differential scale might look like this:
rigid:___:___:___:___:___:___:___:flexible

Science II (1) (2) (3) (4) (5) (6) (7)
interesting:___:___:___:___:___:___:boring
easy:___:___:___:___:___:___:difficult
current:___:___:___:___:___:___:outdated
relevant:___:___:___:___:___:___:irrelevant
abstract:___:___:___:___:___:___:concrete

In the above scales, the adjectives on the left would be called A adjectives and the adjectives on the right, B adjectives. The scaled positions could then be defined as follows:

(1) extremely A
(2) quite A
(3) slightly A
(4) neither A nor B; equally A and B
(5) slightly B
(6) quite B
(7) extremely B

Semantic differential scales are not limited to seven positions. Logically, however, an odd number of scaled positions allows the middle position to reflect an intermediate point between the polar adjectives. Students do have a tendency to overuse the middle position, however. When a definite student commitment toward the "goodness" or "badness" of a situation is desired, then an even-numbered blank is applicable.

While a broad variety of other affective evaluation schemes is available, most are spinoffs of those already mentioned, designed to fit individual needs. Whenever you want the true response of the individual in regard to a particular class or to the curriculum in general, you must expect to make the evaluation completely anonymous. To do anything other than that will elicit responses the student wants the teacher to hear or responses the student thinks the teacher wants.

In schools where the curriculum is quite varied from day to day, and where faculty are not threatened by regular student feedback to the day-to-day activities, student reactions to each class on a weekly basis can be of significant benefit in improving curricula and teaching.

PRACTICE EXERCISE 4:
WRITING EVALUATION ITEMS
FOR AFFECTIVE OBJECTIVES.

Directions: Write an evaluation item at the proper level for each of the following objectives.

1. The student will show his or her reactions to school and home situations by filling out an incomplete-sentence survey that is reflective of the typical school day. (Provide at least six sentence-beginnings reflective of your school situation.)

2. The student will show his or her interest in obeying school rules as evidenced by responses on the following questionnaire. (Design a brief evaluation item that might reflect this objective.)

3. The students will indicate whom they perceive as the leaders in the class as evidenced by their responses to a "Guess Who" device. (Prepare at least six reaction statements reflective of your school or class situation.)

4. The student will indicate his or her agreement or disagreement with certain aspects of this course as shown by responses to an appropriate device. (Prepare one of the following: A six-item yes-no attitude response; a six-item intensity of agreement or disagreement response; or a six-item semantic differential scale.)

5. Write your own objectives, and write the proper evaluation items that reflect the objectives.
Objective:

Evaluation Item:

PRACTICE EXERCISE 5:
SELECTING VALID EVALUATION ITEMS
FOR OBJECTIVES—AFFECTIVE DOMAIN.

Directions: Following are four objectives in the affective domain and evaluation items designed for those objectives. In the blanks below each evaluation item, state whether the evaluation item is valid for that objective. If not valid, on a separate sheet of paper, write a valid evaluation item. Responses to the four items are at the end of the chapter.

1. *Objective:* The student will show an awareness of the works of Shakespeare by identifying at least two Shakespearean plays from a list of ten plays in which at least four of his more popular plays are included.

Evaluation: To the left of the following ten plays, place a check mark for each one which you identify as having been written by Shakespeare.

_____ 1. *Cymbeline*
_____ 2. *King John*
_____ 3. *She Stoops to Conquer*
_____ 4. *Hamlet*
_____ 5. *Macbeth*
_____ 6. *Antigone*
_____ 7. *Everyman*
_____ 8. *King Lear*
_____ 9. *The Tempest*
_____ 10. *Saint Joan*

2. The student will show an interest in reading the newspaper by indicating on an ungraded survey the sections that he or she reads daily.

Indicate the areas of the daily paper that you usually read by placing an X in the blank to the left of that area. Place your name in the blank at the bottom of the list.

_____ a. front page
_____ b. women's section
_____ c. sports
_____ d. local news

_____ e. comics
_____ f. want ads
_____ g. obituaries
_____ h. horoscope
_____ i. advice columns
Name _____

3. The student will form judgments on the life he or she would like to lead by filling out a self-analysis involving reactions to possible life situations as they are affected by the values of money, family responsibility, and desire for recognition.

On the form below, show your reactions to the following influences on life by selecting the blank on the continuum which best reflects your attitude toward that influence.

	Very Important			Very Unimportant	
Money	1	2	3	4	5
Recognition	1	2	3	4	5
Family	1	2	3	4	5
Happiness	1	2	3	4	5

4. The student will show his or her reactions to the lectures on this unit by checking the areas that best apply.

Lecture 1: Depression—Part I

Extremely Worthwhile			Extremely Worthless	
1	2	3	4	5

Lecture 2: Depression—Part II

Extremely Worthwhile			Extremely Worthless	
1	2	3	4	5

Lecture 3: Postdepression Period

| Extremely | | | Extremely | |
Worthwhile			Worthless	
1	2	3	4	5

PRACTICE EXERCISE 6:

1. Which of the following is the least valid reason for providing an evaluation?

a. To indicate a student has achieved an objective.

b. To tell a student whether he or she passed or failed in relation to his or her peers.

c. To show a student where his or her problems might lie.

d. To provide the basis for a grade.

2. From the viewpoint expressed in the chapter, which of the following would be the most prevalent reason for providing evaluations?

a. To provide student feedback.

b. To indicate achievement of objectives.

c. To provide a mechanism for producing grades.

d. To gather input for improving the curriculum.

e. To show a student where he has room for improvement.

3. Which of the following generally reflects the situation when a student successfully passes an evaluation instrument?

a. Teacher is interested, but student is not.

b. Student is interested, but teacher is not.

c. Neither student nor teacher is interested.

d. Both teacher and student are interested.

4. Norm-referenced evaluation

a. is predominant and will probably remain so.

b. is predominant but is losing in popularity to criterion-referenced evaluation.

c. is gathering momentum over criterion-referenced evaluation.

d. is about equal in importance to criterion-referenced.

5. When S and U grades are given

    a. S generally means A or B work.

    b. S always means A or B work.

    c. S means somewhere between A and D work.

    d. S means anything above failing work.

    e. S has little meaning without an accompanying explanation.

6. A standard deviation is a simple means of showing

    a. the relationship of the top student to the rest in the class.

    b. the relationship of the bottom student to the rest in the class.

    c. the relationship of the mean of the class to any other point.

    d. the relationship of the top student to the bottom student.

7. A test is reliable if it

    a. tests what it is supposed to test.

    b. provides the same approximate scores when given a second or third time to the same individual.

    c. is as meaningful to the teacher the second or third time as it was the first time.

    d. will provide the same results no matter who administers the test.

8. Discrimination is the ability of a test to

    a. show which students are good and which are poor.

    b. allow the better students to do better than the poorer students on a particular item.

    c. allow the poorer students to do better than the better students on a particular item.

    d. provide the same approximate scores when given a second or third time to the same individuals.

9. As compared to norm-referenced items, criterion-referenced items are generally

    a. multiple-choice.

    b. more difficult.

    c. less difficult.

    d. expected to be valid, reliable, and usable.

    e. showing relationship to a level of competence.

    f. demanding of a much higher level of performance.

10. The minimum pass level is an attempt to

    a. provide a more realistic basis for a passing grade.

    b. provide a precise basis for a passing grade.

    c. provide general recommendations for consideration of a passing grade.

    d. provide a mathematical formula as a base for a passing grade.

True-False

Please circle **T** for true, **F** for false.

T F 11. Matching items may be used for only the lowest cognitive level.

T F 12. Translation items are generally fill-in-the-blanks.

T F 13. Rigidity in time factors and other controlling factors should be eliminated when evaluating at the synthesis level.

T F 14. When evaluating at the evaluation level of the cognitive domain, the student should not be allowed extra resources for referral.

T F 15. To make an affective evaluation valid, the objective must not be known by the student.

T F 16. With the use of projective techniques, the teacher can expect students to discuss personal areas.

T F 17. A sociometric device has as its primary purpose the identification of students who are either popular or isolates from the class.

T F 18. To be reliable, most affective questionnaires must be given more than once.

T F 19. Semantic differential scales, to provide commitment on the part of the student, should be even-numbered rather than odd-numbered.

T F 20. While regular curricular evaluations are necessary, feedback on less than a monthly basis tends to be underproductive.

EVALUATION

The practice exercises included in this chapter are equivalent practice for the proficiencies which you will be asked to demonstrate in the examination given by your instructor.

ANSWERS

Ex. 1

1. MPL = 49%
2. MPL = 74%
3. MPL = 83%

Ex. 2

While there are no correct answers for this exercise, the student is cautioned to make the evaluation item reflect the objective.

Ex. 3

1. OK—The student is forced to form the past tense.

2. Needs revision. If the definition is to come from memory, a matching question will not work. Here the student is aided. Far better to provide space for the student to write out each definition. One plus for this item is that more foils are provided than correct answers.

3. Needs revision. If the intent is for the student to translate, he or she is again aided by this type of question, being able to compare a number of foils.

4. Needs revision. In a sense the basic items of a balance sheet have already been set up for the student by listing the three main areas. Total construction of the balance sheet, even a simple one, would include the titles named by the student.

Ex. 4

While there are no correct answers, the student is again cautioned to make the evaluation item reflect the objective.

Ex. 5

1. OK—While more than four of Shakespeare's plays are provided, the additional ones are not popular.

2. While the format for the item is adequate, having students sign their names forces them to try to please the instructor, possibly listing more areas of the paper than actually read.

3. Needs to be reconstructed. While value analysis is called for, it is not related to life situations.

4. Could be adequate. Possible change might be the consideration of two check lists for each area, one for information obtained and one for adequacy of presentation.

Ex. 6

1. d   6. c   11. F   16. F

2. c	7. b	12. F	17. T
3. c	8. b	13. T	18. T
4. b	9. e	14. F	19. T
5. e	10. a	15. T	20. F

NOTES

1. Paul B. Diederich, "Short-cut Statistics for Teacher-made Tests," Educational Testing Service, Princeton, New Jersey, p. 23.

2. John A. Green, *Teacher-made Tests*, (Evanston, Ill.: Harper and Row, 1963), p. 141.

3. Paul B. Diederich, "Short-cut Statistics," pp. 6-10.

4. D. Cecil Clark, *Using Instructional Objectives in Teaching*, (Glenview, Ill.: Scott, Foresman, 1972), pp. 76–77.

5. "Setting Standards of Competence: The Minimum Pass Level," The Evaluation Unit, Center for the Study of Medical Education, University of Illinois, College of Medicine (Chicago, 1972), p. 2.

6. Ibid., pp. 3-4.

7. Benjamin S. Bloom, J. Thomas Hastings, and George F. Madaus, *Handbook on Formative and Summative Evaluation of Student Learning*, (St. Louis: McGraw-Hill Book Company, 1971), p. 151.

8. Norris M. Sanders, *Classroom Questions: What Kinds* (New York: Harper and Row, 1966), pp. 129–137.

9. Ibid., pp. 128-129.

10. Bloom et.al., *Handbook of Formative and Summative Evaluation*, p. 238.

11. H. H. Remmers and N. L. Gage, *Educational Measurement and Evaluation*, (New York: Harper, 1955), p. 330.

Index

347